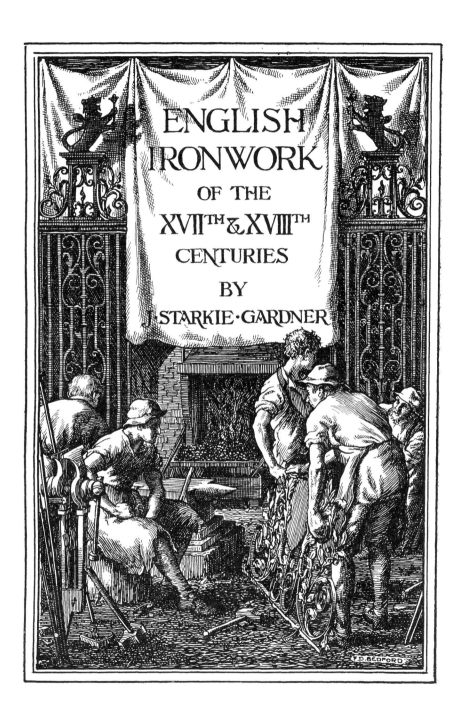

ENGLISH IRONWORK

Frontispiece

GATE IN THE SHEEN ROAD, RICHMOND.

ENGLISH IRONWORK
of the XVIIth & XVIIIth Centuries

AN HISTORICAL & ANALYTICAL ACCOUNT
OF THE DEVELOPMENT OF EXTERIOR SMITHCRAFT

J. STARKIE GARDNER

DOVER PUBLICATIONS, INC.
Mineola, New York

Published in Canada by General Publishing Company, Ltd., 30 Lesmill Road, Don Mills, Toronto, Ontario.

Bibliographical Note

This Dover edition, first published in 2000, is an unabridged republication of the work originally published in 1911 by B. T. Batsford, London and William Helburn, New York.

Library of Congress Cataloging-in-Publication Data

Gardner, John Starkie, 1844–1930.
    English ironwork of the XVIIth & XVIIIth centuries : an historical & analytical account of the development of exterior smithcraft / J. Starkie Gardner.—Dover ed.
       p. cm.
    Originally published: London : B.T. Batsford ; New York : W. Hellburn, 1911.
    ISBN 0-486-41243-1 (pbk.)
    1. Ironwork—England—History—17th century. 2. Ironwork—England—History—18th century. 3. Decoration and ornament—England—History—17th century. 4. Decoration and ornament—England—History—18th century. I. Title: English ironwork of the XVIIth and XVIIIth centuries. II. Title: English ironwork of the seventeenth & eighteenth centuries. III. Title.

NK8243 .G3 2000
739.4'742'09032—dc21

00-060329

Manufactured in the United States of America
Dover Publications, Inc., 31 East 2nd Street, Mineola, N.Y. 11501

TO

SIR ERNEST GEORGE, A.R.A

GRATEFULLY INSCRIBED

BY

THE AUTHOR.

Preface

THE necessity for an historical account of the English Ironwork of the Renaissance has so long been apparent to all interested in art and the history of art in this country, that no apology for this volume is needed.

For nearly two centuries, including the whole period of the Early Renaissance, the art of Ironwork in England lay practically dormant, but with the accession of William and Mary the craft experienced an extraordinary development, which continued to the middle of the eighteenth century. The achievements of this short period form one of the most brilliant phases in the history of English craftsmanship, though many of the best examples are comparatively unknown.

In the present volume an attempt has been made for the first time to discriminate the works of the highly skilled and native craftsmen who produced the finest works in iron the country possesses, and to whom collectively is due the development of a style which we may justly claim as national. It defines the peculiarities by which their several works may be distinguished; while the names of at least the pioneers of the revival of an industry that had too long been neglected are recorded and rescued from oblivion.

The intention of writing a history of the subject in one form or another had been in my mind for many years, and when I was definitely asked by Messrs. Batsford to undertake the task I gladly accepted it and at once set seriously to work upon it. During the course of many years' practical work and study I had accumulated a great store of material in the shape of illustrations of ironwork, notes, etc., and these proved exceedingly valuable as a source from which to draw examples, and as an aid to their classification. I must here also mention my indebtedness to the late Mr. John Norton, who had in the " seventies " spent much of his leisure in sketching the old iron gates in and around London and elsewhere, which were at that time little appreciated and rapidly disappearing. Mr. Norton generously allowed me to trace these sketches and add them to my collection, and they have proved most valuable both in noting those that no longer exist, and in describing and classifying the examples that remain. Mr. Horace Dan, an architect whose photographic work is now known to many, had taken photographs of interesting examples of gates in London and the Home Counties, and he continued this work, so that many of the illustrations in the book are the result of his enthusiastic labours. As the book progressed other photographs and drawings of examples of importance were obtained from various parts of England, and through these much information of exceptional interest and value regarding the life and work of hitherto unknown craftsmen came to light. The book has grown continuously during the intervals of a busy career in the five years that have been devoted to it. Messrs. Batsford have spared neither time nor money in actively assisting the discovery of facts and documents in order to make the work, as far as it goes, complete and exhaustive, so much so that I regard them as joint authors.

The loss or disappearance of very many interesting examples, and the peculiar dangers to which the work is liable through atmospheric influence has disposed me to give detailed descriptions of those that remain, which may in many cases appear needlessly tedious and technical.

Preference has been given to exterior examples, as more accessible, and the most liable to damage and decay.

Preface

Though the limits of the book have made it impossible to deal with every example of importance, sufficient of each type and period have been included, and the handicraft of every known smith is so fully illustrated and described, that it should become possible not only to recognise their individual work, but to date approximately any examples that may come under the reader's notice.

In conclusion, it only remains to express my gratitude to Mr. H. Myddleton of Chirk Castle, Mr. John E. Pritchard of Bristol, Mr. J. R. Wardale, Mr. Beck of Sandringham, Mr. S. W. Bickell of Dulwich College, Mr. E. E. Bland of Kirkleatham, and Sir G. J. Armitage of Kirklees Park, Mr. R. Phené Spiers, Mr. J. Berkeley Cubay, Mr. Stead Mills of Leicester, the Duchess of Rutland, the Marquis of Hertford, Lord Northesk, Lord Harrington, Earl Bathurst, Lord Harrowby, and Sir Henry Bedingfield, to all of whom I am indebted for material information.

To Mr. Walter Spiers, curator of the Soane Museum, I am specially indebted for unvarying kindness and assistance.

In addition to Mr. Horace Dan, the following have contributed photographs: Mr. W. Galsworthy Davie, Mr. C. B. Keene of Derby, Mr. Hope Jones those of Emral, and Mr. J. Simpson those of Leeswood and Eaton. Many architects and draughtsmen have kindly lent their work for illustration, among whom are Mr. W. Niven, F.S.A, Mr. Harold Falkener, Mr. E. Guy Dawber, Mr. A. E. Martin, Mr. H. P. G. Maule, Mr. A. H. Hind, Mr. M. S. Adams, Mr. Heaton Comyn, Messrs. Brewill & Baily, Mr. F. Lishman, Mr. G. J. Poston, Mr. Joseph Seddon, Mr. F. E. Collington, and Mr. T. Garratt. To Mr. Victor Ames I am indebted for photographs and drawings of several of the gates in Norfolk and elsewhere. The proprietors of *Country Life* have generously supplied electros of several most interesting subjects. Mr. Percy Lovell, of the London Survey Committee, has lent figures 91–92, Mr. Garraway Rice the illustration of the monogram of Huntington Shaw, and Colonel Hart figure 2, while the Bodleian authorities have permitted the reproduction of the drawing of Hamstead Marshall.

J. STARKIE GARDNER.

"RIVERHOLME,"
    MAIDENHEAD COURT,
        BERKS.
           August, 1911.

CONTENTS

	PAGE
INTRODUCTION	xxvii
MEDIAEVAL IRONWORK	1
THE EVOLUTION OF GATES	
MEDIAEVAL GATES	10
RENAISSANCE GATES	16
Forecourt and Garden Gates	16
The Garden	27
THE WORK OF JEAN TIJOU, 1690–1710	37
THE SCHOOL OF SMITHS AFTER TIJOU	59
Robert Bakewell, 1707–30	59
The Brothers Roberts, 1719–30	63
William Edney, 1710–40	72
THE ENGLISH SCHOOL OF SMITHS	81
The work of Thomas Robinson, 1697–1720	85
The work of Warren, 1700–20	95
Work by George Buncker, 1720–30	109
FORECOURT SCREENS	116
THE LANDSCAPE GARDENER	125
THE INFLUENCE OE ARCHITECTS	129
GATES BY UNDISCOVERED SMITHS	138
Dated Gates	139
London Gates	140

	PAGE
COUNTRY GATES	175
South-Eastern Counties	175
Counties West from London	184
South-Western Counties	191
The Midland Counties	192
West Midland Counties	198
Counties immediately North of London	199
The Eastern Counties	202
The Northern Counties	206
Scotland	210
Wales	210

RAILINGS, BALUSTRADES, BALCONIES, STAIR-RAMPS AND GRILLES

	PAGE
RAILINGS	212
BALUSTRADES	246
BALCONIES	254
STAIR-RAMPS	261
GRILLES	267

LAMPHOLDERS, BRACKETS, SIGNS AND VANES

	PAGE
LAMPHOLDERS AND BRACKETS	278
DOORWAY BRACKETS	289
INN SIGNS	292
VANES	300
LIST OF SMITHS AND DESIGNERS	321
GENERAL INDEX TO THE TEXT	324

BRIEF SUBJECT LIST OF EXAMPLES ILLUSTRATED

NOTE.—It is obviously impossible to index fully or adequately in this list such general subjects as Gates, Railings, etc., examples of which occur in almost every illustration. The list deals mainly with accessories and details, and even of these examples beyond those mentioned in this list will often be found on the plates of Gates, etc., e.g. there are ornamental panels on every screen illustration.

Roman figures refer to plates, ordinary numbers to the figure numbers of text illustrations, which are *not* referred to under their page references.

ARMORIAL BEARINGS AND CRESTS

	FIG. NOS. OR PLATES.		FIG. NOS. OR PLATES.
Burleigh House	vi	Clandon Park	xxxv
Baptist Chapel, Derby	x	Dulwich College	xxxviii
Etwall Hall	xiii	Much Hadham	lxv
Chirk Castle	xiv	Beddington	71
Leeswood	xv	Design by Tijou	99
Trinity College, Cambridge	31	Stoneleigh	lxxix
Devonshire House	xxxiv		

BALCONIES

Crowley House, Greenwich	lxxvi	Design by Tijou	99
Kirby Hall	96	Seaton Delaval	100
Wallingford Town Hall	97	XVIIIth Century Designs	101, 2
Guildford	98	Boodle's Club, St. James' Street	103, 4

BALUSTRADES

Powis House, Great Ormond Street	43	Cheyne Walk	91
By Tijou	88	Chesterfield House	lxxv
Hampton Court	89, 90	Somerset House	93
Melbourne Hall	lxxiv	Design by Adam	94

BRACKETS: LAMP AND DOORWAY

The Admiralty	130	Adam Designs	134, 5
Micklegate, York	131	Ludlow	136
Tottenham Cross	132	London	137
Stratford	133	Frensham	138

Brief Subject List of Examples Illustrated

DETAILS OF SMITHING (see also MASKS, LEAFWORK, ETC.)

	FIG. NOS. OR PLATES.		FIG. NOS. OR PLATES.
Tewkesbury	26	Wovington	37
By Bakewell	p. 80	Newark	65
Oakley Park	33	Great Ormond Street	78

FANLIGHTS (see also GRILLES)

Designs by J. Bottomley	109–116	Design by Carter	122
Anonymous Designs	117–121	Design by Adam, for Drapers Hall	123
Mansfield Street	lxxxii		

FOLIAGE, ORNAMENTAL (see LEAFWORK)

GARDEN GATES

| Eaton Hall | vii | Scraptoft Hall | 28 |
| Emral | xvii | Exning | xxxii |

GATES

General:	Figs. 1–69, Plates i–lxx	Garden: Eaton Hall	vii
Castle Gates	1–4	,, Emral	xvii
Wooden (in part): Groombridge	5	Scraptoft Hall	28
Sarsden	6	Tudor: Cowdray	8, 9

GRILLES (see also FANLIGHTS)

| Trinity College, Cambridge | 13 | Mansion House | 107 |
| Radcliffe Library, Oxford | 49 | A London example | 108 |

LAMPHOLDERS (see also BRACKETS, LAMP)

Great Ormond Street	lxxi	Crowley House, Greenwich	lxxvi
Grosvenor Square	lxxii & lxxxv	A Design by Adam	125
Chandos House and Portman Square	lxxiii	10, Downing Street	lxxxvii
		Designs by Carter	126
Berkeley Square	lxxxiii, v	Chesterfield House	lxxxviii
Charles Street	lxxxiv	Arched form	127
John Street, Adelphi	lxxxvi	An Adam design	94

LEAFWORK, ORNAMENTAL

By Bakewell	p. 80	Cheveley	xxxiii
Hampton Court	16, III, iv, 17, v, 19a	Tewkesbury Abbey	26
Newnham Paddox	xix	Chesterfield House	lxxv
Exning	xxxii	Studley Royal, Ripon	lxx

MASKS

Hampton Court	iii, 19a	Queen's House, Chelsea	91, 92
Newnham Paddox	xix	Chesterfield House	lxxv & lxxxviii
Oakley Park	33		

Brief Subject List of Examples Illustrated   xvii

MONOGRAMS, ORNAMENTAL

	FIG. NOS. OR PLATES.		FIG. NOS. OR PLATES.
Sheen Road, Richmond	*frontispiece*	Chiswick	53
Burleigh House	vi	Fenton House, Hampstead	54
Hampton Church	p. 58	Stratford	55
Okeover Hall	xi	Queen's House, Chelsea	91
Cheyne Walk	xxxvi	A London Grille	108
Eagle House, Edmonton	l		

PANELS, ORNAMENTAL AND PILASTERS (*see also* BALUSTRADES)

Clandon Park	32	Drayton House	lxxvii, lxxviii
Horse Guards	50	Stoneleigh Abbey	lxxix
London Examples	74–76	Somerset House	93
Great Ormond Street	lxxi	Great Ormond Street	106
St. James' Square	87	An Adam design	125
By Tijou	88	Chesterfield House	lxxxviii
Chandos House and Portman Sq.	lxxiii		

PORCH

Melbourne	viii

RAILINGS (OF SPECIAL CHARACTER)

Powis House, Great Ormond Street	43	Designs by Ware	79, 82
Chesterfield	70	St. James' Square	87
Reigate	72	Crowley House, Greenwich	lxxvi
Reading	73	Mansfield Street	lxxxii
Grosvenor Square	lxxii	An Adam design	125
Great Ormond Street	78	Chesterfield House	lxxxviii

SCREENS, ORNAMENTAL

Traquair Castle	10	Carshalton	xxx, xxxi
Hampton Court	15, iii, 17	Buckingham House	34
Sheldonian, Oxford	12	Ormeley House, Ham Common	35, 36
Wimpole	19	Elvaston	38
Drayton House	20, 21	Powis House, Great Ormond Street	42, 43
Burley-on-the-Hill	22	Designs by James Gibbs	45–7
Leeswood	xv, 22a	"Remnants," Marlow	lx
Eaton Hall	xviii, 24	Newdigate House, Nottingham	67
Newnham Paddox	xix, 25	Houghton	68
New College, Oxford	29	Beddington	71
Wootton, Bucks	xxvi		

SCROLLS, CONNECTING, OR RAMPS

Powis House, Gt. Ormond Street	43	10, Downing Street	lxxxvii
Chesterfield	70		

xviii   Brief Subject List of Examples Illustrated

SIGNS

	FIG. NOS. OR PLATES.		FIG. NOS OR PLATES.
Redbourne	139	Aylesbury	143
Bruton	140	Bedford	144
Mere	141	Bletchingly	145
Harleston	142		

SMITHING DETAILS

Cote Bampton	7	Oakley Park	33
Cowdray	9	Wovington	37
Newnham Paddox	xix	Newark	65
Tewkesbury	26	Great Ormond Street	78
By Bakewell	p. 80		

SPIKES

St. John's, Westminster . . 95

STAIR BALUSTRADES OR RAMPS

Powis House, Gt. Ormond Street	43	High Head Castle	lxxx
Chatsworth	105	Wentworth Woodhouse	lxxxi
Drayton House	lxxvii, lxxviii	Great Ormond Street	106
Stoneleigh Abbey	lxxix		

VANES

Oxburgh Hall	146	Greenwich Hospital	155
Butleigh	147	Bow Church	156, 7
Barlborough Hall	148	Design by Wren	158
Ruscomb Church	149	Rochester Town Hall	159
Lambeth Palace	150	St. Ethelburgha's, Bishopsgate	160
Lucas Asylum, Wokingham	151	Minster Church, Sheppey	161
Rye Church	152	Hedsor Church	162
Town Hall, Guildford	153	Canons Ashby	163
St. Stephen's, Walbrook	154		

VASES, ORNAMENTAL

Leeswood	xv	Chesterfield House	lxxv
Tewkesbury	26, xxi	Mansfield Street	lxxxii
Cheyne Walk	xxxvi	Berkeley Square	lxxxiii, lxxxv
London Examples	83–6	Charles Street	lxxxiv
Much Hadham	lxvi	10, Downing Street	lxxxvii

WEATHERCOCKS, see VANES

WICKET GATES

Examples occur on most Screen Illustrations.

YETT

Glamis Castle 4

TOPOGRAPHICAL LIST OF EXAMPLES ILLUSTRATED

Plates are referred to in Roman numerals; text illustrations in ordinary figures under their illustration numbers, not their page references.

Note.—All references to Suburban districts will be found under "London."

References to names of Smiths, Architects, etc., will be found in a list at the end of the book.

	Plate or Fig. number.	Page where referred to.
ASHBURNHAM HOUSE, *see* Battle.		
AYLESBURY, sign	143	297
BARLBOROUGH HALL, vane	148	306
BATTLE, gate to Ashburnham House	LVIII	182
BEDDINGTON, screen and gates	XXVIII, 71	91, 229
BEDFORD, sign	144	298
BEXLEY, HALL PLACE, screen and gates	XXIX	91
BRUTON, sign	140	295
BURFORD, gates	LIX	186
BURLEIGH HOUSE, entrance gates	VI	46
BUTLEIGH, vane	147	305
BURLEY-ON-THE-HILL, gates	22	57
CAMBRIDGE, gates at Clare College	30	97
,, gates to Trinity College	31	99
,, grille to cloisters, Trinity College	13	35
CANONS ASHBY, vane	163	320
CARISBROOKE CASTLE, entrance	I	11
CARLISLE, High Head Castle, balustrade	LXXX	265

	Plate or Fig. number.	Page where referred to.
CARSHALTON, screen and gates	XXX, XXXI	92
CAST-IRON VASES, to railings	83–86	240
CHATSWORTH, balustrades to garden stairs	105	263
,, design for balcony	99	258
,, entrance gates	LXII	198
CHEVELEY MANOR, see Newmarket.		
CHEVENING, screen	39	118
CHESTER, see Eaton Hall.		
CHESTERFIELD, railing at	70	225
CHESTER-LE-STREET, gates	69	208
CHIRK CASTLE, screen and gates	XIV	64
CIRENCESTER, gates to Oakley Park	33	103
CLANDON PARK	XXXV	101
,, ,,	32	101
COLWICK HALL	LXI	197
COTE BAMPTON, gate	7	21
COWDRAY, SUSSEX, gates	8	23
,, ,, details	9	24
DERBY, gate to Old Silk Mill	IX	60
,, ,, to Baptist Chapel	X	61
,, ,, side gate to	XI	61
DRAYTON HOUSE, forecourt screen	20, 21	53, 55
,, ,, stair balustrades	LXXVII–LXXVIII	264
DUNSTER CASTLE, gate	3	13
DURDANS, see Epsom.		
EATON HALL, gate to kitchen garden	VII	52
,, ,, gates and screen	XVIII, 24	68, 69
ELTHAM, gate	LVII	179
ELVASTON, the golden gates	38	116
EMRAL HALL, bridge gates	XVII	66
,, ,, gates	23	67
EPSOM, gates to the Durdans	XXIV	77
ETWALL HALL, gates	XIII	62
EVESHAM, gate at Merston Green	LXIV	199
EXNING HOUSE, see Newmarket.		

Topographical List of Examples Illustrated

	Plate or Fig. number.	Page where referred to
FARNHAM, gates at the Grange	62	181
FRENSHAM, SURREY, bracket	138	292
GLAMIS CASTLE, SCOTLAND	4	14
GRILLES, designs for, anonymous	117–121	274
GROOMBRIDGE, KENT, gates	5	19
GUILDFORD, balcony at	98	257
" vane on Town Hall	153	309
GUILDFORD, see Clandon Park.		
HAM COMMON, gate to Ormeley House	35, 36	110, 111, 112
HAM HOUSE	I, II	26, 27
HAMPTON COURT, garden screen	III	41
" " " " gates	V	43
" " garden entrance	IV	42
" " design for screen	15	40
" " gate to east front	16	42
" " lion gate	17	44
" " design for gates	18	45
" " mask by Tijou	19a	52
" " balustrade, designs for	88	247
" " balustrade to Long Water	89	247
" " balustrade to South front	90	248
HAMPTON CHURCH, monogram	—	58
HAMSTEAD MARSHALL, design for entrance	11	31
HARLESTON, sign	142	296
HAWKHURST, screen to High St. House	40	118
HEDSOR CHURCH, BUCKS, vane	162	319
HIGH HEAD CASTLE, see Carlisle.		
HIGH ST. HOUSE, see Hawkhurst.		
HOUGHTON HALL, NORFOLK, screen	68	205
KIRBY HALL, balcony	96	255
KNOLE PARK, entrance to gardens	58	177

xxii Topographical List of Examples Illustrated

	Plate or Fig. number.	Page where referred to.
LEESWOOD HALL, screen	XV, 22a	65
,, ,, park gates	XVI	66
LIDGATE	4	15
LONDON—		
ADELPHI, lampholders	LXXXVI	280
ADMIRALTY, lamp bracket	130	287
BERKELEY SQUARE, gate to Lansdowne House	LIV	172
BERKELEY SQUARE, lampholders	LXXXIII, LXXXV	279
BOODLES CLUB, balconies at	103, 104	261
BOW CHURCH, vane	156, 157	311–12
BRACKET at Messrs. Trollope	137	291
BUCKINGHAM HOUSE, gates formerly at	34	108
CHADWELL HEATH, gate to Whalebone Hall	XLIII	152
CHANDOS HOUSE, Queen Anne St., lampholder	LXXIII	244
CHARLES ST., lampholders at No. 41	LXXXIV	279
CHELSEA, Cheyne Walk, Queen's House gate	XXXVI	106
CHELSEA, Cheyne Walk, Queen's House, balustrade to	91	249
CHELSEA, Cheyne Walk, Queen's House, balustrade mask	92	250
CHELSEA, Cheyne Walk, gate to No. 15	LI	163
,, ,, ,, No. 4	52	145
,, gate at Grove House	XLVIII	156
CHESTERFIELD HOUSE, Mayfair, balustrade	LXXV	249
CHESTERFIELD HOUSE, Mayfair, pillar and lamp	LXXXVIII	285
CHISWICK, gate to Latimer House	53	147
CLAPHAM, gate in Old Town	XLVII	156
CROWLEY HOUSE, GREENWICH	LXXVI	253
DEVONSHIRE HOUSE, PICCADILLY, gates	XXXIV	101
DOWNING ST., entrance to No. 10	LXXXVII	283
DRAPERS' HALL, fanlight	123	276
,, ,, lamp brackets	134–5	290

Topographical List of Examples Illustrated

	Plate or Fig. number.	Page where referred to.
LONDON—*continued*.		
DULWICH COLLEGE, gates	XXXVIII	109
,, VILLAGE ,,	XXXIX	110
EDMONTON, gate, Fore St.	L	162
ENFIELD, gate at Burleigh House	XXXVII	107
,, ,, to Goughs Park.	XLI	113
,, ,, in Baker St.	LIII	172
GREAT ORMOND ST., railings in	LXXI, 78	235, 238
,, ,, ,, stair balustrades.	106	266
,, ,, ,, Powis House, gates	43	122
,, ,, ,, Powis House	42	120–1
GREENWICH, Crowley House	LXXVI	253
,, HOSPITAL, vane	155	310
GRILLES, FANLIGHT	117–121	274
GROSVENOR SQUARE, Nos. 12 and 44, lampholders	LXXII	236
GROSVENOR SQUARE, No. 14, lampholders.	LXXXV	279
HAMPSTEAD, gate to Fenton House.	54	149
HANOVER SQUARE, panel	74, 76	234
HORSE GUARDS, screen by Ware	50	134
I'ANSON, MR. E., grille in possession of	108	270
KENSINGTON GORE, gate to No. 24	LII	171
LAMBETH PALACE, vane	150	307
LAMP SUPPORT	127	284
LANSDOWNE HOUSE, *see* Berkeley Sq.		
LEADENHALL ST., gates formerly at No. 20	51	142
LEWISHAM, garden gate	LVI	178
LUDGATE, *see under* LIDGATE *in gen.* Alphabet	4	15
MANSFIELD ST., doorway and grille	LXXXII	275
MANSION HOUSE, grille	107	269
MITCHAM, gate to Eagle House	57	161
MONMOUTH HOUSE, *see* Soho.		
NEWINGTON GREEN, gates	XLIX	160
PORTMAN SQUARE, lampholder	LXXIII	244

xxiv Topographical List of Examples Illustrated

	Plate or Fig. number.	Page where referred to.
LONDON—*continued*.		
POWIS HOUSE, *see* Great Ormond St.		
RAILING PANELS	74–76	234
SACKVILLE ST., lamp and bracket	128	286
ST. ETHELBURGA'S, Bishopsgate St., vane	160	317
ST. JAMES'S SQ., railings to No. 22	87	243
” ” ST., *see* Boodles Club.		
ST. JOHN'S CHURCH, WESTMINSTER, spikes	95	253
ST. STEPHEN'S, WALBROOK, vane	154	309
SAVILE ROW, bracket for lamp	129	286
SOANE MUSEUM, design by Robert Adam	125	282
SOANE MUSEUM, design for vane by Wren	158	313
SOHO SQUARE, screen to Monmouth House	44	123
SOMERSET HOUSE, balustrade to Strand	93	251
SNARESBROOK, gate to Elm House	XLVI	152
SPRING GARDENS, lampholder	124	280
STOKE NEWINGTON, the Old Manor House, panel	75	235
STRATFORD, gate to 6, Forest Lane	55	151
” ” in Romford Road	56	153
” lamp bracket	133	289
TEMPLE, Fountain Court	77	237
TOTTENHAM, gate at Vicarage	XL	113
” lamp bracket	132	288
VASE-SHAPED finials to railings	82–86	240
VICTORIA AND ALBERT MUSEUM, gate in	58	166
VICTORIA AND ALBERT MUSEUM, design for balustrade	94	252
WHITEHALL, Admiralty	130	287
WOODFORD, gate to Grove Hall	XLV	152
WREN, *see* Soane Museum.		
LUDLOW, bracket	136	291

Topographical List of Examples Illustrated

	Plate or Fig. number.	Page where referred to.
MARLOW, GREAT, gates to Remnants.	LX	189
MAXSTOKE CASTLE, gates.	2	12
MERE, sign	141	296
MELBOURNE, porch to summer house	VIII	60
,, balustrade	LXXIV	249
MINSTER CHURCH, SHEPPEY, vane	161	318
MISERDEN PARK, GLOS., gates	64	190
MONMOUTH, see Tredegar Park.		
MUCH HADHAM, gates at the Lordships	LXV, LXVI	201
NEWARK, screen to the Chantry House	65	194
NEWMARKET, gates to Cheveley Rectory	XXXIII	98
,, Exning House, garden screen	XXXII	98
NEWNHAM PADDOX, screen	XIX–XX, 25	68, 71
NORTH CRAY, gate to Church	LV	178
NORWICH, gates to Town Hall	LXVIII, LXIX	203
NOTTINGHAM, gates in Museum	LXI	197
,, screen to Newdigate House	67	200, 201
NOTTINGHAM, gates in screen	66	196
OKEOVER HALL, entrance	XII	61
OXBURGH HALL, vane	146	305
OXFORD, New College, garden screen	29, XXV	87, 88
,, Radcliffe Library, gates to	49	133
,, St. Mary's porch, gates to	63	187
,, Sheldonian Theatre, railing to	12	34
,, Trinity College, gates	31	88, 89
RAPHAEL PARK, see Romford.		
READING, railings	73	233
REDBOURNE, sign	139	294
REIGATE, entrance to the Priory	60	179
,, details of	61	180
,, railings	72	231
RICHMOND, gate in Sheen Road	*frontispiece*	159
RIPON, see Studley Royal.		
ROCHESTER TOWN HALL, vane	159	316
ROMFORD, gates to Raphael Park.	XLIV	152

	Plate or Fig. number.	Page where referred to.
RUSCOMB CHURCH, vane . . .	149 ..	306
RYE CHURCH, vane	152 ..	308
ST. ALBANS, gate to St. Peter's . .	LXVII ..	202
SANDRINGHAM, gates . . .	XLII ..	139
SARSDEN, KENT	6 ..	20
SCRAPTOFT HALL, entrance gates .	XXIII, 27 ..	75, 76
,, ,, garden gate . .	28 ..	77
SEATON DELAVAL, balcony . .	100 ..	259
SHEPPEY, *see* Minster Church.		
SHREWSBURY, gates to Abbey House .	LXIII ..	198
SOCIETY OF UPHOLSTERERS, designs for balconies	101–2 ..	260
STONELEIGH ABBEY, balustrade to steps	LXXIX ..	265
STUDLEY ROYAL, gates . . .	LXX ..	207
TEWKESBURY ABBEY, gates, overthrow	XXI, 26 ..	73
TRAQUAIR CASTLE, gates . . .	10 ..	25
TREDEGAR PARK, gates . . .	XXII ..	74
WALLINGFORD, Town Hall, balcony .	97 ..	256
WARE, ISAAC, designs for railings. .	79–82 ..	239
WENTWORTH CASTLE . . .	41 ..	119
WENTWORTH WOODHOUSE, balustrade	LXXXI ..	265
WIMPOLE, gates formerly at . .	19 ..	46
WOOTTON, BUCKS, screen and gates .	XXVI, XXVII ..	89
WOODSTOCK, sign	145 ..	299
WOVINGTON, gate at	37 ..	114
WOKINGHAM, vane	151 ..	307
YORK, lamp bracket	131 ..	288

Introduction

THE want of any historical account of artistic ironworking in England has long been felt, and it is this the present volume is intended in part to supply. It deals chiefly with one notable period of the art, the dramatically sudden revival accompanying the accession of William and Mary. The possession of richly wrought ironwork at once became the fashion and remained so throughout the reign of Queen Anne. Following the example set by Hampton Court, every important seat or mansion became adorned with magnificent forecourt and garden gates, screens and balustrades, gaily painted in blue and green and gilded, and rivalling the glories then being produced for Louis XIV across the water. Magnificent specimens even now survive in almost every county, notwithstanding ravages of time and the havoc of changing fashions. Yet though these are talked about and sketched and photographed, neither their relative rarity or dates, nor the names and characteristics of the artists who produced them are known. The singularly rapid development of the art and splendid achievements of our smiths at that time are matters of which any other country would be justly proud, but here, in the greatest iron-producing centre of history, our knowledge of them has been as limited as of sun spots. Even our educational authorities have allowed to be set up on the façade of the Victoria and Albert Museum, and to stand for all ages as representing England's chiefest art and craft, a possibly ordinary work's manager, perhaps not even a craftsman, of whom little more than the name is known.

As an unfettered expression of English craftsmanship, stimulated by emulation alone, working freely, and with hardly any help from traditions, this unexampled revival gives much to think over. The arrival from over sea of an exalted patron and a talented French Protestant refugee sufficed to wake the dormant or liberate the pent-up talent of the English smith. Without previous opportunities or education, the skilled labour the Frenchman Tijou required seems to have been at once to hand, enabling him to accomplish work that in every detail has never been surpassed. All his successors bore English names, and almost from the outset he found English rivals, superior in some ways even to himself as designers. Their work is indeed stately in form, admirable in transparency and well arranged balance of light and shade, no less than in practical directness of construction. Though some of the workers must have made fortunes, none took heed, in the truly English spirit, to make either contemporaries or posterity acquainted with their names or triumphs. Are such results possible now, after all our technical training and education, or has the past century of the factory system, centralization and professional control, rendered it impossible? The iron craftsmen, smiths and designers flourished then for some forty years, it would appear, without assistance from the architect or professional. That co-operation would, in the words of Sir Ernest George, have led to still grander results there can be no question. But instead, professional influence banished it almost completely, not only from the mansions, but from the gardens and parks of the noble and wealthy, and the demand was only kept up for a few years longer by the middle-class dwellers in the then suburbs of London and Provincial towns. History is like to repeat itself, for hardly has the present-day smith been trained to emulate the works of his predecessors, than he seems once more destined to find his occupation gone. Cast-iron geometric neo-grec treatments of the ruler and set square, less consistent than those of the early nineteenth

Introduction xxix

century, form the railings and balconies even to our richest and finest buildings, while gates to our parks, devoid of English character and owing little to the blacksmith, are to be handed down as the best that English talent of the first or second decades of the twentieth century could devise.

Though many of the charming old examples of gates and balustrades are here described or illustrated, the work is but half complete. It has been found impossible to treat the whole subject within the limits of a single volume. This present one is therefore restricted to objects the most liable to deterioration or destruction through exposure, leaving the rest, which are more sheltered within doors, to a future time. Though now much more appreciated by owners and the public generally, and likely to be preserved, the destructive agencies are unhappily not time and weather alone. The demand for old ironwork, which inevitably accompanies appreciation, has caused it to be greedily bought, and in many cases "faked" by the dealer to enhance its price, which has often become many times its value. Severed from its surroundings and associations, it hardly appears that much real sentiment can attach to old iron apart from beauty of design, and if new work is skilfully executed few experts can distinguish between old and modern. The greatest danger, however, lies in injudicious restoration, for examples subjected to the process entirely lose their interest and place in the art of the past.

The finely embossed leaf-work and masks, and other interesting features are either abolished as beyond the powers of the "restorer" to repair or reproduce, or they are travestied and lose the distinction and artistic touch which enables the work to be ascribed with certainty to its original designer. It will be seen in the following pages that some of the grandest examples have been defaced through ignorance and want of perception of the characteristics of the artist who originally produced them. In this connection the writer will be pleased to advise where the restoration of ironwork is contemplated. Old work is also often condemned as beyond repair, while it rarely is so in fact. In the Victoria and Albert Museum are the unique twelfth century hinges of St. Alban's Abbey, rescued and presented at the writer's request, and found to be in perfect condition. The thirteenth century grilles from Chichester, similarly displaced by " restoration " and rescued for the Museum, might, though dilapidated, have been repaired and held their place in the cathedral for centuries to come. Of the vast quantity of fine seventeenth and eighteenth century ironwork swept out of our churches during the " Gothic revival " and broken up or exposed to weather in gardens, it is impossible to speak. That this work is as yet adequately represented in our museums cannot be said, since no specimens of the work of any of the distinguished smiths, the subject of these pages, is known to be preserved in them.

There had been an almost complete collapse of decorative smithing in England between the fifteenth and seventeenth centuries, the more remarkable since it was then at its zenith in Germany, Spain and the Low Countries, and ours had always been famed for its iron production. When Britain first takes its place in history, though Cæsar supposed it to contain little iron, in some districts iron ring money and weapons were in use long before the Romans appeared. By the end of their occupation it was extensively used for a variety of purposes, including highly civilized appliances. It flourished as a craft during our Anglo-Saxon period, when no armed force entered the field without its complement of smiths. To smite and to smith are synonymous terms, and probably the familiar surname became well established when the call for the smith was constant in camp and field. With the Norman host a great complement of " Ferrers " arrived, their distinctive appellation, changed to farrier, being still maintained and specially attached to those having to do with horses. Later sobriquets, as Coalburn, Cokeburn, Chaffer, Naylor, and Goff, the Welsh for Smith, also carry back to smithing. In those days the smithing of weapons of offence and defence, horse trappings, implements of agriculture, tools, chains, anchors and such like must have provided ample employment and rendered the smith independent of merely decorative work, which at last fell far below the level of that produced on the continent. A brief sketch of decorative smithing in mediaeval days will be found on pages 1–8. In the days of Henry VIII the craft fell to its lowest ebb, when foreigners smithed for him, cast his cannon, made his armour, weapons, and gold and silver work. These were so honoured that on the public meeting at Greenwich of Henry and Anne of Cleves in 1539, the merchants of the steel-yard held the post of honour next the park pales, and beyond them were ranged those of Genoa, Florence, Venice and Spain. They enjoyed their privileges till Elizabeth closed the steel-yard.

The Production of Iron in England.

The Britons must have possessed the art of calcining the surface bog ores and pans, probably reducing them in underground chambers by a blast depending on the strength and direction of the wind. A small spongy mass would result, unusable until consolidated and the cinders and scoriae extruded by beating. Foot-bellows introduced later enabled the furnaces to produce daily blooms weighing about one cwt. The imperfect nature of the process and the length of time it was carried on are seen in the thousands of tons of slag and cinder since profitably smelted. More powerful bellows worked by water-wheels followed, doubling the production and extracting a greater proportion of the metal, but still producing the iron in the form of a bloom or spongy mass. The process of melting and casting iron practised in the Weald for a brief period and lost was revived when Henry VIII sent some of his foreign bronze founders to essay the casting of iron there. After this the foundries melted the ore by stronger blasts and fluxes and began to produce at the rate of two to three tons of iron daily in the modern form of pigs, which also passed through the fineries and forges before becoming merchantable. The sole fuel used in all these processes was wood-charcoal, causing the rapid disappearance of woods and forests. Elizabeth hardly checked this by enactments and limited monopolies. Meantime the blacksmiths, the actual workers in iron, used small sea coal in their forges. as more economical. Unemployment followed on the scarcity of wood, Dud Dudley estimating in 1626 that about 20,000 smiths and naylers living round Dudley were " ready to steal or starve."

In the period covered by our pages there probably still remained the 400 furnaces and iron mills of the Weald, some 200 in Wales, and as many in the Midlands, which latter must even then have been rapidly monopolizing the trade. The ore was melted by the aid of fluxes and supplied by the furnace masters in the form of pigs, about the size of billet wood, whence it passed into the fineries or chafferies for purification, or the pigs may have passed direct to the forges, where they became malleable under the great helve or tilt hammers, generally a separate business. Finally the iron was rendered merchantable in the slitting and rolling mills, where charcoal only was used, whence it was sold by the iron masters to the iron manufacturers in bars, rods, or plates. These worked it up into the various implements, etc., for which England had by the time of William and Mary become celebrated. The manufacturers used no charcoal, but only pit coal, and were persons of middling fortune, except the nailers who were in the lowest rank of life. In regarding the older work contrasted with the new we should consider how great must have been the expenditure of time and patience by the smith merely to bring the iron from the old to the present merchantable state. The resulting irregularity added a charm that modern work rarely possesses, while enhancing its cost. The heaviest part of the old smith's task is now accomplished at the mills before his modern descendant needs to use the hammer, since his iron is delivered to his orders in a vast variety of sections ready refined and even tempered to his use. Every needful thickness of plate or sheet iron, bars, round, square or oblong, of all required dimensions and of several qualities are now delivered at his door.

PROPERTIES OF THE METAL AND PROCESSES OF WORKING.

It is perhaps hardly necessary to remind our readers that the importance of the blacksmith to the community is in the first place due to the peculiar and valuable properties of iron and its abundance. If iron were one of the rarer, instead of the commonest of all metals, cost might limit, but not end its use. Neither the engineer, shipwright, builder, miner, quarryman, soldier, sailor or agriculturist could dispense with it, cost what it might. Happily it may be used by all for every purpose and in vast masses, if need be. Iron alone among metals can be "welded," that is separate pieces may be united by hammering at a relatively low temperature. Its strength, tenacity and hardness are increased by the process of tempering, or more profoundly by converting it into steel, effected either by impregnating the mass with a small percentage of carbon in closed chambers by heat, or by the direct admixture of ore containing carbon. Nor do these unique properties affect in any way those it possesses in common with other metals, for it can be cast, carved, chased, hammered, rolled, drawn, pressed, punched, embossed, stamped, inlaid, polished, turned, planed, sawn, filed or drilled.

In conclusion a few words on the craft of the blacksmith may not be out of place. The salient characteristic is that his chief operations are hurried ; he may ponder and think over important works, but once undertaken he must strike while the iron is hot, the heat and glare in his eyes, amidst showers of sparks, while the telling blows are delivered by assistant hammermen. His results under such conditions cannot fail to be more or less impressionist, and hence perhaps they appeal so strongly to the artistic sense. The interior of the smithy, though dark and grimy, seems dear to the poetic mind, and the work begets a spirit of sturdy independence in its votaries. The craft itself is fascinating not only from its antiquity and primitive methods, but in the importance of its results. Indeed the art as practised now can differ but little from that of the far off days of fabled Cyclops, Thor or Vulcan, and the tools used by St. Dunstan, said to be preserved at Mayfield, hardly differ from those of to-day.

The smith's plant is simple and consists of an open hearth or forge, wherewith to heat the iron, furnished with bellows to create and a hood or chimney to quicken the draft and convey away the fumes; also a trough of water to quench the heated iron, and an anvil on which to hammer it. The small tools are an assortment of tongs, chisels and punches of various sizes; and a stout leather apron as a protection from sparks violently extruded by the blows, completes the equipment. Coke broken up, screened and washed to free it from impurities which would affect the quality of the iron, is now the fuel in lieu of charcoal.

The iron is delivered in bars about 16 feet in length, and plates; the former of many sections, round, square, or oblong, and of many sizes. The least are classed as nail-rod, hoop-iron, and wire, and are done up in bundles. There are several qualities from low grades imported from Belgium, to the expensive Lowmoor and charcoal iron. The cheaper is apt to be granular and brittle, while the better is fibrous and tough. Intermediate qualities, made in England and branded to denote the grades are ordinarily used. The quality depends on that of the cast pigs or ingots from which the bars are made, but still more on the puddling which converts the iron from cast to malleable, and on the hammering previous to rolling.

While heated, iron is softer and more pliable than lead, and in this state two or more pieces can be welded together, in other words made one by a few smart blows of the hammer. This joining of various pieces can be carried to any reasonable extent, so that smaller objects, whether of refined simplicity or great elaboration, and even considerable works, may be completed without any further process. While normal rigidity is temporarily lost under heat, bar iron is made with slight effort to take the form of scrolls and curving lines, and we thus in every age find the scroll a principal element in decorative smithing. This property has in fact dictated the form of the anvil from remote antiquity: it bears a flat, oblong surface above, produced into a sharp conical beak in front, over which the bars are bent. Scrolling is the simplest operation but the volutes end variously, either merely rolled or with solid centres, said to be "snubbed," or beaten thin and spread, called "fish-tailed," or rolled round a short bar and produced spirally, or beaten on edge into a flat central disc.

Scrolls are usually to some extent clothed with leaves, the simplest of which are cut from plate, waved or crinkled along the margins, and welded to the stem. The most elaborate are based on the classic acanthus richly modelled and indented, in stout sheet iron, and welded. These only occur on the richer work, and in England not prior to William III. In the tufts of bay and other leaves seen so frequently in our examples, the leaves are fashioned from bar iron and welded piece by piece to the stems, and then to each other, until the clusters are complete. A simpler way is to flatten the end of the bar into the semblance of a leaf twisted over, but such leaves are only used singly or in pairs, and in later work. Balustered forms and moulding in relief are usually hammered between top and bottom tools or swages, in which the required form is sunk in intaglio. The hot iron is compressed between these by sledge hammer blows.

Objects built up of many separate forgings, such as gates, require to be fitted, which is accomplished without heat and mainly by tenons and rivets, and by halving and inlaying bars which cross, or passing one through the other. To this end holes can be drifted through the bars while hot by the smith, causing slight lateral swellings, which may have suggested the more elaborate process of insertion, by welding, of wider pieces with carefully prepared angles and squared holes for the passage of each bar. The modern and simplest way is to punch pieces clean out of the bars by hydraulic pressure while cold. Examples comprising all these processes will be found among the illustrations.

MEDIAEVAL IRONWORK

Mediaeval Ironwork

A BRIEF sketch of the development of decorative iron in England during mediaeval times may be of interest as an introduction to the consideration of later work, though this cannot be complete, since so little of the ironwork, with which our Cathedrals and Abbeys once almost certainly abounded, has been suffered to remain; the majority of them are now destitute of the gilded and elaborately coloured screens and gates which formed in mediaeval times a beautiful feature of their brightly decorated interiors.

The tenacity of iron led very early to its use in strengthening doors, the most vulnerable parts of buildings, when their capacity for resisting was of the utmost consequence to the inmates. Its use for this purpose remained almost undiminished throughout the troubled centuries of our mediaeval history. As with ships, doors continued to be made in England of oak, the strongest material to hand, until the possibility of producing them wholly of iron was realized. Probably no door of Anglo-Saxon date is preserved, but careful delineations of them exist in pictures and sculpture which show that strap hinges with diverging scrolls, of simple and conventional type, were in common use. In some rare cases they are reinforced by a more elaborate system of scrolls and straps, introduced both for decorative effect and to bind the planks of the door more effectively together. Rich results were obtained, for the ironwork in these cases was probably gilt and laid over some scarlet material or pigment. No sudden change followed the Norman invasion, doorways remaining practically the same except that they were increased in size.

In time the system of reinforcing and enriching doors with defensive scroll or geometric work in addition to the hinges, became general, not only to the outsides, but to the insides of doors as well. The iron was gilded and laid over skins dyed scarlet, or sometimes azure. Tradition has it that the skins were of sacrilegious Danes, and doors have been found actually covered with human skins, like a door in Worcester Cathedral, and four of the doors in Westminster Abbey. Still, existing examples of ironwork applied to the interiors of doors are by no means numerous. Among the finest examples are the doors to the Chapter House at York, those to Worksop Priory, and the doors removed from the Chapel of Henry III to the adjacent St. George's Chapel at Windsor. Treasury and sacristy doors were especially strengthened, and in the crypt under the Chapter House at Wells is a most interesting thirteenth century door completely sheathed externally with iron, reinforced with decorative straps intersecting at various angles. Evelyn, visiting Bury St. Edmunds in 1672, observed "the gates are wood but quite plated over with iron," yet examples of this are so rare that it could at no period have been a general practice with us. Almost the same result was obtained by setting bands of interlacing hoop-iron closely together. In Central Europe, however, doors of important churches were commonly sheathed with iron in the fifteenth and sixteenth centuries, decorated with diapers of heraldic devices, tinned or gilt on brightly coloured grounds. No doubt this custom either had an independent origin, or, more probably perhaps, was derived from doors of Northern Italy and the nearer East.

Of more interest is the origin of the open-work lattice gate constructed entirely of iron, which may have existed in ancient Rome, or been brought into existence in early mediaeval times in Italy. The construction of some of the early Italian gates suggests that the lattice binding and hinges were found to make serviceable gates without any wood.

But probably the use of gates wholly of iron was led up to more directly at a somewhat later period, and became general. The shrines and altars of Christian Churches were railed off almost from the time of Constantine, at first by wood or stone, later by bronze or iron. In the twelfth and thirteenth centuries choirs and chapels became protected by highly decorative grilles. Especially was this the case in Italy, France, Germany and Spain, where they at last culminated in the majestic and magnificent *réjas* of Spanish cathedrals. Parts of all these had to be hinged to allow passage way, and thus iron gates, whether in screens or fixed to stonework, became familiar objects in ecclesiastical buildings.

Our earliest existing iron gates, in Winchester Cathedral, date from about 1093, and once protected the high altar and shrine of St. Swithin from the swarming pilgrims who entered the body of the church. They consist of a stout rectangular framing filled up by scrolls of a design which later extended to France and Spain. That similar protection existed to the high altar at Canterbury is clear from the graphic account of Becket's death in 1170. A gate of scrolled iron still closes St. Anselm's Chapel there, dating from about 1333. Edward I was a considerable user of iron, the still remaining grill in Westminster Abbey having been made to his order in 1294 by Thomas de Leghtone. Four years previously he had paid Master Henry of Lewes for the no longer existing ironwork to the tomb of his father, Henry III, and he also employed Alexander le Imaginator to make the ironwork for the monument containing Queen Eleanor's heart in the church of the Friar's Predicant in London. The accounts further disclose that he caused some at least of the Eleanor crosses to be protected by iron railings. An existing grill in St. Alban's Abbey, protecting the shrine,

Mediaeval Ironwork

also falls within his reign. This is formed of fourteen strongly framed panels filled with bars which intersect each other diagonally in each alternate panel and rectangularly in the remainder, the bars being half-inch half-round, placed back to back and secured together by large decorative rivets. The frames are moulded and there is a delicate border of quatrefoils. But one choir grill of iron remains complete in England, at Lincoln, and consists of massy frames entirely filled with delicate C shaped scrolls, produced like similar examples abroad, in the twelfth century. Remains of a thirteenth century example removed from Chichester Cathedral during a " restoration " are now in the Victoria and Albert Museum, together with a gate of intersecting bars with the spaces filled with quatrefoils. A pair of early fifteenth century gates shut the choir from the south aisle of Canterbury, of geometric design derived from a wooden trellis.

A gate of more elaborate construction closes the chantry of Henry V in Westminster Abbey, made to the order of Henry VI in 1431 by Roger Johnson of London. It consists of an open diaper, also designed from a wooden trellis, with an architectural filling to the arch above, formerly richly coloured and gilt with royal heraldry. A similar but more rudely worked trellis design closes certain openings in the choir at Salisbury, and remains show that the same design was used at Christchurch, Hants. These geometric designs are of different technique to those which preceded them. Doors constructed in various ways of bars crossing or interpenetrating at right angles may be seen at Warwick in the Beauchamp Chapel, the crypts at York, Arundel and other churches. A beautiful chancel screen, of fifteenth century architectural design, also exists at Arundel. But by far the most splendid iron gates existing in England are in St. George's Chapel, Windsor, to the right of the altar over the spot where Edward IV was buried. They are 7 feet high with lofty hexagonal piers, designed in the richest style of late fifteenth century architecture, and were still gilt when seen by Gough the antiquary. Tradition is probably correct as to the work being part of the sumptuous monument to commemorate Edward IV, who was greatly lamented; they were perhaps ordered during his life. It resembles work by Josse Matsys of Louvain, a distinguished craftsman in his day. A second and probably somewhat later specimen of Low Country work, possibly from the same atelier, is not dissimilar, except in the more florid and naturalesque intertwining branches filling the arch, which match in some respects those of the famous Antwerp well cover: these gates close Bishop West's Chapel in Ely Cathedral. Near them, closing Bishop Alcock's Chapel, are sedate-looking English gates of about 1488, of vertical bars, half of which tenon into the top frame with tracery between, the rest stopping short and ending in fleurs-de-lis riveted between two hinge-like battlemented straps; while between two horizontals at the base, through which all the bars pass, are small quatrefoils. This gate is practically of approved modern construction, except as to the central horizontal rail, and has stood the test of four centuries without a sign of failure or decay. The evolution of these mediaeval examples is of great interest, but to trace the story fully the similar gates remaining in Italy, France, the Netherlands, Germany and Spain would have to be considered, countries with which our history was at one time or another intimately connected.

Our period of decorative ironworking did not outlast the fifteenth century, though the sixteenth century was the most expansive elsewhere. The feudal fortress was passing away, and our Tudor kings and queens lacked neither riches nor enterprise, and loved to display their wealth and artistic leanings. Their patronage of artists and craftsmen from all parts of Europe was lavish, and they were the first in England to create splendid dwellings of modern type, adorned with statues and fountains and surrounded by gardens and parks. It would have appeared safe at the time to predict that the opening century would prove a red-letter one for the workers in iron and steel in England. Yet while its beginning saw our churches full of fine ironwork only waiting apparently to share with architecture in further developments, ironworking actually remained with us for two centuries a dwindling and dormant industry.

Abroad, on the contrary, especially in the vast empire of Charles V, the grandest creations in iron were being produced. The marvellously intricate threaded and thistle work in which the Teutonic smiths revelled, the finely designed fluted armour of Maximilian, and the superbly embossed and damascened suits made in Augsburg by the sister craft for kings and emperors; and above all perhaps the astounding throne of chiselled iron made in the same city for the Emperor Rudolph and now at Longford Castle, all belong to the sixteenth century. Spain simultaneously produced the glorious *réjas* or choir screens, each eclipsing the rest, in which the smiths delighted to introduce forgings of ever-increasing size and difficulty. North Italy too continued to produce screens and grills and gates, while surpassing even Germany in the beauty and strength of its embossed and damascened armour and arms; so that Tuscany, the Milanese, and Venetia shared with Augsburg the supply of the civilized world. In France a decline is visible, for the locksmiths alone maintained and added to their reputation. Yet while the iron and steel crafts were flourishing and at their zenith in the rest of Europe throughout the sixteenth century, no century is more barren in England of works in iron or steel.

To form a comprehensive idea of the decorative defensive ironwork of the sixteenth century, far-away towns of North Italy must be visited. In Venice, Verona, Pisa and Lucca the windows of important residences were safeguarded by iron bars, and grills of great beauty fill the semicircular openings of palace gateways. In Spain windows are sometimes handsomely grilled, and in a few towns entrances to houses of any pretence are provided with richly wrought gates in front of the ordinary doors. Throughout Germany too most elaborate iron defences to doors and windows were in vogue, while the crafts also revived with our nearer neighbours.

In England it was otherwise. The prolonged Wars of the Roses were being waged at the doors of our smiths. They were sinewy men, and to join the fray may have seemed to them in those days but an interlude of their calling. Perhaps in the end they were cropped as completely as their noble patrons, for no armourers and few native-born smiths seem to have been left in England when the final peace came with the triumph of the Tudors. The succeeding generation may have been disheartened by the numbers of skilled Italian and other craftsmen who flocked over to fill their place. Under Henry VIII foreigners monopolized almost all the art work then required. During this century moreover the dwellings of the nobility and merchant princes passed from an excess of defensive precautions to an opposite extreme of almost ostentatious self-reliance. In any case, neither then nor when taste later affected an academic classic, nor indeed while the Palladian influence of Inigo Jones prevailed, was there any revival, and few decorative gates, railings, balusters, balconies, or window grilles were required from the English smith.

THE EVOLUTION OF GATES

Mediaeval Gates

IN churches the ironwork, whether used for strengthening woodwork, or for gates and grilles, was employed for a twofold purpose: to protect and also to contribute to the general decorative effect. Prior to the Norman Conquest contemporary illustrations show that the same ideas prevailed for domestic work. After the momentous day, when the Normans suddenly subjugated a numerous and warlike population, the luxuries of living and intercourse of civilization ceased, for the conquerors were compelled to live practically in intrenched camps, which became impregnable fortresses, whence they could strike and where they could take refuge. When revolt of the conquered was no longer feared, the conquerors quarrelled and the castle became even more grim and forbidding, for it was now exposed to more determined and systematic attacks. The keep was the dwelling, and held the family, the treasure house and the chapel, all that was dear, precious and sacred. Around it was a space environed by embattled walls and towers of immense strength and thickness, loopholed for missiles, and surrounded by a deep moat or at least a formidable trench. These in many cases were made even more secure by an outer system of walls and bastions, such as may be seen in Dover Castle. The entrance was the one vulnerable spot, and to render this secure every device ingenuity could suggest was resorted to. When cities were licensed to fortify, the defence of their gateways was equally of moment and became so complete, that though clever stratagems to rush them while opened for

Mediaeval Gates

traffic might succeed, or they might be opened by treachery from within, it was otherwise less dangerous to attempt to scale or breach the massy walls than to give the assault direct to the gates. These were religiously closed at a given hour, and the belated wayfarer was excluded for the night.

Unless the castle was perched, like Bamborough, on an inaccessible rock, the securest defence to the gates was the drawbridge. Whether a fortress dwelling commanding the road, like Alnwick, or a moated castle of a lesser baron in the shelter of a hollow, the drawbridge was at once the sole means of access, which could instantly be cut off by raising it, when it became a shield of immense strength in front of the entrance, impervious to missiles. Behind this were the massive oaken gates, bolted and barred and studded with iron, and, even more reliable, the portcullis, shod with iron and working in deep grooves, drawn upward by iron chains into the chamber over the gate. There was always one and sometimes more of these, and they were let drop so suddenly as to merit the name of " cataracts."

FIG. I. THE CASTLE GATE, CARISBROOKE, GUARDED BY A PORTCULLIS.

Adventurous enemies attempting the gates were sometimes entrapped by them. The portcullis was held in such consideration that it became adopted as one of the chief badges of the Tudor sovereigns.

It is unlikely that any of the very few still in use are originals, but with the gates it is otherwise. Those to Carisbrooke (Fig. 1), of the fifteenth century, with hinges and wicket, are shown, and also the more unusual pair to Maxstoke (Fig. 2), sheathed externally with overlapping plates of iron strengthened by horizontal bars, a protection according to Dugdale added by the Earl of Stafford, about 1432, with the Stafford knot and arms seen on the middle band. The fine and perfect doors to Dunster Castle (Fig. 3) present a complete lattice work of iron within and without of stout iron bars, fixed by large and numerous rivets to the wood, which thus becomes of secondary importance, and prepares the way for the "yetts."

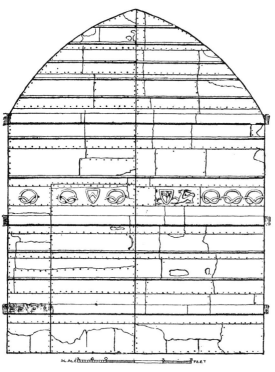

FIG. 2. CASTLE GATE SHEATHED IN IRON, MAXSTOKE. PROTECTED IN FRONT BY A PORTCULLIS. DATE ABOUT 1432.

Later, iron gates in some cases took the place of the portcullis as second or third defences, and they equally permitted, if need be, the defenders to cross weapons with the assailants without a sortie. Leland, writing about 1538, mentions that Raby and Durham castles were provided with exceedingly strong gates of iron, and there was also an iron gate opening from the Tower to Tower Hill. In England they were called yat or yeat, and were to be found to many dwellings in the marches bordering Wales. But it is along the northern marches, exposed perpetually to raids

FIG. 3. DOORS TO DUNSTER CASTLE, SOMERSET.

until England and Scotland were united, that they are chiefly to be found. Upwards of two score still exist, known as yetts, and a list of them was published by the Society of Antiquaries of

14 English Ironwork of the XVIIth and XVIIIth Centuries

Scotland in 1883. The stout horizontal and vertical bars pass through each other alternately so as to afford the maximum of resistance. Even the churches on both sides the border had them until

FIG. 4. THE DOOR AND THE YETT AT GLAMIS CASTLE.

Mediaeval Gates

James I ordered them to be destroyed. They are plain lattice work and though no decoration was wasted on them, they are picturesque in their rugged strength, and the massive swellings where the bars interpenetrate create a not unpleasing chequer, as may be seen by visitors ascending the staircase to the Regalia in Edinburgh Castle. The illustration shows a door to Glamis Castle, reinforced by a yett (Fig. 4). They were opened in token of surrender. A curious illumination to De Commines' copy of Froissart shows an iron Lid gate, a name given to a small postern with a gate swung overhead like a lid, as Mr. W. J. Loftie informs us. It is represented open for a procession of knights and dames, and the pivots on which it swings are clearly shown. The costume is about 1450. It recalls Bishop Alcock's gate at Ely, date about 1488, for it is of round bars, with shorter fleur-de-lis ended bars between.

FROM AN ILLUSTRATION OF THE MS. COPY OF
FROISSART. MADE FOR P. DE COMMINES.

Fore-Court and Garden Gates in Renaissance Times

IN the palaces and mansions, colleges and other foundations built during the reign of Henry VIII, the single entrance was adhered to and generally opened directly on to the highway. The dormitories and domestic offices completely enclosed one or more courtyards, and the family dwelling was at the end farthest from the gate-house, with its guard-room or porter's lodge. This reproduced in a way the outer and inner ballia of a castle, both of which had to be traversed in order to approach the keep or family dwelling. The complete privacy of the castle was maintained, as well as its security, by massive oaken doors well bolted and barred. Such are the houses of Knole, Hampton Court, or Eton College, built in the sixteenth century, while others, like Northumberland House, had but one courtyard. These closed courts prevailed until Dr. Caius, when building Caius College in 1565, directed that the south side, away from the high-road, should never be enclosed "for fear the air should become foul." It was therefore only closed by a wall of moderate height with a gate in the centre. This was the first inception of the fore-court. A want of dignity must have been felt by those used to buildings approached through several courts, and we soon find walled courts added in front, which led to houses being built away from the highway in the midst of their own domain. Bacon laid down that a perfect house should possess not less than three courts, a plain green one or fore-court, walled; a second court with its walls embellished with turrets or other ornaments, and an inner court surrounded by cloisters roofed with lead. Where there was ample ground bass-courts were built to stables and farm buildings, while gardens, orchards and pleasure grounds of various sorts were equally walled in for privacy and protection. These were grouped, the garden at the back and the rest adjoining, so that the house was completely environed by a system of walled enclosures. All these communicated by gates, first high and of wood when security and privacy were the great desiderata, but as ideas and fashions changed the wooden gates were lowered in the centre after an Italian fashion, and a cresting of iron spikes added to keep them defensive. Later their wooden panels were sometimes pierced or replaced by vertical iron bars, at first the upper ones but later the lower ones as well, and finally the entire framing became replaced by iron. The wooden construction was adhered to in the iron gates of the first half of the seventeenth century, and for a time the far superior construction of mediaeval gates was completely forgotten. With the lowered gates and Italian taste came the stately stone gate-piers capped with balls or vases; and the courts, often raised one above another by steps, were paved and adorned with fountains and laid out with grass plats, so that coaches could enter the outer courts, but not set visitors down at the front door. It seems that first the gates of the outer court were widened to admit these, and then the inner gates; while other gates in the side walls appear to give more direct access to the stables. The introduction of coaches certainly influenced the dimensions of courtyard gates. The Earl of Arundel of the time of Mary is reputed to be the first who rode in a coach in England, and Lord Grey de Wilton the first to import a coach into England, while Marshal Bassompierre, when French ambassador, was the first to ride in England in a coach with glass windows. To the Duke of Buckingham was owed the introduction of the great travelling coach and six. With these the time-honoured tradition which secluded the dwelling by surrounding it on all sides with high-walled courts and gardens began to pass away, and an increasing desire for ostentation was checked not only by the innate refinement of Charles I, but later by the Revolution. After the Restoration we find massive stone piers removed in favour of pilasters of open ironwork, and the front walls of brick or stone lowered for half their height and replaced by railings of iron. Finally the entire fronts of fore-courts were bowed out, with high and transparent iron railings on low stone-copings.

These changes can be followed in the engravings of country seats of the late seventeenth and early eighteenth centuries, in which the general forms of the rails and gates are easily recognized. In the earlier all the gates still appear of solid wood, but under Charles II the wooden panels are occasionally pierced geometrically. Garden gates were of lattice, wood or iron, and one such is represented to a fore-court at Burney House, Nottinghamshire, 1677. Hide Hall and the Hoo in Hertfordshire, 1700, have the old-fashioned wooden gates with crestings of iron fleurs-de-lis, but most others are lowered towards the centre like a reflected arch, with their spiked crestings more or less decoratively treated. Several examples still remain in London. A replacement of the solid wooden panels of gates by bars of iron is seen, and there are attempts to make these decorative by waving or twisting. At Groombridge Place is a fine pair of gates (Fig. 5) of heavy wooden framing filled with vertical iron bars and surmounted by a cresting of sharp spikes, rendered decorative by an occasional fleur-de-lis: a second pair there of the same form is deeply interesting, being wholly of iron. The finest gates of this kind are those closing the Warburton Chapel in St. John's Church, Chester, very decorative and in perfect preservation. The numerous stately stone piers of Canons Ashby, surmounted by obelisks elevated on scrolls, and by family crests, held gates of

Fore-Court and Garden Gates

wood, two or three of which remain, one curiously framed and filled in with iron bars. Iron was also associated with wooden gates in various other ways. Over the fine doors at Blickling

FIG. 5. WOODEN GATES WITH IRON BARS AND CRESTING AT GROOMBRIDGE PLACE, KENT. LATER XVIITH CENTURY.

is an open timber semicircular grill, the spaces filled by iron fleurs-de-lis. Gates to Brewers' Hall in London have an upper story of vertical iron bars. Kennet's *History of Ambrosden and Burcester*, 1695, shows the fore-court to Sir William Glynne's house, commenced 1675, closed by triple gates, of which probably only the centre one opened, all of wood except large panels of twisted iron bars under a moulded beam with fleur-de-lis iron cresting. The palings at either side look as if of wood shaped into spearheads above. Sarsden (Fig. 6), in the same book, built 1640, is remarkable for palings of wood of the usual form, with gates to match, the stout stakes of wood alternating with bars of tightly twisted iron with

FIG. 6. ENTRANCE GATES AND RAILINGS TO SARSDEN, NEAR CHIPPING NORTON, DRAWN IN 1695, THE FRAMING AND ONE-HALF OF THE VERTICAL BARS OF WOOD, THE REST OF IRON—NOW DESTROYED.

elaborate fleur-de-lis heads. Many such combinations are shown in Chauncey's *History of Herts*, 1700, and we must conclude that wooden gates to fore-courts were retained in many cases from choice, because best suited to English tradition and requirements, and in others to save expense. Iron gates were in use abroad at this time, especially in Italy, Germany, and Spain, countries with which travelled Englishmen were familiar. Though seldom

Fore-Court and Garden Gates

pictorially represented until the end of the seventeenth century, their existence in England is occasionally mentioned, and they were evidently used here when conditions required them, just as wooden gates are used to-day when iron gates are unsuitable.

It is strange, however, considering the excellent construction of mediaeval iron gates, to find that some remaining of the times of Elizabeth or James I are much more primitive, and smith-craft must have sadly retrograded. Gates (Fig. 7) existing at Cote Bampton in Oxfordshire, though entirely of iron, are constructed, like others of the same date, in all respects as if of wood, all the spiked vertical bars being riveted between horizontal hinge straps like the planks of an old church door. The twisted bars surmounted by very large fleur-de-lis or broad spear-headed spikes alternating with smaller plain spiked bars present a striking effect.

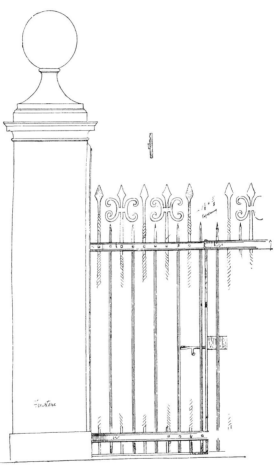

FIG. 7. IRON GATES AT COTE BAMPTON, OXFORDSHIRE.

A somewhat older pair close the Abbey porch at Cirencester, about 8 feet 2 inch wide and 8 feet 6 inches high and some 2 feet lower in the centre. The hinged straps between which the vertical bars are secured, are moulded and beaten into short scrolls, and taper as if intended for wooden doors, and are about $2\frac{1}{8}$ inches wide, $\frac{3}{8}$ inch thick. One pair of straps is fixed a little above the centre, the other near the base, while a third pair curved form a top horizontal between which the twenty-two verticals rise, their spikes, short and plain, alternating with boldly designed fleurs-de-lis. The spaces between are $4\frac{1}{4}$ inches from centre to centre, each alternate bar tightly twisted, $1\frac{1}{4}$ inches diameter, the rest 1 inch in diameter and roughly octagonal. The back standards finish in scrolls, and all the verticals tenon into a flat bottom-bar 2 inches wide and a bare quarter of an inch in thickness, a short spike between each presenting a primitive form of the later dog-bar. Gates of somewhat similar construction close the porches of Llandaff and Hereford Cathedrals. These are later, and the only important differences are that all the verticals are cut in two by a double lock-rail with scroll filling of tulip leaves and four-petalled rosettes, and they finish without passing through the top horizontal. There are no dog-bars, and the back standards are not scrolled, but separate scrolls are riveted to them giving the same appearance. In place of spikes, a cresting of somewhat defensive scrolls and leaves is riveted to the top bar at Hereford, but is absent at Llandaff, though the two gates are evidently by the same maker. These gates in front of church doors were required after the Reformation, when doors were kept locked between the services, to prevent access when opened for necessary airing, especially where there were porches.

By far the most important gates of Elizabethan or early Stuart date are those to Cowdray House (Figs. 8 and 9), which, unless made up in part from older iron standards and bars from Battle Abbey, certainly form the earliest known screen entirely of iron comprising double and single gates and fixed panels between stone piers. Like those of Groombridge they may owe their existence to the proximity of Wealden forges. The main gates, 10 feet wide and 8 feet high, were hung from rich standards 2 inches in diameter,

FIG. 8. IRON GATES TO COWDRAY HOUSE, SUSSEX, WITH FIXED SIDE PANELS AND A WICKET, IN THEIR PRESENT CONDITION.

with Gothic caps and bases and mouldings on the front and backs; fifteen or twenty years ago they opened over quadrants. On either side are fixed panels, each about 4 feet 6 inches wide, identical with the gates, and beyond these on one side a wicket gate 4 feet wide to match, the whole width thus extending to 23 feet. The vertical bars of which these are composed are $\frac{7}{8}$ inch in section, riveted diagonally between the top and bottom horizontals, and spaced $4\frac{3}{4}$ inches from centre to centre. The top horizontal and the single lock-rail are 2 inches wide and about $\frac{5}{8}$ thick, finished with cable edgings. Above and below the latter, and below the top rail are fringes of C scrolls between the verticals, $\frac{7}{8}$ wide and $\frac{1}{4}$ thick, thinned off and finished with solid ends. All the bars are riveted into the plain bottom rail, as well as between

24 English Ironwork of the XVIIth and XVIIIth Centuries

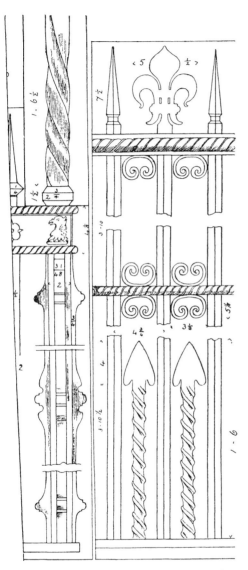

FIG. 9.   DETAILS OF COWDRAY GATES.

each, short twisted spikes with ends flattened like harpoons for dog-bars. A cresting of alternately plain and fleur-de-lis spikes is riveted along the top to look as if the bars passed through it. It is a peculiarity, common to all these gates, that the smiths seemed oblivious of making the vertical bars penetrate through the horizontals as in mediaeval work. These gates were sketched and measured many years ago, in the south wall of the Park, with the fine old standards and hangings complete (Fig. 9); they were still practicable with the standards mutilated until a few years ago, but are now brought up to the roadway, the gates made fixtures, a new wicket added, and the old standards discarded (Fig. 8).

Gates of iron retaining the central dip are frequently represented in engravings as carrying very large shields of arms, which must have opened in an awkward way—like the Victorian cast-iron

Fore-Court and Garden Gates

FIG. 10. GATES TO TRAQUAIR CASTLE, SCOTLAND.

gates to Kew Gardens. Entrance gates have always presented favoured sites for coats of arms, which denote at once the family and rank of the owner. The shields were at first merely supported by a pair of scrolls, but the tendency developed towards a richer treatment. Few now exist, and as the lowered centre practically merely lessened the strain on the back standards and presented no other advantage, it was soon abandoned.

The gates to Traquair Castle (Fig. 10) present a good example of the treatment of gates in the time of James II. The next step proved a most important one, and speedily led up to a much grander and more stately conformation of the entrance gates. The shields and their now elaborated scrolled supports were severed from the gate tops and placed above them on an independent fixed and rigid bar, which not only acted as a stretcher between the piers, but completed the framing of the gates, so that henceforth gates of importance opened between fixed panels and under an overthrow. Their later development, on well-defined constructional lines, necessitated by the increasing grandeur of the designs, was inevitable. The simple shield of arms ceased to suffice, and the crest, coronet, supporters and motto were required to be displayed in addition, necessitating a more elaborate and pyramidal system of scrolled supports. Such top-hamper could not be carried on any reasonable single bar, and the base of the overthrow took the form of a latticed girder, or two bars braced together by scrolls. This required corresponding piers for support, and led to the four-sided and H-plans, which for symmetry were also provided with pyramidal tops. These aspiring pinnacles led, like the pinnacled buttresses and *flèches* of Gothic architecture, to a lofty perpendicular treatment. But this is anticipating. The gates to the northern entrance of Ham House (Plate 1), follow closely in design the contemporary wood-framed gates with iron bars: they are, however, entirely of iron, and consist of a massive framing of thick plate iron with four

Plate I.

NORTHERN ENTRANCE GATES TO HAM HOUSE, SURREY.
The House built by Sir T. Vavasour in 1610.

Plate II.

WEST GATES TO HAM HOUSE.

equal panels, the two central of these opening, the others fixed. They consist of ¾-inch vertical bars set diagonally which, unlike those previously described, pass through holes in the horizontals. The holes are drifted, that is driven through the bars by punches while hot, the iron being merely displaced instead of cut out clean and removed as in later processes, the resulting difference being a swelling of the bar at every hole. Both ends of the bars are flattened and bent over, and riveted to the plate iron of the framing. The heavy back standards finish above in small onion shaped finials. The overthrow is a single horizontal bar furnished with a row of long and plain spikes. Simple, lofty, and dignified, these gates appear the more impressive between their great stone piers capped with globose vases. These are perhaps not very much later than the house, built by Sir Thomas Vavasour in 1610. There are south gates (Plate 11) of the same dimensions, constructed like the north gates, but with less massive framing and a plain bar for overthrow, surmounted by a round shield of arms and coronet supported by scrolls. There are fringes of scrolls to the horizontals and arrow-pointed dog-bars with scrolls on either side fixed between two plates vertically placed instead of a bottom bar. The fringe of larger scrolls below the top-bar, and of smaller above and below the lock-bar, and the dog-bars give a richer if more modern effect. The overthrow comprises scrolls supporting a finial of drooping tulip-shaped flowers over the gates and plain and waved spikes over the panels. Gates and panels are between massive stone piers of Italian design. A third pair not illustrated has been engraved by Mr. D. J. Ebbetts in *Decorative Wrought-Iron Work*.

THE GARDEN

In all these fore-court gates there seems no wish to conceal but only to keep out intruders. Garden gates were smaller and less ambitious.

The garden gate is seen at its best when providing a picturesque break in the long high and mellow garden wall of brick or stone, or in tall clipped hedges of yew or privet. They combine agreeably with stone terraces and steps, and among fountains, figures, and vases, decorative iron gates and balustrades find their appropriate place. In the modern gardens, if judiciously placed, they enhance the beauty of the vista, the brilliancy of the flowering plants and green of the lawns, and provide a welcome foil to dense masses of shrubs. The history of the garden has been ably dealt with by many writers and need only be referred to here in respect to iron gates. When the mansion was situated, both in England and France, between the fore-courts in front and the formal garden at the back, many gates were required. The formal garden itself was a legacy of Roman civilization, for the Roman garden was closed in by walls or hedges and plentifully adorned with porticos, fountains, statues, vases, and arbours, and trees clipped fantastically by the *Topiarius*. Neither were grills and gates of bronze or iron unknown to the Romans, who possibly used them in their gardens, though no delineations of such exist.

Though none could possibly have survived the destructive Germanic invasion of England, the earliest gardens recorded, after the country had settled down under Plantagenet rule, are formal, with fountains, shady walks, arbours, seats, flower-beds of intricate design, walled in by clipt hedges, iron hurdles, trellises, or wattle-work. The notices of them are scanty, but a few of the illuminated manuscripts show glimpses of their arrangement. The garden of Woodstock is mentioned because Henry I kept a menagerie in it, including a favourite porcupine, and his nephew, Henry II, made it the site of Fair Rosamond's bower. A precept of Henry III, in his twenty-fifth year, to his keepers of the Palace of Woodstock required them to " cause an extension of the iron trellises on the steps leading from our chambers to the Herbarium." The citizens of London already enjoyed in this reign the gardens of fruits and herbs to their villas, as well as of roses, the ever popular flower since the days of Rome. A description of the gardens at Windsor exists from the pen of James I of Scotland, while a captive to Henry IV. He saw them hedged and railed with alleys, bowers, groves, mounds on which were garden houses, and the sweetest flowers. The Italians of the sixteenth century were laying out formal gardens to the splendid villas, Albani, Pamfili, Ludovici, building for dignitaries of the Church, and gardens in England expanded considerably under their influence. These were replete with well-trimmed hawthorn, privet, and hazel, if not also with box and yew, and diversified with shaded walks, mazes with cypress trees in their midst, fountains, statues, vases, sundials, summer and banqueting houses, in short with all the coolness, shade, and mystery of the Italian originals noticed by Du Cerceau; to which were added the old English lawns and bowling greens, nothing being more pleasant to the eye, as Bacon said, than green grass kept finely shorn. To the Italians were handed over by Henry VIII the extensive formal gardens and orchards laid out by Wolsey, and a few years later they laid out the gardens of Nonsuch, which contained marble and bronze fountains and obelisks, and other curious devices. A picture at Hampton Court of the family of Henry VIII affords a glimpse of his garden there, with trim parterres and the King's beasts on posts striped with the Tudor white and green like barbers' poles. The Duke de Najera speaks of the garden at Whitehall in Queen Mary's time as extremely well laid out with high corridors and walks on each of its four sides, and within them busts of men and women, children, birds, monsters, and other figures, both above and below. We know that Francois I had adorned and laid out the gardens of the Louvre with statuary. The almost contemporary Theobald's Gardens were surrounded entirely by water and comprised a garden house full of statuary and a banqueting house, besides the usual statues, pyramids, labyrinths, columns of marble, stone and wood, and so on. James I attracted to England André Nollet, the last of three celebrated gardeners of the name, and the French influence then becomes noticeable. He exchanged with Lord Burleigh his house at Hatfield against Theobald's, on account of its famous gardens, which were exciting considerable interest at the time, essays being written on them by Bacon and others. History is silent as to the existence of beautiful iron gates in the formal gardens of the Tudors, but such magnificent displays of summer or banqueting or garden houses, terraces, temples, and cloisters as there were at Moor Park, Herts, by Sir Richard Temple, or at Wilton by Isaac de Caux, must, we may suppose, have comprised decorative gates. Their disappearance is due in the first place to the destructive effort of the Puritans. The detailed surveys they made previous to selling the royal domains in 1649, show that a stone balustrade led up to iron gates at Worcester Park, where there were several other pairs between brick or stone piers. A picture of a garden in needlework at Stoke Edith Park in Herefordshire presents as handsome a pair of iron gates in the foreground as any that could have been produced at the time on the Continent. Not dissimilar to these, but larger and with arching top (Fig. 11), are the remarkable gates seen in the drawing signed " Sr. Balthazar Gerbier Baron Douty Fecit," and inscribed " The Great Peeres at Hamstead Marshall," a house near Newbury, Berks, built in 1662 for Lord Craven in the style of Heidelberg, but of which no trace now exists. " Heidelberg " accounts for the extraordinary piers, of the dimensions of garden houses, and possibly for the design of the gates, though these comprise the initials, coronet, fleurs-de-lis, and dagger of the Cravens. No other drawing so signed is known, and the gates are interesting as a design for florid ironwork of the first years of Charles II. Some such piers are represented in Kip's view of 1707. The Restoration brought with it a revival of gardening. The creations at Versailles were not unnoticed here. Evelyn expresses

The Garden

FIG. 11. DESIGN FOR GATES AT HAMSTEAD MARSHALL BY SIR BALTHAZAR GERBIER. FROM A COLOURED DRAWING IN THE BODLEIAN LIBRARY.

admiration for the garden gates at the Château de Maisons near Paris, by the celebrated Daniel Marot, who published designs for them in 1658. They are still to be seen in the Louvre, polished and parcel gilt, closing the Galerie d'Apollon. Lord Essex sent his gardener, Rose, to study the gardens of Versailles, and King Charles annexed him on his return. The celebrated painter Verrio was employed to lay out the gardens of St. James', Greenwich, and Hampton Court Palaces, for years attributed to André Lenôtre, architect and gardener to Louis XIV. Though never in England the latter's influence here was enormous, and led to a most extensive use of iron gates. Views of Badminton show fine entrance gates to the avenue $2\frac{1}{2}$ miles from the house, and others were left behind before the fore-court was reached by visitors. The bass-courts, bowling green, pleasure grounds, kitchen and fruit gardens were all walled and entered through iron gates. Besides these were the geometrically planned bosquet, with a maze and fountain, and at the end of every main path leading from these were wide gates, opening into avenues which radiated for several miles in every direction. In Kip's view of Wrest in Bedfordshire thirteen pairs of iron gates may be counted, but these were later. In 1666 we gather that the views of Hugh May, the architect and controller of parks at Windsor, were not very extensive. He agreed with Pepys that our gravel and turf were better than any abroad, and admired a little mixture of statues and pots, which might be handsome and hold flowers or green. Fruits were to be grown separately in walled gardens and flowers in little plots by themselves. In 1669, however, Charles was laying out avenues and gardens at Hampton Court and in 1670 Wren was called on to repair the fences and make new gates there, on which £2,700 was spent, under the direction of the Surveyor, William Young. They disappeared without illustration or comment, so were probably not very beautiful. Evelyn, with his progressive ideas, influence, and devotion to gardening, may have helped to introduce a better taste for ironwork. When taken by Lady Sunderland to see Lord Northampton's seat in 1688, where they were enlarging the garden, he saw nothing of interest except the iron gate opening into the park, "which indeed was very good work, wrought in flowers and painted with blue and gilded." A note in Miss Fiennes' diary, quoted by Reginald Blomfield in his *Garden Book*, also speaks of gates painted blue and gilded. This decoration was adopted in Holland in the Royal Gardens at Loo. As to parcel gilding of gates, Leigh Hunt observes at Holland House, "it relieves the sombreness of the iron, and being confined to the ornamental portion of the work, gives it a kind of golden efflorescence." T. Gibson * wrote an account of gardens in 1691, and describes a broad gravel walk leading to the highway at East Barnet, as ending in "a pair of broad gates with a narrower at either side, open at the top to look through small bars, well wrought and well painted and a great ornament to the garden." All that had previously been seen in gardens was completely eclipsed by the magnificent screen of wrought iron set up by Jean Tijou in the Fountain Garden at Hampton Court for the pleasure of Queen Mary and William III. Nothing so extensive existed elsewhere in Europe, and nothing in wrought iron so rich and florid has been produced for any garden since.

It is singular that neither Inigo Jones nor Wren made much use of ironwork in their buildings and it does not appear that the taste for it was fostered by our celebrated architects as it was in France, where work of redundant richness was being produced during the last half of the seventeenth century, perhaps originally influenced by Rubens. With the relations prevailing between the two courts the French taste for fine ironwork must sooner or later have been shared by us. Wren was "prying into trades and arts" as he wrote home from Paris in 1665. The existing work of Louis XIII, and the later superb gates, railings, and balustrades of Louis XIV were already in position in the Palais Royal,

* *Archæologia*, vol. xii., p. 181.

34 English Ironwork of the XVIIth and XVIIIth Centuries

Bibliothèque, at Fontainebleau, and in many of the churches; work such as had excited the admiration of Evelyn sixteen years before. Wren was no doubt impressed, but he showed no desire to produce similar works at home.

On the contrary, the Ashmolean, built in 1677, either by Wren or T. Wood, an architect of whom little is known, possesses a pair of contemporary gates of geometric design. The top bar dips and its two ends are scrolled, and one of the meeting bars rises high in a spike

FIG. 12. RAILING TO THE SHELDONIAN THEATRE AT OXFORD, BY WREN, 1668.

with crescents. A little below the top is a horizontal bar, the space between filled with vertical bars and short spike between each, well riveted to the top and the lower bar. The larger half of the gates is below the horizontal, each panel consisting of a lozenge, subdivided by two diagonals crossing in the centre through an oval, all the spaces being occupied by spikes. A later and much better gate on the same lines has fleur-de-lis spikes, narrow pilasters and crested top. Very few examples of ironwork by Wren exist earlier than William III. The railings to the Sheldonian Theatre at Oxford (Fig. 12), completed in 1668, are interesting as associated with a building erected by Wren only two years after his return from Paris. The bars are lofty and straight, the horizontal bar low down, and perfectly

FIG. 13. ONE OF THE GRILLES TO THE CLOISTERS OF TRINITY COLLEGE LIBRARY, CAMBRIDGE, BUILT BY WREN, 1678. THE IRONWORK BY PARTRIDGE, A LONDON SMITH.

plain but for a scrolled finial to the higher central standard of each bay. The great stone piers between them, terminating in heads of sages,* are a landmark to visitors in Oxford. Loggan's engraving shows them to be contemporary with the building, a picture of which forms a well-known tail-piece to the seventeenth century title-pages of the Clarendon Press. A pair of gates about 9 feet high of the same construction and without ornament still remain in the corridor behind the rich entrance gates of the old Clarendon Press.

A long stretch of very similar railing, with fleur-de-lis to the central standards, formed a screen in an unexecuted design for remodelling the forecourt of Wadham College, engraved by M. Burghers probably about 1690–1700, and republished in the Oxford Almanack for 1733? The piers were surmounted by vases instead of heads of fauns, and the lower part of the gates was of four scrolled bars diverging diagonally from a central shield of arms.

The handsome cloister grilles and gates under the library at Trinity College, Cambridge (Fig. 13), built by Wren in 1678, are the work of Partridge, the London smith, who received £400 for them and the staircase. They consist of five horizontal panels, each subdivided unequally into three. Three are filled with vertical bars and fringes of C scrolls with waved centres; the rest with scroll work and peculiar leaves of three designs varying in richness. The design of the staircase, though taken from Tijou's book, was also executed by Partridge.

* The existing busts are new.

FIG. 14.   PORTRAIT OF TIJOU BY HIS SON-IN-LAW, LOUIS LAGUERRE.   FROM THE ORIGINAL CRAYON DRAWING FOR THE FRONTISPIECE TO TIJOU'S "BOOK OF DESIGNS," IN THE POSSESSION OF THE PUBLISHER.

The Work of Jean Tijou, 1690-1710

THE arrival of the Prince and Princess of Orange in 1689 must be regarded as a momentous event in the history of English smithing, for in this year appears the great designer of richly worked iron, "MONSIEUR" JEAN TIJOU (Fig. 14), who enjoyed an exclusive royal patronage to the fullest extent throughout the life of Queen Mary. He was probably a French Protestant refugee in the Netherlands who came over in the royal train, but as to this nothing is actually known. His daughter was married in the church of St. Martin's-in-the-Fields to the French artist, Louis Laguerre, who was also buried there, as well as a Mrs. Ann Tijou, who died in 1708, and a male Tijou without Christian name who died in 1709, and were presumably members of his family. Three of his name remain in

Soho to the present day. His own place of burial and residence are unknown, neither has any will come to light. There is no trace of his having worked in France, and he has never been claimed as a compatriot by French writers. Neither is there any existing work in the Netherlands particularly suggesting Tijou, though some of the engravings of châteaux show lofty and impressive iron screens to the fore-courts and gardens. One thing is certain, that Tijou's ironwork was associated with Wren's buildings almost from the moment of his arrival, for Wren had retained the Royal appointment as surveyor, and began almost at once to build the addition to Hampton Court. Only one year after the arrival of the Prince and Princess, Tijou, who must have possessed remarkable energy, rendered his bill for six iron vanes, " finely wrought in Leaves and Scroll worke," £80, and the rich iron balcony to the Water Gallery, furnished and decorated expressly for Queen Mary to reside in while the palace was building, and taken down in 1701, as it interrupted the view of the river.

There are reasons for believing that Tijou's florid ironwork was not to Wren's taste, and that he was no willing patron, for while he extols Grinling Gibbons in his memoirs, he never even mentions Tijou, and Tijou in the dedication of his book of designs equally ignores Wren. The estimates and bills, both for the work at Hampton Court and St. Paul's Cathedral, were presented direct to the Crown or to the cathedral authorities without the usual vouchers or certificates from Wren, the architect. Also the indoor work at Hampton Court, presumably left in Wren's hands, comprising the King's and Queen's back staircases, the King's privy stairs, the Princess', Lord Portland's and others, are as plain as Wren could have desired, and though by Tijou, are without trace of the beaten leaf-work of which he was lavish.

Notwithstanding which, so rapidly did commissions fall to Tijou that in 1690 he rendered a second bill for the garden screen. This is preserved in the Record Office, among the Audit Office accounts, and is quoted by Law : " To John Tijou for 2 pair of great iron gates with 2 other little gates on each side thereof, for 8 square pillars of ornaments, 12 panels for the circle of the Fountain Garden at Hampton Court, with ornaments, iron, and workmanship included, and for 10 pilasters between the panels, £755 7s." In Gibson's note on gardens made in the year following, 1691,* Hampton Court Garden is a large plat " environed with an iron palisade round about next the park, laid out with walks," etc. The " Fountain Garden " of Tijou's bill can only be the large semicircle opposite the east front, still known by the same name, planned and enclosed by Charles II, who took the ground from the Home Park, and which Evelyn notes, July 16, 1689, " a spacious garden with fountaines was beginning in the parke at the head of the canal." It had only five fountains and three broad walks, two leading to the great avenues in the park, and the third direct to the terrace overlooking the Long Water, where it ends. The design in Tijou's book was not carried out exactly, for he shows narrow gates and no wickets, nor are the pilasters square (Fig. 15). The two pairs of great iron gates with wickets and eight square pillars of ornament, are those which shut off the two broad walks continued into the park as avenues, and, as stated in the bill, then formed a part of the screen of the Fountain Garden, when it separated the garden from the park, as noted by Gibson only one year later. It has since met with vicissitudes.

Mr. Law states in his exhaustive account of Hampton Court, on the authority of the gardener Switzer, that from the death of the Queen late in 1694, little work was done until the burning of Whitehall Palace early in 1698. Work was then resumed with vigour. The Fountain Garden was redesigned by Daniel Marot, "*Architecte de sa Majesté Britanicque,*" and considerably enlarged in 1699, when Talman was required to make estimates for lead pipes, £987 14s., for the outer row of eight additional fountains, and for 1,442 feet of iron rails to be done on both sides the Fountain Gardens, £2,132 16s. The screen had no place in the new design,

* *Archæologia*, vol. xii., p. 181.

40 English Ironwork of the XVIIth and XVIIIth Centuries

and must then have been removed to its second position at the end of the Privy Garden with one fountain, which extended from the south front to the river. Sutton Nicholl's engraving of 1695 makes

FIG. 15. A PILLAR OF ORNAMENT AND GATES DESIGNED BY TIJOU BEFORE 1690, FOR THE SCREEN OF THE FOUNTAIN GARDEN AT HAMPTON COURT.

it quite clear that it was not in the Privy Garden in 1694 when the Queen died. The great gates were not removed with the screen, but occupy in Kip's views a similar position in the new boundary line and still separating the two broad walks from their continuations

Plate III.

A PANEL FROM THE SCREEN AT HAMPTON COURT.
(*Made for the Fountain Garden by Tijou.*)

Plate IV.

EAST FRONT OF HAMPTON COURT CENTRE GATE LEADING TO GARDEN.
By Tijou.

as avenues into the park. Kip's views of 1708 and later show the screen overlooking the river, where there was probably one gate in it, which merely opened onto the foreshore. Ralph Thoresby must have seen them in this position in 1712 when he notices " these curious balustrades which separated the Park from the gardens," which in fact they practically still did, though not directly," and were painted and gilt in parts." No doubt part of the £832 expended on masonry in the Privy Gardens, when the Fountain Gardens were enlarged, was for the reception of the screen (Plate III). It is necessary to be thus explicit as some confusion regarding the first position of the screen exists, even Mr. Law believing it to be made for the unimportant position in the Privy Gardens and afterwards removed to the more important site. At the time or soon after its removal the Privy Garden was sunk 10 feet, and the Water gallery and mount taken down to open up the view, and terrace walks were raised. At some subsequent period the screen was again removed, perhaps by "Capability" Brown when gardener to George III. It was described to the Society of Antiquaries by the Hon. Daines Barrington in 1782, when " the magnificent gates and rails of iron " extended " parallel to the Thames for 600 yards, broken at intervals of 50 yards with twelve gates 4 yards wide and 7 feet high. The design of these rails is elegant and most capitally executed. The harp, thistle, garter, etc., are introduced as ornaments." * The intervals were filled by a plain spiked railing with elegant arrow-headed dog-bars, perhaps removed from the east front of the Palace, and by plain gates 12 feet wide. Panels of cast-iron railings replace the parts removed in 1865, when the large decorative panels were transferred from this somewhat meaningless position to South Kensington Museum, and later distributed among other museums. Within the last few years they have been re-erected in the Privy Gardens and somewhat injudiciously "restored" by the Office of Works, in the belief that this was their original position.

* *Archæologia*, vol. vii., p. 113.

42 English Ironwork of the XVIIth and XVIIIth Centuries

FIG. 16. ONE GATE OF THE TWO PAIRS OF SIDE GATES, *Drawn by* H. P. G. MAULE.

The design in each of the twelve panels (Plate III) of the screen centres round a square frame displaying some royal emblem, as the cypher of the King and Queen, the rose, thistle, harp, fleur-de-lis and garter, supported by two large scrolls of bold acanthus and rosettes, finishing above in Tijou's well-known cock's-heads and acanthus, and surmounted by a mask over a table with drapery. Each panel with its pilasters is 10 feet 6 inches high and 13 feet 4 inches broad. The pilasters present a vertical treatment of scrolls ending above in curved and moulded architraves under an imperial crown and acanthus. Almost half the detail in Tijou's engraving is omitted in execution, both improving the design and reducing the cost.

The three fine gates (Plate IV) in the garden or east front of the Palace present another example of Tijou's richest work, and as they stand within the shelter of the triple arch, they remain in perfect preservation. Each consists of an oblong panel half the height of the gate, over a wide and richly worked lock-rail, with a square panel beneath; the central gates being the richest. The upper panels are of scrolled design, round an oval almost hidden by acanthus and flowers; the lock-rail is as rich, and the square panel below repeats four times a scrolled design radiating from a centre, all being in rectangular frames joined at the angles by short diagonals. The side gates are similarly, but less richly treated. One is illustrated with the scantlings and dimensions set out (Fig. 16). Above the gates is a lintel of scrolls and acanthus. They are included in Tijou's bill of 1694 for £1,153 12s. 6d., which also comprised several plain staircase balustrades. Like all Tijou's work they are seen to be even richer in the book of designs, than in execution.

Two more pairs of gates are shown in Sutton Nicholl's engraving of 1695 in the high wall continuing the line of the east front, between high piers with large vases. The engraving indicates four equal panels of rich work all framed like the gates just described, and with wide lock-rail. The top dips slightly and is spiked. They no longer exist, unless one is now at Eaton Hall, and are not included in the book of designs of 1693.

A third work of great magnificence is the pair of gates and wickets until recently in the line of railing separating the Long Walk from the Home Park (Plate v). These are no doubt one of the two pair of gates of the garden screen, and the Lion Gate may be the second pair very much restored. They open within a framed border filled with a lozenge pattern of scrolls and tulip leaves, beneath a rich overthrow supported by a massive-looking but plainly moulded cornice between lofty pilasters. Each gate is formed of a large panel with oval centre, from which diverge four scrolls clothed with acanthus and water-leaves and completed by plain bars. The lock-rail is filled with a design of broken scrolls, and the lower panel is composed of scroll-ended bars in pairs. All are framed in rectangles of duplicated bars connected at the angles by diagonals. The overthrow on the wide and moulded transom consists of an open shell and acanthus base, under a royal crowned circle with the monogram W.M.R., the cypher of William and his consort, supported

FIG. 17. DRAWING OF THE LION GATE, HAMPTON COURT. *Measured and Drawn by* W. NIVEN.

Plate V.

ONE OF THE PAIRS OF GATES OF THE SCREEN TO THE FOUNTAIN GARDEN, HAMPTON COURT.
By Tijou.

Plate VI.

ENTRANCE GATE TO BURLEIGH HOUSE, STAMFORD.
By Tijou.

The Work of Jean Tijou, 1690–1710

by broken scrolls with rich acanthus (Fig. 17). The flat pilasters are filled with simple scrolls repeating in pairs on either side of a central bar with lily leaves between, surmounted above the moulded transom by a pyramid of scrolled acanthus with a curious wrought openwork vase for finial. A graceful buttress of festoons and broken scrolls and fine acanthus leads down on each side to the plainer wickets with their shorter pilasters. They are of fine design and differ little from the engraving of 1693, except as to extra height, but have recently been much "restored." An identical pair, known as the Lion gates, was put up by George I between the colossal stone piers erected by Queen Anne as an entrance to Bushey Park, which so dwarf them that Defoe speaks of them " as pitiful low gates." One other royal gate appears in the design book surmounted by the imperial crown and palm branches (Fig. 18). The two sides differ, and seemingly neither were executed, unless the designs were for the three iron gates made for the Queen's

FIG. 18. TWO DESIGNS FROM TIJOU'S BOOK, 1693, POSSIBLY MADE FOR THREE IRON GATES ON THE QUEEN'S SIDE OF HAMPTON COURT, NEXT THE PARK, NOW LOST.

46 English Ironwork of the XVIIth and XVIIIth Centuries

side next the Park for £360, as appears in an existing bill of 1694.

An engraving of the fine gates for Burleigh House near Stamford (Plate VI) is also in the book of designs. They still close the inner court, and under the shelter of an arch are well preserved. The semicircular over-grill bears a large coat of arms, the golden garb between lion supporters, surrounded by rich acanthus and moulded scroll work. It differs little in execution from the engraving and

FIG. 19. GATES DESIGNED BY TIJOU, 1693, ERECTED, AS REPRESENTED ON THE RIGHT SIDE, AT WIMPOLE IN CAMBRIDGESHIRE, FOR THE EARL OF RADNOR; NOW DESTROYED.

dwarfs the gates. In the latter the moulding of the bars and scrolls and more difficult forgings are suppressed, though the lines remain the same. A large pair of fantastic carriage gates in Tijou's book (Fig. 19), treated differently on each side as to the finials are recognizable in Kip's engravings of Wimpole, but have long since been destroyed, probably by Kent.

In publishing a book of designs Tijou followed a custom in vogue in France and Germany but not at that time introduced into England. The inscription on the frontispiece that it was on sale at the author's in London, but without any address, proves that Tijou's work emanated from London, and that he at least considered himself a well-known personage. It seems very clear that soon after his arrival he was under the immediate patronage of Queen Mary, who took great interest in his work and probably ordered it personally on her own initiative. If this were so it would account for much. In return Tijou paid her the graceful compliment, as it then was, of portraying her as Minerva reclining, attended by Vulcan, Mercury, Saturn, Amorini, and a group of the Arts. The man in Fig. 14, in redingote and cravat, with strongly marked features and long hair and heavy moustache, who is closely inspecting the work of four brawny smiths, is probably a portrait of Tijou himself, by his talented son-in-law, Laguerre. The rest of the plates were engraved by well-known Dutch and Flemish artists of the day: Van Somer, Van der Banck, Van der Gucht, and P. P. Bouche, who were from Antwerp and Amsterdam. That Tijou set out his own work is proved by a charge made in 1695 by Hopton, a joiner, " for gluing of boards for Mr. Tijoue to draw ye Iron Screen upon, and also for Mr. Gibbons " for the seats in the choir, all in St. Paul's Cathedral. There can be no difference of opinion as to Daniel Marot's influence on Tijou's designs. This distinguished artist had fled to Holland in 1685, and was appointed architect to the Prince of Orange in 1686. While there he published six plates of designs for iron-work, on which many of Tijou's were based. Nothing approaching to these rich designs for balustrades, balconies, screens and gates had been seen in England before, and the immense and indeed revolutionary influence they exerted on the craft is perfectly evident. Tijou was no doubt a practical embosser, and himself executed the masks (Fig. 19A), which are most artistic. The smith might reproach him for the marked partiality he showed for his own craft, embossing; their forgings being almost concealed by the wealth of acanthus, rosettes, masks, draperies, eagles'-heads, etc., which he introduced in profusion whenever he had a free hand. Later he seems to have been more restrained, but he never had claims as a practical smith, for many designs in the book are irrespective of construction or technique, and impossible of execution. The considerable discrepancies between the published designs and the work as actually executed, were probably as much to avoid these technical difficulties as to lessen the excessive cost of execution. As a rule the changes and omissions added to the dignity of the work, and were there not evidence that Wren held aloof from Tijou, it might have been supposed that they were suggested by the great architect, for whose buildings almost all were produced.

Besides the gates and garden screens, the book comprises the design for the fine balustrade to the King's staircase at Hampton Court, the actual construction of which was delayed by the Queen's death till 1699. An interesting feature is the moulded iron handrail, the new fashion of mahogany handrails not having then reached us from France. It also includes the stair balustrade and balconies for Chatsworth then building under the direction of Talman for the Lord Steward, created Duke of Devonshire in 1694. This work must also have been commenced, like that at Hampton Court, soon after Tijou's arrival, for Laguerre was there in 1689, joined by Verrio, 1690. Here too Wren surveyed the work in 1692, for which Tijou received £528. Beyond these are a few practical designs for stair balusters, one of which was selected in 1691 for Wren's building at Trinity College, Cambridge, and executed apparently by a London smith named Partridge, and several others for signs, *enseignes* as they were called, panels, finials and a curious capital for a column, which were of no practical value to the metal worker. We thus find that the bulk of the work illustrated was commissioned and most of it executed within three years of Tijou's setting foot in England, and there was there-

The Work of Jean Tijou, 1690–1710

fore little necessity to include speculative designs with a view to future commissions, as in the case of all later design books published in England.

After the burning of Whitehall, when the King became anxious to complete Hampton Court as a residence, the works were pushed on with the greatest activity, and Tijou received his largest commission, though for different work to that given to him by the Queen. In December, 1699, Talman, as we have seen, was required to make an estimate for railings for the Fountain Gardens, along the east front of the Palace, as shown in Kip's view, 1,442 feet long, with 172 panels, to weigh 45½ tons 4 cwt. 0 qrs. and 6 lb. of iron, to be charged at 5d. per lb., the total cost, excluding coping and £100 for painting, being set down at £2,132 16s. Tijou contracted to supply 1,484 feet, at 5d. per lb., but his bill was rendered for £3,675, and was thus apparently a gross overcharge, as it should on Talman's estimate have come to no more than £2,194 18s. 6d. A balance of £1,889 1s. 6½d. was the subject of appeals and petitions, which, if truly stated, show that Tijou, with all the Royal patronage, had not, during his thirteen years of trading, made art metal-work pay. Tijou's work for Hampton Court ceased. On the death of the King, in 1702, his account was still unpaid. Queen Anne was loath to pay creditors for work executed for Hampton Court in the late reign, and though much importuned she does not seem to have settled this balance. She cared little for Hampton Court and seldom went there, and hardly any work was done there during her twelve years' reign. Tijou's career can be followed at St. Paul's Cathedral, the building accounts of which are preserved. He had employment there for seventeen years, still almost independent of Wren, and through it can be traced some tendency to more sober and dignified design, inevitable where there was little restraint at the outset.

Tijou's work at St. Paul's finished in 1711, when he pressed to have his account settled up, in terms which lead to the inference that he was not even then, after twenty years of work, in easy circumstances. It would have been interesting to know something more as to the extent of his ateliers, his residence, and family. As to the names of craftsmen who actually assisted in the work there is no claim extant by any smith. Huntington Shaw from Nottingham has, however, been made posthumously to usurp the credit, but there is absolutely no mention whatever in the building accounts, memoranda, letters, or documents of any other kind, of this name, and it seems therefore very unlikely, in the case of a man since made so famous by guide books and museum labels, that he ever was a master craftsman. The basis for assigning the credit of Tijou's work, against every kind of evidence, to Shaw is a tablet in Hampton Church, which formed part of a large and fantastic marble monument, 12 feet high, erected in the churchyard against a wall by Benjamin Jackson, Queen Anne's master mason at Hampton Court, apparently as a labour of love, for he was left sole executor. Shaw died in London in 1710, aged 51, and the inscription ended " he was an artist in his way," leaving half the tablet vacant to commemorate his widow, who was presumably to be buried with her husband in the churchyard in due course. This was the only inscription when Lyson transcribed it: " he was an artist in his way," but when the church was rebuilt in 1833 the monument was destroyed except the tablet, which was scraped, cleaned and fixed inside the church. The vacant space on the tablet presumably being thought inartistic, the additional words were added, " he designed and executed the ornamental ironwork at Hampton Court Palace"; a gratuitous assertion, for it is not even known that Shaw was a smith, and Nottingham, from whence he came, was not then, and never had been, a school of artistic smithing.

Mr. Garraway Rice, a well-known antiquary, examined the tablet in 1895, and published his conclusions in the *Archaeological Journal* for June of that year. It was only in the year 1908 that the crowning injustice to Tijou's work and memory has been perpetrated, by the inclusion of the mythic Huntington Shaw to represent smith-craft, among the statues of men supposed to have influenced British art, adorning the façade of the new buildings of the Victoria and Albert Museum. The Board of Education at least are perfectly aware of the fact, as Mr. W. Matchwick was officially instructed to inquire as to the authorship of the garden screen from Hampton Court, and his report was printed and numbered "[313] 25-7. '83." Speculation as to the nature of Shaw's work is of course idle in the absence of any known facts.

This, though the greatest, is not the only injustice the memory of Tijou has suffered. Some of the plates of ironwork in Batty Langley's *Treasury of Design*, 1740, are copied from Tijou's designs without the slightest acknowledgment; they are merely signed T. Langley, Sculpsit. These with the rest are described " as 22 designs of ironwork of the most exquisite taste, from which many curious enrichments may be composed, for the embellishment of cabinet works, ceilings, etc." Engravings from the original copperplates taken to Paris were also issued under the title " *Livre de Serrurerie de Composition Angloise, contenant plusieurs Dessins pour les Maisons Royales, etc., Lesquels ont été exécutez à Londres.*" At first Tijou's and the engraver's signatures remained, but other copies show that they were later erased and simply replaced by " L. Fordrin exc." The latter was the son of a notable smith responsible for some of the ironwork for the Palace of Versailles and the Trianon, and author in 1723 of a work on it of remarkable beauty.

By help of his book the identification of Tijou's work is plain sailing, and the work at St. Paul's is identifiable by the building accounts preserved in the Cathedral library. The style and craftsmanship of a few others proclaim their author. During his career he had opportunities of meeting Vanburgh, an officer of His Majesty's Works, and two of the most easily recognized gates may have been commissioned by him. A pair of gates at Eaton

Hall (Plate VII), leading to the kitchen gardens, may have been brought from the east front of Hampton Court, and differ little from the side gates of the triple entrance still there, except that the design of the upper panel repeats four ways as well as the lower, and the lock-rail is narrower. They have also a central vertical border and two side borders repeating exactly those used in the Lion gates (Fig. 17). A distinctive character is given by a defensive top. The design finishes horizontally above, but the back standards are carried up and scrolled round a very large rosette, from which proceeds a second top bar dipping to the centre, into which handsome spikes are riveted, recalling, and having the same object as the much older gate tops outside Hereford Cathedral.

FIG. 19A. MASK BY TIJOU FROM THE GARDEN SCREEN AT HAMPTON COURT.

The resulting spandrel spaces are filled with a broken scroll and smaller rosette. The gates to the Clarendon Printing Press have the same *motif*, but the lock-rail panel is omitted, and the design of the upper panel is bi-symmetric as at Hampton Court. The semi-circular grill above, though rich with acanthus leaves and festoons, is nearer to one at Drayton House than to Tijou's Burleigh example. Between gates and grill is a curious frieze of four compressed quatre-

Plate VII.

GATES AT EATON HALL, CHESTER.
By Tijou, perhaps brought from Hampton Court.

The Work of Jean Tijou, 1690–1710

FIG. 20. THE FORE-COURT GATES TO DRAYTON HOUSE.

foils and two small panels, with the highly characteristic rectangular frames joined diagonally. The pair from Bridewell, now in the offices in Bridge Street, Blackfriars, are very similar, but lighter. The bottom panels repeat the Oxford design, a rare instance in Tijou's work, but the upper panels are much higher, and consequently of more complex design, centring in an oval shield of arms. These were presented to the new chapel at Bridewell by Sir William Withers in 1713, and may be by a later hand. The Clarendon gates are shown in Williams' *Oxford*, circa 1723, but must have been erected before Vanburgh completed his work there in 1712.

Of other work, part of which may reasonably be attributed to Tijou, that at Drayton House stands foremost. The whole of it has recently been illustrated by Mr. Baily Murphy in *English and Scottish Iron-work*. Much but not all of it was made to the order of the Duchess of Norfolk, who had married Sir John Germain in 1700. Her coronet and arms appear on the overthrow above the gates to the fore-court, with acanthus foliage and rosettes on either side, a rich and massive work with the scrolls moulded as at Burleigh House and also resembling the overthrow of the gates in the Long Walk at Hampton Court, the pattern of the pilasters of the latter also being used for the borders of the Drayton gates (Fig. 20), which are otherwise plain except for fringes to the horizontals and the handsome dog-bars. The existing wicket gates match, but their overthrows are lighter and have been stripped of their embossed work in some process of restoration. The central stone piers form another link with Hampton Court, being almost identical with those of the famous " flower-pot " gate, no doubt adapted from those of the Villa Albani at Rome, but surmounted by large eagles. The façade is completed by handsome railings, which extend 60 feet on either side, with scrolled pilasters and pyramidal tops. The interesting drawing by Buck (Fig. 21) shows this fine screen in its original position about 170 years ago. A second pair of gates close the kitchen garden, in which panels and scraps of German Renais-

FIG. 21. DRAYTON HOUSE AND FORE-COURT, FROM A DRAWING BY BUCK IN THE SECOND QUARTER OF THE EIGHTEENTH CENTURY.

sance ironwork, roughly put together by some local smith, have been incorporated, and they dip to the centre between lofty pilasters of English design, dated 1699. The gates filling the arched entrance to the Bowling Green are evidently by Tijou. They are relatively plain, their horizontals fringed, a scrolled border under the overthrow, and scrolls filling the place of dog-bars. The overthrow fills the arch, and consists of a delicately interlacing monogram of the Duchess, under her coronet and over a drapery, supported by broken scrolls on each side, moulded on the face, and with the peculiar acanthus tufts and rosettes in the overgrilles at Burleigh (Plate vi). Gates to the south avenue are without an overthrow, a rare instance at this time, and the front bars not being carried up, the leafy scrolls on the top are without support; between the lock-rails are circles, and narrow scrolled borders form the front stile. They hang from scrolled pilasters with pyramid tops, set between massive stone piers of Italian design, richly carved and supporting leaden vases. A great stretch of panelled railing, with scrolled pyramids over both panels and pilasters, flanks these on either side. The gates formerly to the East Avenue are also without overthrow, but each is surmounted by its own pyramid of scrolls, like those in Tijou's original design for the garden screen at Hampton Court, while the piers recall those of the wicket gates in the Long Walk there. Mr. Murphy has called attention to most of these similarities in the Drayton House work to that of Tijou; and being ten years later than most of that at Hampton Court it may be intentionally plainer, though embossed enrichments in sheet iron soon perish if neglected, and are seldom replaced in "restorations."

At Burley-on-the-Hill is a pair of imposing gates and wickets (Fig. 22), between lofty fluted stone piers, surmounted by griffins. The overthrow has two bases, the upper of horizontal plain panels and the lower of running scrolls, under a high pyramid finishing in a coronet and a rectangular panel with delicate monogram, both over

The Work of Jean Tijou, 1690-1710

FIG. 22. GATES TO BURLEY-ON-THE-HILL, RUTLANDSHIRE.

58 English Ironwork of the XVIIth and XVIIIth Centuries

tasselled drapery. On either side are scrolls with acanthus and sprays of bay leaves. The gates beneath are plain, with four slender vertical panels and a lock-rail of scrolls, below which are scrolls, taking the place of dog-bars, like those of the Bowling Green gate at Drayton. The wickets match and slope downwards to minor piers and thence to the level of the railings.

The monogram H.M.S. here produced is peculiary interesting from its connection with Huntington Shaw and his wife Mary. It is from the railing of the monument to him formerly in Hampton Churchyard, destroyed in 1833, now in the possession of Mr. Garraway Rice, F.S.A. Not the least charming of the innovations due to Tijou are the delicately interlaced monograms, in place of heavy shields of arms in the overthrows of gates. This feature is already seen in Daniel Marot's designs, and had been much used by English locksmiths in their key bows.

The School of Smiths after Tijou, 1707-20

Robert Bakewell

WE have seen that Tijou undertook and actually produced an enormous amount of exceptionally magnificent work which required a large and able staff of highly skilled craftsmen. No delay took place between the royal commands and setting about their execution, and he must therefore presumably have brought his own ironworkers with him, possibly members of his own family, for he could hardly have found them ready to his hand in England. He may have trained Englishmen to this kind of work later, for there were English smiths who followed Tijou's manner even while he was living, and acquired it so thoroughly that they must presumably have been long in his employment.

Earliest among these is Robert Bakewell of Derby, who produced the wrought-iron front to the garden house at Melbourne for Thomas Coke in 1707. The idea was no doubt suggested by the trellis-work arbours of the same form which were popular in England and France, but no such structure had been attempted in wrought iron. The accounts are extant, and he is seen to have received £130 for the work. His work, though designed in the spirit of Tijou's, is crisper and more modern-looking, and is usually much lighter. His leaves are more definite and graceful than those of any smiths who followed. He makes frequent use of the cockle and scallop shell, which are well modelled, but his masks are wholly devoid of the expression and dignity of Tijou's. There are other distinctive peculiarities, as the use of a single waved bar for the filling of narrow panels. Without great ambitions, Bakewell had unquestionable taste and sense of proportion. His principal works are in All Saints', Derby, where he made the great Cavendish screen and the altar rail; several gates, etc., in Derby, Nottingham, and Stafford, and the gates and railings for the Guildhall at Worcester.

His earliest work seems to be this arbour at Melbourne (Plate VIII), consisting of a dome, about 9 feet in diameter, of open scroll work and branches in panels, alternately of oak and laurel, with a sun in front, and surmounted by a birdcage-like cupola. The dome rises from a small rectangular chamber of masonry without other roof, the horizontal spandrels being also filled with scrolls, the whole forming an unceiled roof of iron to the porch of a small garden room, approached by steps, without gate or door. Over the entrance is an overthrow disfigured by a large and ugly mask and drapery, with the supporting pilasters of plain vertical bars ending in clusters of turned knobs, and between them a handsomely designed panel with a garland of laurel and rosettes, scrolls and drapery, finishing in a crescent. Slightly in advance are two narrow pilasters excellently treated, supporting an architrave of ovolo filling. A letter preserved at Melbourne from Elizabeth Coke acquaints the Rt. Hon. Thomas Coke that the arbour is finished and that Bakewell has got a shop fitting up at Derby. " He is so miserable poor, I believe he cannot remove till he has some money." The work had made great progress in August, 1707, and was stated by Bakewell to be finished in the following February, " all but the setting up." It was not actually so till 3 years later, April 8, 1711; two days later the bill was paid. A long interval elapsed between this and his work in All Saints' Church, Derby, for which he received £500 in 1722. In 1717 he made the gates to the old Silk Mill in Derby (Plate IX) for John Lombe, who was poisoned at the early age of twenty-nine by Italian workmen jealous of his enterprise. Nothing could be more artistic than these semicircular-headed gates of plain vertical bars, to which he has given a richly worked overthrow of most picturesque form. A scrolled border is surmounted by one of open shell pattern, like that to Tijou's Long-Walk gates, and over

Plate VIII.

PORCH TO GARDEN HOUSE, AT MELBOURNE, DERBYSHIRE.
By Robert Bakewell 1711.

Plate IX.

GATES TO THE OLD SILK MILL, DERBY.
By Robert Bakewell, 1717.

Plate X.

AT ST. MARY'S GATE, DERBY, NOW THE BAPTIST CHAPEL.
By Robert Bakewell.

Plate XI.

SIDE GATE TO THE BAPTIST CHAPEL, DERBY.
By Robert Bakewell.

these are three scrolled pyramids with acanthus, the centre one enclosing a circle round a charming monogram of J.L. twice repeated and interlaced. The overthrow is supported by well-designed pilasters containing panels of scroll work. Another important work in Derby was produced for Alderman Pegg, who built what is now the Baptist Chapel at St. Mary's Gate (Plate x). A pair of large, severe gates, chiefly of vertical bars, are set in a frame or border of almost geometric design. Over this is a pyramid of somewhat massive richly foliated scrolls with shield, crest, and acanthus ornament. Four strong upright bars, with a fine scroll panel between, form the pilasters, which finish above in four solid spheres. Beyond these are two narrow panels of high railing, and lastly two stone piers. A side gate to the same building (Plate xi) is plain with a semicircular top of large open shell design. The arched overthrow consists of a border with geometric filling, and a simulated keystone of iron bars; under a shield with draperies and turned finials, buttressed by broken scrolls, and carried on pilasters of vertical panels, formed of rectangular frames with diagonal ties and waved bars for centres. A pair of plain gates with elliptical top, formerly at Mill Hill House, Derby, are without overthrow, as in a pair at Drayton House, but have a horizontal border of the same panels and two large acanthus scrolls above without bars carried up to support them.

Several of Bakewell's works exist in different parts of the county. At Tissington there is a plain but finely wrought gate set in a wall, and opening between pilasters under a framed arch of scrolls. At Okeover Hall not far off is a very fine pair, with elliptical top, of good design and perfect workmanship (Plate xii). The overthrow is a depressed arch with border of the characteristic panels under a rich pyramid of scrolls, comprising an intricate monogram within a circle, draperies on either side, a shell and acanthus and tendrils. The pilasters have large panels scrolled and with converging lines, and the gates are plain with single lock-rail and arrow-headed dog-bars. Beyond the pilasters are panels of railing to match (page 226), between stone piers with vases, of the same design as those to the fore-court of Devonshire House in London, the general effect being similar to the gates there and at Clandon (Plates xxxiv and xxxv). Other interesting gates are in the gardens. At Etwall Hall (Plate xiii) on the road to Melbourne is another pair of plain gates between vertically treated iron pilasters, surmounted by drapery and a spray of tulips. The overthrow is treated horizontally, under a fine but restrained pyramid of scrolls, comprising a shield over a draped table and crest; and the scrolls are clothed with acanthus and rosettes, enriched with tendrils, fleur-de-lis and flower-spray finials. Buttress scrolls lead down to short bays of railing between stone piers. Another fine pair of gates with semicircular head, the typical borders, and a rich pyramid above in the manner of the Silk Mill gates, and pilasters crowned by large vase-like finials of open work bars, is at Irongate Park, Cannock, Staffordshire. There is also a good pair of gates with elliptical top at Willoughby House, Nottingham, very characteristic of Bakewell's work. A much more imposing pair of gates by Bakewell, of large size, was brought out of Derbyshire and erected first at Saville House in Leicester Square, then a royal residence, and later at Penshurst by the first Lord De Lisle. They resemble the Cannock gates, but are much wider, with large and rich overthrow, comprising the pheon and coronet, and monograms over the wickets, with acanthus, tendrils and finials. The four massive pilasters are surmounted by the characteristic vases worked in bar iron on one plane, and the rest of the details are like those of the Cannock gates.

The Town Hall, Worcester, was built in 1721–3 with a recessed centre and two projecting wings, having a courtyard closed by railings and gates produced by Bakewell. In these the most distinctive feature is the pair of massive rectangular iron piers, 9 feet high to the moulded cap, with domed top formed of scrolls bent to

Plate XII.

ENTRANCE TO OKEOVER HALL, NEAR ASHBOURNE.
By Robert Bakewell.

Plate XIII.

GATES TO ETWALL HALL, MELBOURNE, DERBYSHIRE.

the shape, and at present supporting a pair of street lamps. A panel of converging scrolled bars as at Okeover, but more elaborate, forms the centre of the pier, the sides being simpler. Between the piers is an elliptical overthrow filled in exactly as that of the Penshurst gates and with similar scroll work above. Next the gates are decorative pilasters of repeating design, from which are hung plain gates with single lock-rail, fringed above, and spear-headed dog-bars. A long stretch of railing, described with others, page 226, with panels and wickets at either end completes the screen, which has recently been not only restored but reconstructed.

THE BROTHERS ROBERTS

We hear of the brothers Roberts in 1719, the gates at Chirk Castle, on the borders of Wales, being perhaps their first considerable effort. From their work it may be supposed that they were under Tijou and worked at Drayton House, and the pair of gates there with German interlaced work possibly suggested the peculiar interlacing patterns they introduced at Leeswood and Eaton Hall. They may also have worked with Bakewell, as they use the same ornament. They show a marked preference for massive piers, square in plan, with heavy-looking caps and bases worked in sheet iron, and were among the first to forge balustered bars in the Spanish manner. Their second commission may have been the grand screen to the fore-court at Leeswood, with elliptical arched gates in the French taste, plain, under a rich overthrow. The high panels on either side with gabled pediments are strikingly original, and scarcely attempted by others. A pair of minor gates, and railings in the park are less imposing, but of excellent design. Both these are among the very few in England that have never been removed or tampered with. Work of these craftsmen is also to be seen at Wrexham and Oswestry churches. Their gates at Emral are dainty, but much slighter and ill-constructed. Their grand gates at Eaton Hall and Newnham Paddox are the only instance of two works by the Roberts' strikingly resembling each other. All these might have been produced within ten years, for their work seems to have been confined to Cheshire and the bordering counties, and their commissions to have come from local magnates, and not for buildings in course of erection.

Their work is more easily recognized by its grand and ambitious scale and unusual outlines than by details. They made great use of sheet metal, as the acanthus with eagles' heads, draperies, masks, scallops, etc., also of rectangular frames to panels with diagonal ties (sometimes merely with waved bars for centres like Bakewell's), and the solid swaged vase-shaped finials, or vases built up of bars and sheet iron, or worked in the flat from bars. More individual are the borders seemingly of tassels, the interlacing knots, and the large loose sprays of bay leaves and flowers.

For the name of these smiths we are indebted to Mr. Myddleton, the owner of the ancient castle of Chirk, near Llangollen, who has ascertained from his family accounts that his gates (Plate XIV) were made for Sir Robert Myddleton, by two brothers, local smiths named Roberts, for the price of £190 1s. 6d. They now form part of the fine existing screen, 103 feet long. This was probably the first important commission given to the Roberts', who produced a most ambitious work, comprising massive square piers with acanthus capitals and solid-looking entablatures and bases of sheet metal, copied from stone mouldings. The sides are filled with panels of scrolls and bars with foliage, with heavy balustered bars below. They were perhaps made thus heavy to carry leaden wolves brought by sea. Between the piers and gates are two broad panels of scroll and leaf design, of a larger scale and distinctly inferior to the gates. The grandiose overthrow stretches from pier to pier, and consists of a base of two bands of foliated scrolls, the upper one heavily moulded and with a large mask, and pyramids of scrolls over the panels. Over these again is a third band of stiff leaves and masks under an

Plate XIV.

THE FORECOURT GATES, CHIRK CASTLE, DENBIGHSHIRE.
By the *Brothers Roberts* 1719.

Plate XV.

SCREEN TO LEESWOOD HALL, NEAR MOLD, FLINTSHIRE.
By the Brothers Roberts.

FIG. 22A. THE SCREEN AT LEESWOOD HALL.

elaborate arch of scrolls and flowers enclosing a shield and helmet, with scrolls, acanthus and eagles' heads, and with delicate sprays of laurel on which birds are perched. The gates consist of an upper and a lower panel and borders, elaborately worked in the manner of Tijou. The wickets and railing are simpler, and were added by the present owner in 1888, when the gates were brought back to their original position, shown in a drawing of the Castle by Buck, after being relegated, since 1770, to a distant part of the domain. Consideration of cost did not restrain the brothers Roberts from displaying their capabilities to the full, and no work of the grand scale of theirs had before been seen in the western counties. They bear the date 1719.

Their next great work was probably the magnificent screen in front of **Leeswood** Hall (Plate xv), not far distant, near Mold in Flintshire. It is known as the " white gates," to distinguish it from a second screen in the park, known as the " black gates of Mold," and it was made for Sir George Wynne. In 1782, not a very appreciative period, it was placed by the Hon. Daines Barrington, when writing of gardens, as " the most magnificent and extensive ironwork next to that at Hampton Court." The screen consists of four square and massive piers with solid domed tops and bases, surmounted by a large vase and spray of flowers and panels of scroll design with interlacing ornaments. The overthrow is arched, with a border of intersecting bars and scrolls, centring in an escallop, and another of short vertical bars and husks supporting a pyramid with arms, crests and drapery, and with scrolls, rosettes, acanthus, and flower sprays on either side. The gates are plain with elliptical top, the lock-rail of horizontal panels with waved centres, and spear-headed dog-bars with pilasters of vertical ornament on either side. More striking than the gates and rivalling them in effect is the range of two lofty double panels to the right and left. The panels are plainly treated and each subdivided by three finely worked pilasters with finials, supporting a frieze of interlaced work and scrolls, over which are balusters supporting two broken pediments of rich work with dolphins, the family crest.

The "black gates" (Plate XVI) resemble the "white gates," but with less elaborate detail. The piers are H in plan with a semi-circular top, and a shell design and solid flask-shape vase on an open pedestal, and with panels of interlacing below. An elaborate buttress scroll leads down to railings only half the height of the piers. These are of vertical bars with simple pilasters, and pyramid tops, and spear-headed and scrolled dog-bars, all distinctive of the Roberts' work. Turned finials, tassels, waved bars, water leaves and tendrils are freely introduced.

The gates at Emral (Plate XVII and Fig. 23), also in Flintshire, which, like the house, have been neglected and fallen into decay, differ considerably from other known work of these artists. A pair of low gates with side panels and piers have pyramidal tops, and are filled with light flowing scrolls forming a sort of tracery centring in an acanthus crocket. Their miniature piers are H plan, and have the usual solid acanthus caps and bases, with small wrought vase finials and scrolled panels. The large gates between lofty stone piers are of vertical bars with a narrow panel of scrolls, which also centre in a salient and

Plate XVI

PARK ENTRANCE TO LEESWOOD, MOLD, FLINTSHIRE.
By the Brothers Roberts.

Plate XVII

THE BRIDGE GATES AT EMRAL, NEAR BANGOR, FLINTSHIRE.
By the Brothers Roberts.

peculiar acanthus crocket; the lock-rail and pilasters are similarly scrolled, and the latter have pyramidal tops. The large overthrow rests on a single moulded bar, and comprises a broad shield and mask, rosettes, and two graceful sprays of laurel, supported by fragile scrolls, which notwithstanding added supports, have been blown

FIG. 23.   GATES AT EMRAL IN FLINTSHIRE, BY THE ROBERTS.

over by the wind. A similar pair to a lodge, illustrated by Randolph Caldecott, has been sold.

Gates and railings to Carden Hall, near Malpas, are in somewhat the same manner, but with several original features, the crocket forming the centre of the gate panels at Emral forming the centre of the overthrow here, in place of a shield of arms. The over-

68 English Ironwork of the XVIIth and XVIIIth Centuries

throw is light and of similarly weak construction. On either side are stout railings with curious open drops and scrolled dog-bars. A pair of gates at Mere Hall near Droitwich are between square pillars with solid-looking caps, supporting large open-work vases, but are themselves relatively simple with high overthrow.

Eaton Hall was built by Sir John Vanbrugh in 1690 for Sir Thomas Grosvenor, and Kip's engraving of about 1700 shows its courts, gardens and roadways closed by gates of a very plain description. It is only in the 1740 engraving (Fig. 24) that the fine forecourt gates by Roberts' became a prominent feature. These are seen to consist of four noble square and massive piers, with low solid ogee-domed tops and open vase-like finials, and solid bases. Their rich panels have interlaced centres with shorter and simpler panels above, which serve for caps. The gates are plain, with semicircular head, panelled lock-rail and dog-bars as at Leeswood. They open in a fixed frame, consisting of two richly worked and scrolled pilasters and spandrels with large acanthus leaves, supporting an overthrow resembling that at Leeswood, with a fine pyramid of scrolls and acanthus arranged round an oval shield, upon a table with drapery and monogram surmounted by a talbot crest and various finials. On either side are lofty panels to match, but with great circles of radiating design surmounted by scrolls, finials, and acanthus. These are seen to form the entrance to a spacious fore-court with semicircular front, closed by simple railing with panels at intervals, on a dwarf wall. Later they formed an entrance to the Bretton drive, and were afterwards relegated to the Pulford lodge, at the end of a three-mile avenue opening to a lane. Skidmore re-erected them for the first Duke of Westminster when the old piers were heightened and several new ones added, with the two wickets and lofty railings (Plate XVIII).

No less magnificent than the original gates at Eaton Hall, and greatly resembling them, are those now at Newnham Paddox (Plates XIX, XX, and Fig. 25), Lord Denbigh's seat in

Plate XVIII.

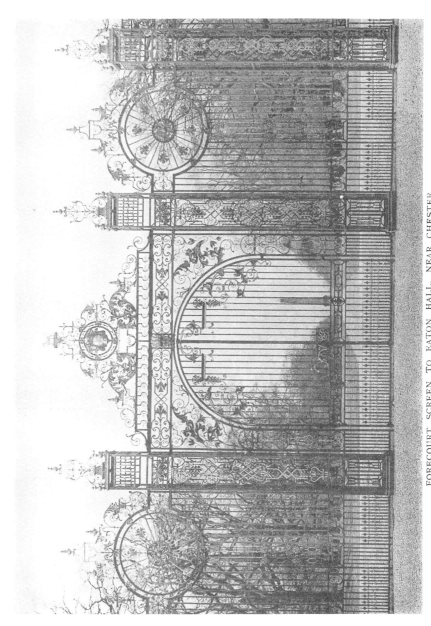

FORECOURT SCREEN TO EATON HALL, NEAR CHESTER.
By the Brothers Roberts.

The Brothers Roberts

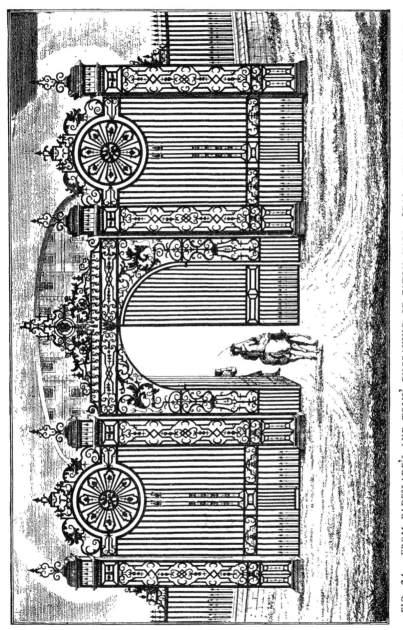

FIG. 24. FROM BADESLADE'S AND TOMS' ENGRAVING OF EATON HALL, 1740. THE GATES AS LEFT BY THE ROBERTS BROTHERS.

Leicestershire. As at Eaton, they consist of four lofty and massive square piers, 18 feet high and 2 feet in diameter, with caps of acanthus, open panels, solid tops of ogee outline and tall finials of plain vases with bunches of flowers and moulded bases; as a special feature each pier has a garland of flowers and foliage. The gates, 13 feet high, are plain as at Eaton, with elliptical head, and vertical pilasters of scrolls on either side. The overthrow follows the ellipse, and is otherwise like that of Eaton and Leeswood, and has a high pyramid remarkable for its spirited design and treatment. The shield of arms is within a spread eagle with coronet and double crest, and large acanthus leaves and eagles' heads, escallop shells, etc., on either side. Two smaller scrolled pyramids flank these and support two wyverns. The side panels repeat the design of the gates except in their large circles, 6 feet in diameter, of radiating ornament under pyramids of scrolls, with mask and monogram like those of Eaton. Subsequent additions are the wicket gates between pilasters, with narrow panels and elaborate overthrow, which, while ostensibly matching their important neighbours, are complete in themselves on a much smaller scale, with no regard to their juxtaposition. Though a certain want of scale between the parts of the Chirk Castle gates is apparent, we still recognize there a grandeur and harmony which makes the Roberts' work exceedingly impressive. Perhaps the Roberts' had relinquished business when the wicket gates were requisitioned, for they appear to be by Bakewell, who was doing his best work in 1727. The gate heads are semicircular, and filled with the exact shell design used by Bakewell in the side gate to the Baptist Chapel in Derby. The lower border and the mask of the overthrow are those of the Silk Mill gates. The square piers are of plain vertical bars with Doric capitals, but carried higher by peculiar flat pilasters of acanthus and rich openwork vases, as in his work in All Saints', Derby. This may account for the tradition that they were made in Derby embodied in "The Severn" by

GATE AND PART OF SCREEN TO NEWNHAM PA[DDOX]
The larger work by the Roberts Bro[thers]

Plate XIX—XX.

MONKSKIRBY, (Removed from Shrewsbury).   From a Wash Drawing by A. E. MARTIN.
aller by Bakewell.

FIG. 25. GATES AT NEWNHAM PADDOX, BY THE ROBERTS BROTHERS, THE SMALLER WICKETS BY BAKEWELL, OF DERBY.

Thomas Harval, 1824: "The iron gates of entrance into the grounds are of eminent beauty and magnificence; they were made at Derby, and are said to have cost £1,000." At this time they were on the roadside of Berwick Park, near Shrewsbury, the seat of Thomas Powys, having been moved from some other position in consequence of the construction of a new road. They were sent to Norwich for "restoration," and while there were pronounced to have been made by the Coalbrookdale Company about the year 1720. They have also been regarded as Spanish and Russian. The gate now at Shrewsbury (Plate LXIII, page 198) is also by the Roberts'.

WILLIAM EDNEY

A search kindly made by Mr. John E. Pritchard, F.S.A., has brought to light the name of William Edney, a notable smith of Bristol. The fine ironwork in several churches of the city had revealed the existence of an accomplished smith, who, like Bakewell in the midlands, made free use of rosettes, acanthus, and other embossed work, following the lines of Tijou. He had probably worked on the choir screens of St. Paul's, but he was distinctly Tijou's inferior in knowledge of the principles of design and in artistic powers. While Bakewell's leaf-work is always fine in technique, accompanying the lines of the scrolls in a graceful manner, Edney's acanthus leaves sometimes diverge abruptly from the stems, and the most original of his designs are amateur. His most important work is in St. Mary Redcliffe Church, and is of the rich character of Tijou's work in St. Paul's. The accounts show that he made the gates to the chancel in 1710, for £60, and two pairs of gates at the side of the chancel for £50. He found much employment in Bristol, in several of the churches, notably in the Temple Church, and that of St. Nicholas, and in city buildings, the gates of the Exchange, not completed till about 1740, being apparently by him. William Edney must thus either have worked for a full

Plate XXI

GATES TO TEWKESBURY ABBEY BY WILLIAM EDNEY,
MADE FOR LORD GAGE IN 1734.

Plate XXII

GATES TO TREDEGAR PARK, NEAR NEWPORT, MONMOUTHSHIRE.
By William Edney.

William Edney

thirty years, or the gates may have been brought from an earlier building, or a successor was left imbued with his traditions. The gates to St. John's Hospital in Warwick resemble those in Queen's Square, Bristol, and like the rail to the Leicester tomb in St. Mary's, Warwick, are characteristic of Edney. The hospital gates were for many years overgrown with ivy, and the entire overthrow and some of the enrichments have rusted away. Edney is probably also responsible for the fine pair of gates presented to Tewkesbury

FIG. 26. PARTS OF THE OVERTHROW AND PIER CAP OF THE GATES TO TEWKESBURY ABBEY. BY WILLIAM EDNEY.

Abbey by Lord Gage in 1734 and which carry the owner's monogram, delicately worked in an oval, under a baron's coronet (Plate xxi and Fig. 26). The piers are square and massive, 10 feet high, with solid looking sheet iron caps 3 feet high, and bases 17 inches high, heavily moulded, with a curious disregard of architectural proportions. Below the cap is a sort of composite capital with volutes and battlemented enrichment with rosettes. The panels are chiefly of vertical bars with water leaves, and towards the base are two strong tie bars, arched on the front and back and passing round the piers, which are surmounted by two large wrought vases of open work with solid square domed covers and fluted bodies. The gates are curved elliptically above and consist of five vertical panels of scrolls and six pilaster-like spaces between, empty but with acanthus capitals, none passing below the scrolled lock-rail, this space being reserved for plain vertical and arrow-pointed dog-bars. The overthrow follows the curve of the gate top and consists of a scrolled border between moulded bars with a large mask in the centre. Above is a pyramid with broken moulded scrolls, acanthus, and on each side of the oval with monogram are laurel sprays and a dolphin's head set at right angles, from the mouths of which proceed acanthus leaves. At the summit is a large square shield with the Gage arms and coronet, awkward looking because unsupported by scrolls. The mask, acanthus capitals of the gates, and the enrichments to the capitals and panels of the piers have been lost in a recent " restoration."

The gates forming the north-west entrance to Tredegar Park, Monmouthshire (Plate xxii), present a superb work, undoubtedly by William Edney. They consist of four square and massive-looking piers, of almost the same design, the inner ones which support the carriage gates being on a larger scale. Their salient features are the over-massive and disproportionate Corinthian capitals, solid and clothed in applied acanthus leaves, under a crown of scrolls with tufts of laurel leaves as finials. The filling is a repeating pattern of scrolls with much acanthus, and the bases are plain and architectural. The gates are high and entirely of scrolled panels with acanthus, repeating twice in each gate, below a narrow horizontal border with rosette centres. The lofty pyramid of the overthrow rests on a base of a lozenge and baluster pattern, with acanthus husks and mask, the central feature being a scrolled flèche bearing a small escutcheon of arms and finishing in a tuft of flame-like twists as at Warwick. Elaborate stepped buttresses of scroll-work and acanthus, support this and bear arrow-pointed finials. The wickets have buttress-like overthrows with acanthus and a festoon, over scrolled bases. The gates are tall with semi-circular panels of bi-symmetric scroll-work, over rectangular panels between two horizontal borders. A scroll pattern repeats twice below the lock-rail with circles for centres. Though evidently based directly on Tijou's work, nothing could be more characteristic of Edney, recalling his work in St. Mary Redcliffe, Bristol. They exhibit most of his characteristics, every part being suffused in acanthus and revealing both his strange dislike to regions of plain vertical bars and predilection for massive square piers with exaggerated Corinthian capitals, and the close-set tufts of laurel and twisted flame-like finials. The general effect is, however, always majestic and commanding.

The Maxstoke Castle gates are original in design, and may be by Edney, but are relatively unimportant. The gate to Scraptoft Hall, Leicestershire (Plate XXIII and Figs. 27–8), is more certainly his, and comprises two wide pilasters, with a filling of rich lyre design and acanthus, surmounted by a pyramid, comprising a small wrought vase under an arch of scrolls and acanthus; between these is the large pyramid overthrow resting on a long horizontal panel with mask for base, and a shorter panel with leaves above. The centre of the pyramid is a vertical scrolled panel, comprising a circle with radiating filling, a large rosette, bold acanthus leaves, and a crest for apex, on each side being large buttress scrolls with acanthus leaves and turned vase finials; beneath in the centre the single gate is arched with scrolled spandrils and a circle of radiating design in a vertical panel above the lock-rail, and repeating panels of scrolls below with short arrow-pointed dog-bars. On either side under the overthrow are fixed vertical panels of richly scrolled bars with waterleaves in pairs. The railing bars finish in small arrow points, and the dog-bars are scrolled at the base; with pilasters

76 English Ironwork of the XVIIth and XVIIIth Centuries

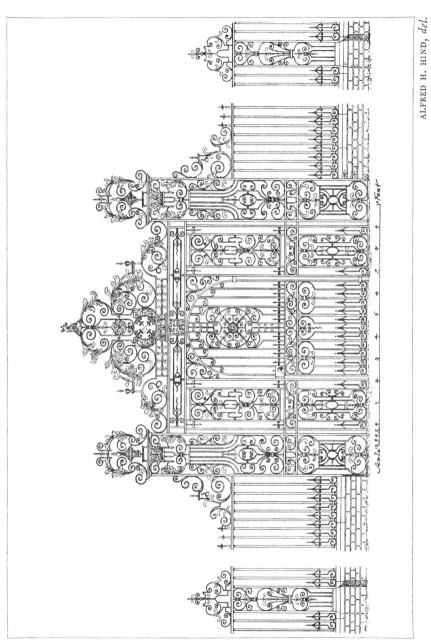

FIG. 27. THE MAIN GATES AT SCRAPTOFT HALL.

ALFRED H. HIND, *del.*

Plate XXIII.

GATES IN SCREEN TO SCRAPTOFT HALL, NEAR LEICESTER.
By *William Edney*

Plate XXIV.

GATES TO THE DURDANS, NEAR EPSOM, REMOVED FROM "CANONS" EDGWARE.
Probably by William Edney.

of scrolls and pyramid tops at intervals. A low but beautiful wicket in the garden (Fig. 28) is square, with a large centre rosette and scroll design repeating four times with a narrow vertical panel on either side and rich top; between fixed pilasters with lyre filling,

FIG. 28. GARDEN GATES AT SCRAPTOFT HALL, NEAR LEICESTER, BY EDNEY.

and buttress scrolls of laurel sprays and eagle-headed acanthus over them abutting on stone piers.

The entrance to the Durdans, near Epsom (Plate XXIV), might also be by Edney, for though the gates and railings are plain, the acanthus, laurel sprays and finials are not unlike his work. These gates were made for Canons, and still bear the Chandos motto, " Maintien le Droit," under the raised table with tasselled drapery which was formerly surmounted by the ducal arms and coronet. They were probably brought to the Durdans in 1747 with other fittings by Alderman Belcher when Canons was pulled down. Tijou is believed to have worked there with his son-in-law, Laguerre, and Grinling Gibbons, and the design, though poor, is perhaps his, though he left England before it was carried out. The work may therefore have been executed by one of his pupils, perhaps by Edney. The gates are treated vertically, each bar ending above in a tassel, and every alternate one in a pair of water-leaves and scrolls over the lock-rail. The tassel is an essentially French feature, and appears in a design by Tijou, and in one of Gibbs' designs for forecourt screens. A few scrolls and water-leaves form a sort of centre to each gate with the monogram J.E. interlaced. The dog-bars are arrow-pointed with scrolls below, and both the lock-rail and the base of the overthrow are of horizontal bars with scroll ends. Over the latter is Tijou's well-known gadroon pattern with a small mask for centre, on which is seated a low pyramid of scrolls with acanthus and eagles' heads and sprays of laurel, which are quite unlike Tijou's. The piers are four-sided, the fronts and backs with rich lyre filling, and their pyramid tops wide and convex.

The Durdans has seen many changes since originally built by Lord Berkeley with materials from Nonsuch in 1669. It was for some time rented by Frederick, Prince of Wales, and later named the Elms. The existing crest on the gates is that of the Heathcotes. They were formerly between brick piers, but recently the railings were added by Lord Rosebery to form a garden screen.

The gates to Quenby Hall, evidently by the same hand as those at Scraptoft, are even more remarkable. Mr. Stead Mills, who measured and drew them, has kindly ascertained that they origin-

William Edney

ally formed the front entrance to the Hall, and were presented by the owners to the Leicester Infirmary, where they were for many years. Becoming dilapidated they were presented to the Leicester Museum, where they still are exposed to the weather. The piers are square on plan, the panels repeated on all four sides, of rich design, and have been shortened at the base, as observed by Mr. Mills. Scrolls at each angle overhang, representing the volutes of an Ionic cap and over these is a high four-sided pyramid of scrolls and acanthus with masks. Inside there are pilasters of scrolled and geometric design, and the pair of gates have a cruciform design in the upper part, two horizontal borders of a plain bar, with square panels at each end of four equal scrolls proceeding from a rosette, and scrolls with spikes in place of dog-bars. The overthrow is also unusual, and apparently bears the arms of the Ashby's. The work is probably a very early and prentice production by Edney, and has suffered by removals and time.

Shobdon Court, near Leominster, possesses a fine fore-court with a screen, perhaps by Edney, comprising entrance gates between massive stone piers with engaged columns, and great lengths of railings on low stone walls on either side. The gates are lofty, with a deep drop fringe to the top-bar and S scrolls in pairs between each vertical bar above and below the lock-rail, with short arrow-pointed dog-bars. The overthrow is relatively poor in design, but comprises several pairs of large and bold, finely embossed acanthus leaves. In the centre is a large monogram, J.B., in an oval, the centre finial being a spray of laurel and the lateral finials flame-twisted tufts over S scrolls and water-leaves.

Gates at Missenden Park (Fig. 64), have the same arrangement of bars as in the gate at St. Mary's, Oxford (Fig. 63), and stiff sprays of laurel in the overthrow. The former are said to have come from Holland Park, as is also a rich single gate with pilasters and overthrow taken from North End House, Twickenham, to Wovington in Sussex (Fig. 37, p. 114). The gate design might be by Tijou himself, and the wide and handsome pilasters and tall overthrow added later. It presents the same stiff clusters of laurel and tufted flame finials emerging from water-leaves seen in Edney's work, and a monogram in a rectangular panel. Nearly identical clusters of laurel characterize the high and richly scrolled overthrow of the gates at Bulwick Hall, Northants. A light interlacing monogram T.C. in a moulded circular frame forms a centre to this over a mask, acanthus leaves, and family crest. The filling of the piers and the scrolled border above are as at St. Mary's, Oxford (Fig. 63), and the gates are plain with long drops to the horizontals, a scrolled lock-rail, and very peculiar dog-bars which are shaped into ellipses and circles below the arrow points. Murphy, who has illustrated these gates, states that they were erected between 1710 and 1720, and are regarded traditionally as the work of a blacksmith from the neighbouring village of Deene.

The English School of Smiths

WE have now traced the work of Tijou's great disciples, who early in the eighteenth century created the demand for richly-wrought iron work in the Western and Midland counties, which they parcelled out and worked between them as if by mutual arrangement. None of their work appears to have reached London, and the unhappy disappearance of Tijou left him without a successor in the Metropolis. Henceforth London was supplied by Londoners, and as no craftsmen of great ability or taste appeared in the Northern, Eastern, or Southern counties, the fine work required was sent from London, while the rest was trusted to the local blacksmith.

Chief among the London men was Thomas Robinson, who first adopted a distinctive English style, differing materially from Tijou's, whose contemporary and serious rival he remained for at least fourteen years.

While in the case of Tijou smith-craft was subordinate and used principally as a means of displaying wonderful embossed work, particularly the masks, which were probably by his own hands and full of artistic expression, with Thomas Robinson it was far otherwise. In his work embossing is sparingly used and not very adroitly. The shields of arms were imposed by the patron, and these necessitated subordinate masses of acanthus or drapery to balance, which seem to be introduced for this and no other purpose. Robinson and Tijou worked in St. Paul's Cathedral for several years, and the former must have been impressed with the hopelessness of any competition in the large embossed work, in which Tijou excelled.

Apart from the extravagant use of embossed work, the distinction between Tijou's work and Robinson's, as seen in St. Paul's, is the elaboration of grand designs on the one hand and simplicity on the other, partly because the great works were given to Tijou and the less important to Robinson. The work at St. Paul's finished in 1711, and it is in this year that Robinson seems to have had his first opportunity of designing and producing work on the same grand scale as Tijou. Instead of following and developing Tijou's lines, as others did, he adopted at New College, Oxford, a distinctly vertical treatment for his work, while Tijou followed the more horizontal lines of classic architecture. Perhaps Robinson was influenced by the perpendicular architecture that surrounded him at Oxford. The effect of height in his gates, and restraint in keeping the richer parts relatively subordinate, render his compositions distinct and very pleasing, and these became the characteristics of the English School. The proportions preferred by Robinson prevail in the gates of Trinity College Oxford, Belton, Harrowden, Beddington, Hall Place Bexley, Carshalton, Loughton, Wootton, Bloxham Park Lincoln, and the Close Lichfield, though possibly all of these are not by him. Robinson worked at Hyde Park Corner, and probably his descendants survived in the firm of iron founders, who only finally relinquished business when their premises were required for Victoria Station. A firm of ironworkers continuing to trade throughout the eighteenth century would have needed to change their output from smith's work to founder's.

Though we may feel some certainty as to the earlier, bolder, and thus more characteristic works of Robinson, it is not so with the more average work required for the numerous houses then building for wealthy merchants and professional men in and around London. Here the craftsman or mechanic easily passes from one employer to another, especially in the trades allied to building, engaging himself while there is work to be done, and moving on in times of slackness. He would thus learn and carry all the peculiarities in forging and style from one workshop to another, or possibly set up workshops of his own, which, in the case of smithing, require no great outlay. The difficulty in recognizing the work of different smiths is enhanced by the number of new forms of scrolls, finials, drops, dog-bars, etc., introduced by Tijou and his followers, as at Drayton House, where many smiths must have worked, almost all of which became and remained the common and accepted and traditional elements of English smith-craft. If new fancies, enrichments, or combinations were thought out and practised by one smith, his work when erected was open to the gaze of all, and the novelties speedily assimilated. To pronounce any piece of London wrought iron-work as that of some particular maker is as hazardous as to assign old silver or pewter to particular craftsmen in the absence of marks. Such identifications as are here attempted must therefore be accepted in many cases with reserve.

Of Partridge, the London Smith who executed the grilles and gates to the cloisters, and the staircase balustrade of the new Library of Trinity College, Cambridge, receiving payments 1691–92, we know practically nothing. Tijou's book was published shortly afterwards for the benefit of smiths, and included the design for the stairs.

Thomas Coalburn shared the work in St. Paul's with Tijou and Robinson, making some of the large window frames with " grotesques." The names of other smiths whose work is little known will be mentioned later.

Nothing is known of " Mr. Warren " but that on August 24, 1715, he was paid the sum of £8 4s. 6d. for erecting the gates at Clare College. This entry was noted by the Rev. J. R. Wardle, a Fellow of Clare, when making researches for the history of his College. There is no other mention of his name, but in those days the smith so invariably set up his own work that it may be assumed for the present that Warren was also the maker of the gates. Mr. J. W. Clark, the Registrar of the University, has also noted that it was ordered, July 20, 1714, " that a convenient iron palisade and gates for the gardens, gates for the bridge foot, and entrance into the college . . . shall be set up." The piers for two of these already existed with wooden gates, having been prepared some years before by Robert Grumbold, a mason and designer who undertook architectural work for the College. All three gates still exist in good condition and present remarkable differences in their designs. The fine and massive stone piers are spaced as if for a carriage drive, but the gate is narrowed by two lofty fixed panels, leaving little more than a third of the opening for ingress. Over all is an overthrow with the College arms. It seems that a wicket of the full height was over heavy, for it was cut down and a new grille fixed over it. The garden gate is similar with fixed side panels and overthrow still intact. The gate for the Bridge, without stone piers, is by far the lightest and the most elegant.

From the style and variety of detail introduced by him it would appear that Warren worked at Drayton House, whence many of his details are derived, and possibly with Robinson as well.

There are two gates near Newmarket which have affinities with the Clare Bridge gate. One at Exning House seen from the road is especially graceful, and others are in the gardens. The second is at Cheveley Rectory, no doubt removed from the Manor House opposite, where it was probably erected by a Duke of Rutland. Both are distinctive, owing to the peculiarly tall and narrow pilasters with rich but very attenuated lyre fillings.

Warren's greatest work, if really his, was undoubtedly the magnificent gate made for Horseheath on the extravagant scale of everything there. The gates at Clandon Park, Devonshire House, Kirkleatham, and Aldermaston, none made apparently for the positions they now occupy, are also sumptuous works. The salient characteristics are the intertwining laurel leaves and berries on long stems and tendrils, and the introduction in later work of small square panels of simple radiating ornament. The piers generally associated with these and the overthrows are massive. As in Robinson's work, the masks are small and cast, in either brass or bronze.

George Buncker is so far only known from his having made the gates for Dulwich College in 1728. His details show that he had probably worked with both Robinson and Warren. Few if any important works were required at this comparatively late date, but Buncker seems to have been well employed about London and its environs, as his handiwork appears in several gates above the average in merit. Among the peculiarities he affected are the flame-tuft finials, composed of clusters of short twisted spikes welded together to form finials, first seen at Drayton House, the beaded ends to welded bars with the appearance of seed spikes, the light dog-bars and finials with barbed heads and button points with twisted ends, and the closely set and rather stiffly arranged laurel leaves. None of these forms, however, are entirely confined to Buncker, who scarcely ranks with Robinson or Warren. There are smiths of this somewhat uncommon name still working in London.

The Work of Thomas Robinson

Robinson's first work in St. Paul's still exists. His rail for the morning prayer chapel, made in 1697, was 43 feet long, and according to his bill contained 121 hollow spikes and balls, and 136 plain spikes and scrolls, and 4 doors with hinges and bolts and locks, at 10d. per lb., £104 9s. 0½d. Under December 5 of the same year Evelyn notes that it was the first Sunday on which St. Paul's had service performed in it since it was burnt down in 1666. The railings are remarkable for the fine tall leaf-shaped heads standing upon discs over the hollow balls, which are of stout sheet metal beaten out in sections and brazed together; the standards having similar tops on a larger scale surmounted by spikes. It is clear that no cast work was at that time introduced into railings, which were forged throughout. The term "ingenious," the highest praise in the vocabulary of the day, was already deserved at this time.

Tijou had been working for St. Paul's Cathedral since 1693, and was getting for the massive window frames 6d. per lb., and for the " Grotesk barrs " 4s. per foot, his total for this year being upwards of £380. In 1699, whether Tijou failed to supply the requirements or for other reasons, four windows had been given to Thomas Coalburn, at Tijou's price of 6d. per lb., and four to Thomas Robinson, who undertook them at 5d. per lb. These continued presumably to divide the windows, for in 1703 each presents a bill for three windows at 5d. In 1704 Robinson produced the rail for the arch at the north-west corner of the dome for 10d. per lb., and in 1706 the "iron rail to stand before the consistory" at 9½d., £100 11s. 7d.; in 1708 £300 for the balcony round the lantern; in 1710 a panel for a balcony in dome at 6d., and in 1711 1,000 feet of chain for the lights, iron fences and gates for the north portico and the west end, and for the Chapter House. In this same year Ayliffe, a contemporary and a fellow of New College, Oxford, noted that the screen and gate to the new court of his college was set up by " that ingenious artist, Mr. Thomas Robinson, of Hyde Park Corner " (Fig. 29). We find his gates and piers of lofty proportions and wonderful lightness, his pyramids more aspiring, and his whole effect vertical rather than horizontal, as in Bakewell's work, and his proportions graceful and slender, yet full of dignity, rather than massive and grand as in the Roberts' work. He almost invariably obtains an effect by introducing a horizontally panelled base, sometimes of great depth,

The Work of Thomas Robinson

FIG. 29. SCREEN IN THE GARDENS OF NEW COLLEGE, OXFORD, BY THOMAS ROBINSON OF LONDON, ABOUT 1711.

under the pyramid of the overthrow. Among many peculiarities are the free use of delicate water leaves with waved edges, giving a beaded look, and occasionally of looped tendrils. These and the general lightness, excellent balance, and the disinclination to use sheet work, and a certain want of mastery over it, are characteristics by which Thomas Robinson's work may be recognized. On these assumptions the gates of New and Trinity Colleges Oxford, and the Belton and Beddington gates may be regarded as typical examples, at least of his later work.

The New College screen (Plate xxv) represented in Williams' *Oxford*, 1723-33, has been illustrated by Baily Murphy. Walford states that it came from Canons.* The new quadrangle is open to the garden, and the screen stretches 90 feet across from wall to wall, the gate forming the centre of a semicircular sweep, with breaks and a lesser sweep on either side. The piers are square on plan and 15 feet high by 1 foot 6 inches wide, and end above in a pyramid of scrolls set diagonally and finishing in a cluster of roses, the panels filled with scrolled bars. Inside these are pilasters, each of four vertical bars, with fleurs-de-lis over the lock-rail and arrow-pointed dog-bars below with scrolls and leaves. The gate consists of two vertical panels of scrolls above the lock-rail and one four-centred panel below. The overthrow supported by the pilasters comprises a horizontal panel, 2 feet deep, of diverging bars and scrolls, and a pyramid, 5 feet high, centring in the arms, garter and motto of William of Wykeham, the Founder, whose mitre forms the apex. Embossing is confined to a very few acanthus leaves and a mask and two small lions' heads below, but slender water leaves and husks are used very freely. The railing, 7 feet high, matches the pilasters, unbroken by horizontals, and with a rich cresting of scroll pyramids and pilasters at intervals (p. 228). The gates at Trinity College, Oxford, appear to be by the same hand and their date 1713. Defoe wrote of these, " At the entrance and end of the great walk that goes through

* *Greater London.*

Plate XXV.

GATE IN THE GARDEN SCREEN, NEW COLLEGE, OXFORD.
By Thomas Robinson.

GATE AND PART OF SCREEN TO WOOTTON HOUSE, BUCKINGHAMSHIRE.
Probably by Thomas Robinson.

Plate XXVI. XXVII.

the garden of Trinity College, Oxford, are very noble iron gates which leave a prospect open to the whole east side of the college." The positions they occupied in the gardens are well shown in Williams' view. The entrance gates are between lofty triangulated stone piers surmounted by three stone vases, with wing walls arched for the wickets and a turret on either side. They hang between richly worked iron piers with pyramid tops and side panels, and are lofty and plain with scrolled lock-rail. The overthrow has a rich border of foliated scrolls and high pyramidal top with the College arms. The gates to the quadrangle formed the centre of a high screen of railings, and no longer exist. The entrance gates to the garden still remain with their original stone piers, but without the wings and wicket openings, but are otherwise much as they were, except that the curved panels on each side are now straight and without the pilasters of ornament which formerly enriched them. The iron piers are quadrangular, 18 inches wide and a foot deep, the scrolls of the finials set diagonally. The overthrow is deep, with a band of scroll-work like that to the piers, with a central pyramid 6 feet high, embracing a large rectangular shield of the College arms with scrolls of acanthus, water leaves, laurel, tendrils, and a mask, with the crest for apex. The gates are plain with scrolled lock-rail and fleur-de-lis and arrow-pointed scrolled dog-bars.

The gates opening on Broad Street are simpler and heavier, and almost entirely new, with the possible exception of parts of the overthrow and the pilaster panels. The piers are built to match those of the garden. In the fore-court is a wicket gate with piers and railing of about the date of those to the garden.

A magnificent set of fore-court gates and railings is preserved at Wootton in Buckinghamshire (Plates XXVI and XXVII), between four imposing stone piers surmounted by large carved vases. The central gates are plain with scrolled and panelled lock-rail, under an overthrow with a deep horizontal panel of scrolled bars of the Oxford type under a pyramid of scrolls, which enclose a shield of arms and palm leaves. On either side are panels matching the gates, with a wicket under a semicircle of radiating ornament, and pilasters between. Above each panel, pilaster and wicket, is a pyramid of scrolls with acanthus leaves and turned vase-shaped finials. Railings and panels on a dwarf wall form an extensive sweep on either side of the gates. A gate to the kitchen garden has a small but much richer overthrow of acanthus.

Belton House near Grantham possesses a remarkable series of fore-court screens, two of which belong to the house, while a third has been brought from a neighbouring mansion. They are all by the same artist and in the manner of those at Oxford. Two have coronets and must presumably be later than 1718, when Sir John Brownlow was created Viscount Tyrconnel. Badeslade's view of Belton shows a large fore-court with semicircular front and iron railings, with the lofty gates now closing the courtyard on the west front. These are much on the plan of the Trinity College gates but wider. Two fine pilasters with acanthus capitals and scrolled pyramids with the Brownlow crest connect with the overthrow by a moulded bar, over which rises a pyramid of scrolls around an oval shield with the Brownlow arms and drapery without the coronet. The gates are plain, with scrolled lock-rail, and horizontal panels at the bottom, these taken probably from the overthrow and included in the gates in a reconstruction, thus increasing their total height from about 10 to over 12 feet. The nine bays of railings separated by pilasters are in Badeslade's view reduced to four, and the existing pyramidal crestings have been added (p. 230). A second pair, between high stone piers surmounted by shields and coronet lion supporters, close an avenue a mile from the house, and may be in their original state. The arms of the family are repeated in iron in the overthrow of the gate. The railings on each side have pilasters supporting a crest or coronet. The third gate, brought in 1743 from Hough, now forms an entrance to the Wilderness. The arrangement

Plate XXVIII.

GATES IN THE SCREEN TO BEDDINGTON HOUSE, CROYDON.
By Thomas Robinson.
(For illustration of Central Shield of Arms, v. page 229).

Plate XXIX.

GATES IN SCREEN TO HALL PLACE, BEXLEY, KENT.
By Thomas Robinson.

resembles that of the New College screen at Oxford, a lofty wicket gate between high pilasters with magnificent overthrow, flanked by a stretch of railing on either side with handsome pilasters. These abut on stone piers with vases, and there are finely forged ramps at each end.

Beddington (Plate xxviii), once famous for its orangery, still possesses splendid gates of the same lofty and slender type. Those to the western front are the finest, and consist of two piers crowned by pyramids, and a wide overthrow of scrolled bars between, beneath which are a gate and two equal panels, separated by pilasters. Upon the overthrow are important pyramids of scrolls with acanthus and solid finial vases, until recently with an immense shield of the Carews with their antelope supporters and crest (Fig. 71). The gate and side panels have each a panel of scrolls, scrolled lock-rail, dog-bars and fleur-de-lis fringes. The railings on either side are lofty, with pilasters and pyramidal cresting. There is also a north gate and a corresponding south gate, which looks older and bears the monogram of Sir Nicholas Carew. On either side are panels of railing to match and a pilaster with pyramidal top (p. 230). A fine screen with a pair of gates closes Hall Place, Bexley (Plate xxix). The gates have each a central and vertical scrolled panel, scrolled lock-rail with fleur-de-lis fringe and arrow-pointed dog-bars. The pyramid overthrow rests on a border of scrolls and comprises acanthus and laurel leaves, a monogram of interlaced R's, drapery and crest. The iron piers are of stout vertical bars with moulded caps and vases, and a panel of open work. There are lower wicket gates, with smaller piers, and crested railings on dwarf walls beyond. The several fore-court gates to Harrowden Hall, Northamptonshire, recently restored by Lord Vaux of Harrowden, are also in Robinson's style, without embossed work. They are lofty and plain, with scrolled lock-rail and arrow-pointed dog-bars, between handsome pilasters with moulded oval centres and pyramid tops, and there are fixed panels beyond : the pyramidal overthrow rests on a horizontal base of scroll-ended bars, between stone piers carrying lead figures and with railings beyond, all of restrained and excellent design.

The imposing gates and screens of Carshalton Park (Plates xxx and xxxi) appear to be by the same hand as the bastion railings at Hampton Court. The great relative height of the four-sided iron gate piers, their simple and dignified severity, plain architectural caps and bases, and the open crown and cast and turned finials, are identical, except in size. The pyramidal tops of the gates resemble some to screens in St. Paul's, except that the scrolls of the latter are almost concealed by the profusion of acanthus, while in the Carshalton screen embossed work is used most sparingly.

A careful examination of the details renders it almost certain that they also are the work of Thomas Robinson. The screen, 113 feet in length, consists of a magnificent set of gates and wickets, all of one height and design, between lofty and massive four-sided architecturally designed piers of iron, of vertical bars, upon a wider base of the same. The caps and bases are plainly moulded and look very solid, and the piers terminate in a crown-like finial of eight bent bars uniting above in a very large cast turned knob. (Plate xxxi). The base of the wide overthrow between them is formed of eight panels of horizontal scrolled bars relieved by eleven masks of fauns. It is penetrated by the two gate pilasters, with richly worked lyre panels, finishing above in arching tops and three solid vases. The gates are under a large central pyramid of scrolls, of four stages, sparingly enriched with water and bay leaves and tendrils, with a circle in the centre filled with the Scawen shield of arms and crest above. Lesser pyramids are over the wickets with monograms of T.S. in circles. All the gates are plain with scrolled lock-rails and fringe, and scrolled and arrow-pointed dog-bars. On either side is a wide and lofty

Plate XXX.

SCREEN AND ENTRANCE TO CARSHALTON PARK, SURREY.
By Thomas Robinson.

Plate XXXI.

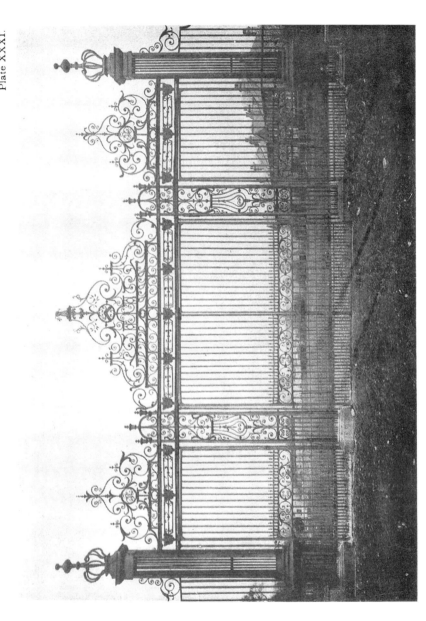

ENTRANCE GATES IN SCREEN TO CARSHALTON PARK, SURREY.
By *Thomas Robinson.*

bay of railing on a dwarf stone wall, the top bar deflected to receive a scrolled pyramid. Beyond these is a high pilaster of four heavy bars with lyre filling, solid cap, and high scrolled finial, finishing with three solid vases of different size. The screen terminates with a much longer bay of the same railings with a simple pyramid break in the centre. The long range is between grand piers of richly carved Portland stone, 17 feet high, surmounted by superb lead figures of Artemis and Actæon. The central gates and a bay of railing are illustrated by Ebbetts, but the grandeur of the whole can only be realized when seen in perspective.

In Lyson's account of Carshalton, it is stated that a part of the original manor was purchased by Sir William Scawen in 1712, and a second part perhaps later. Sir William died in 1722. Thomas Scawen, Esq., formed the design of building a magnificent house upon it, adding to it the manor, known as Stone Court, or Gaynesford's Place, in 1729. According to Mr. George Clinch, who has recently written a brief memoir on the subject, the Thomas Scawen above mentioned was Sir William's younger brother, and an Alderman and Governor of the Bank of England, knighted in 1714. Since the plans and elevations were made for Thomas Scawen, Esq., they were presumably prepared for him before the year of his knighthood.

The house for which these gates and screens were made was never built, but the plans and elevations for it, engraved in 1723, were published in James Leoni's translation of Leon Batista Alberti's *Architecture* in 1755. The iron screen is not represented among these, so that if it had already been erected it perhaps did not interest Leoni, or it was put up after the designs were engraved. Future research may settle the question.

The old gates to Loughton Hall, figured by Ebbetts, are plain between two wickets which exactly match. The single lock-rail is fringed with button spikes with waved ends and water leaves. This fringe is repeated under the top horizontal, but with blunted points, and the dog-bars have large arrow heads and small lateral scrolls. The overthrow rests on horizontal panels with a central mask, and comprises three pyramids of scrolls and water leaves, the central one enriched with J.E.W. in monogram in a rectangular frame, acanthus leaves and rosettes, two remarkable fan-shaped sprays of laurel, and finials. The gates and panels are fixed between wide brick piers surmounted by large and well modelled leaden stags. These fine gates recall the central gates and side wickets at Carshalton, their proportions, height, severity and details being nearly identical. The horizontal border below and the overthrow is also in the same proportion, but comprises only one instead of several masks. The pyramids above, though of different design, show similarity. When published by Ebbetts, he considered them to date from about 1680, but their real date is probably not earlier than 1710.

The splendid gates of Bloxam Park, in Lincolnshire and recently removed to Scotland, consist of the pair of gates, wickets, pilasters, and overthrow, all of lofty proportions and richly worked, between stone piers, with panels of brick, and surmounted by vases. The gates have between the verticals an upper and a lower fringe of waved points, between leaves, scrolled lock-rails, and arrow-headed dog-bars with button and twisted points, with a swelling and pair of leaves. The overthrow is a very lofty pyramid, similar to that over the New College gate at Oxford, but of richer and finer design. It rests on a horizontal border, and comprises an oval with the monogram R.M. over a drapery, and the peacock crest, supported by broken scrolls with finials, acanthus, tendrils and laurel sprays. The uprights forming the tall pilasters are doubled, H plan, with lyre filling, the high capitals Corinthian, of acanthus leaves and flower husks with curved and moulded entablatures surmounted by vases with masks round the centres and waved finials. The tops of the wickets dip to a semicircle to receive small pyramids of scrolls and acanthus. The whole design is charming, and the monogram and crest that of Lord Robert Manners.

The Close at Lichfield is remarkable for its fine wrought iron gates near the West gate, evidently by the same artist. Each gate has next the meeting bar a fine vertical panel of lyre shape, and between the verticals, below the top horizontal, drops each of three converging bars with button and twisted point, as seen at Belton. There are also high spikes with button and twist points over the lock rail and **C** scrolls below, and arrow-pointed dog-bars with the usual swelling in the shaft. The high pyramidal overthrow on a horizontal panel has a stepped rectangular panel with scrolled J.S.C. in monogram and high flèche with scrolls ending in a flame-tuft for centre, supported on each side by scrolls and an arch with acanthus leaves. The pilasters are richly worked, of lyre shape, recalling those of Bloxam Park, except that they terminate in high **G** scroll pyramids. A second pair of gates close by, though on the same lines, are lower and less imposing, though of equally rich work.

The Work of Warren

We look to our venerable Universities with their numerous colleges, almost all presenting traces of antiquity and of the well-nigh constant additions made to them from their foundation to the present day, not only for an epitome of the development of architecture in England, but incidentally for that of iron-working. But the colleges were built round quadrangles and have maintained the mediaeval tradition of the single entrance overlooked by the porter's chamber. Their gateways were not closed by grates or grilles of iron, through which belated students might clamour and parley, but by solid oak doors, many of which still exist with their original ironwork, hinges, locks, bolts and bars complete. The gardens attached to them were small with high walls without access from the street, and only towards the end of the seventeenth century the extension across the river of the grounds of Trinity, Clare, and St. John's Colleges at Cambridge, necessitated bridges and avenues, and iron gates to close them.

Clare College, Cambridge, possesses the fine series of three gates. Two were to be placed between existing stone piers, made by the Grumbolds, to replace gates of wood; but those to the bridge are far more beautiful, and show fine craftsmanship and appreciation of the materials. Their effect is that of a triple gate with three pyramid overthrows and plain pilasters, only the centre panel being hinged (Fig. 30). All are of plain bars with a narrow scrolled lock-rail, having scrolled and arrow-pointed bars above it, continued alike across the panels and the pilasters; while the curious looped, scrolled and arrow-pointed dog-bars below, and the wide border of diverging scrolls with a small lion's mask for centre above, forming the base of the overthrow, are interrupted by the pilasters. These are plain but with a scrolled filling below and a square quatrefoil panel above. Of the overthrow, the central pyramid is concave in outline, ending above in a pair of bulging acanthus scrolls and small flèche, while the lower part is filled by branches of long bay leaves around a small oval of arms with scrolls and acanthus leaves. The lateral pyramids are simpler and convex, and beyond their pilasters are high railings, returned at right angles, with quite plain wickets opening to the meadows.

The entrance to the College has the impressive carved stone piers with vases by Grumbold. The gate is low between vertical panels, now opening under a semicircular grille of radiating design. One horizontal passes under the grille, forming the gate top, and through the side panels, and another forms the lock-rail, all with fringes of scrolls and fleur-de-lis spikes; a third with moulded spikes divides the space below the lock-rail, the lower part being filled with scrolls as at Drayton and Burley-on-the-Hill, in place of dog-bars. A heavy moulded bar above the

FIG. 30. THE BRIDGE GATES TO CLARE COLLEGE, CAMBRIDGE.

semicircular grille and another a little higher, with a scroll filling between them, form the base of the overthrow. The central of three pyramids consists of moulded scrolls of convex outline with acanthus, supporting a large oval shield of the College arms and a finial. The third gate is of similar outline to the last but with simpler details, both contrasting by their relative severity with the more graceful gate to the bridge ; this greater restraint may perhaps be owing to the proximity of the massive stone piers.

To the same hands are due another charming triple gate at Exning House, near Newmarket (Plate xxxii), consisting, as at Clare, of a centre and two corresponding side panels, with arched tops and pyramid overthrows, and four tall pilasters, the whole between stone piers. The gate and panels are plain with scrolled arrow-pointed dog-bars and simple lock-rail, with fleur-de-lis spikes. The pilasters are attenuated, with richly worked lyre fillings, but the charm of the gate lies chiefly in the overthrow of five pyramids, the central of these surmounted by three drooping sprays of flowers growing from vases, and as light and graceful as the peacock's crest. Two others surmount the centre pilasters, which have solid looking draperies and scrolled acanthus below. The three main pyramids have centres like grids, buttressed and surmounted by convex scrolls and heavy acanthus. These gates now abut on the road and afford a view into the gardens, where there are other simpler gates with charming pilasters and overthrows. A pair of high gates at Cheveley, near Newmarket (Plate xxxiii), are by the same smith, and also set between very lofty and attenuated pilasters, with similar lyre filling and pyramid tops, the scrolls of these being carried down on either side below the narrow moulded caps. The gates are plain with narrow scrolled lock-rail, fleur-de-lis fringes, and scrolled and arrow-pointed dog-bars. The overthrow rests on a wide horizontal base filled with the Tijou pattern of scrolls and water leaves repeating in pairs, seen both at Hampton Court and Drayton House, and its pyramid consists of two horizontal stages of scroll-work with scroll buttresses and a large central group of long-leaved branches of bay leaves round a small lion's mask

GARDEN ENTRANCE, EXNING HOUSE, NEAR NEWMARKET.
By Warren.

Plate XXXIII.

GATES AT CHEVELEY RECTORY, NEAR NEWMARKET.
By Warren.

The Work of Warren

FIG. 31. GATES TO TRINITY COLLEGE, CAMBRIDGE.

exactly as in the Clare Bridge gates. Large buttress tops of scroll-work extend over the wicket gates, and down to the railings. These fine gates quite unrestored are now at the Rectory, and were probably removed from Cheveley Hall, when a residence of the Dukes of Rutland.

Trinity College, Cambridge, was fortunate in securing the gift of magnificent gates (Fig. 31) from the Hon. Henry Bromley, brought from Horseheath, the fine seat of the Lords Montfort. The date is unknown, but the mansion was enlarged between 1687 and 1707, and possibly they were made as early as 1700. Their richness, dignity, and solidity recall the work of the Roberts of Chester, but they present none of their peculiar characteristics, and owing no doubt to the late date of the gift, about 1733, no very similar work is in the neighbourhood. The gates are severe with scrolled lock-rail, and fringe of fleur-de-lis with button and twisted arrow-headed points and scrolled dog-bars. The overthrow is an exceedingly rich pyramid of two concentric arches, the inner of acanthus and the outer of husks and scrolls, each with flanking buttresses, over a horizontal base of scroll-work. Its central features are a drapery with symbols of the Trinity and a shield of the College arms within the acanthus arch, and a small mask and smaller drapery above, which probably supported the Bromley crest. The buttresses to the inner and outer arches are flat-topped with scroll supports and acanthus, and plain vase finials, large branches of laurel with tendrils filling the spaces between. The bars are moulded in section and the scrolls finish in massive ends boldly produced in spirals for two or three inches on both sides. The piers are of H section formed of six strong vertical bars with exceptionally richly worked lyre filling between them; the caps are low, and deeply coved, of acanthus leaves surmounted by pyramids of scrolls and converging bars with the outlines of truncated cones. The wickets and their slightly lower piers match the gates, with buttress overthrows of scrolls and

Plate XXXIV.

GATES TO DEVONSHIRE HOUSE, PICCADILLY, REMOVED FROM HEATHFIELD HOUSE.
Probably by Warren

Plate XXXV.

GATES TO CLANDON PARK, NEAR GUILDFORD.
Probably by Warren.

The Work of Warren

acanthus, and beyond on each side is a range of arrow-pointed railings terminating in handsome pilasters.

The fine interior gates in some of the colleges do not fall within the scope of the present volume.

Two similarly rich gates are probably by the same hand, though perhaps a little later in date. One of these was at Chiswick, brought, as Mr. Phené Spiers has now ascertained, from Lord Heathfield's house at Turnham Green, and quite recently to Devonshire House, Piccadilly (Plate XXXIV), and the other is at Clandon Park and believed by its possessor to have come from Naples. These gates are practically almost replicas, but the former has an elliptical and the other a round arch top. Those brought from Chiswick have wickets, and at Clandon (Plate XXXV) there are railings on either side (p. 230). Both are of plain bars with wide lock-rail formed of scrolls within circles, a fringe above and arrow-pointed dog-bars below. A square quatrefoil panel on each side appears to support the arching top. Tijou's gadroon and acanthus leaf border forms the base of the overthrow, framing the arch, with a small mask in the centre, and in one case supports the arms of the Cavendishes and in the other those of the Onslows, under broken pediments. Buttress scrolls with acan-

FIG. 32. PILASTER OF RAILING AT CLANDON PARK.

thus and large waved branches of laurel and tendrils support these. The lofty piers terminate in high acanthus caps with scrolled finials over them, and a lyre filling and small masks resembling those at Trinity, Cambridge. The wickets at Devonshire House have horizontal tops and fine pyramidal overthrows; and the Clandon railings join to the piers with buttresses of scrolls, and have pyramid crestings and noble pilasters, one of which is illustrated in Fig. 32. Mr. Phené Spiers has learnt that the Devonshire arms replace those of the Earl of Egmont, who occupied Lord Heathfield's house from 1765 to 1771, and were added by Messrs. Feetham when the Duke bought the gates and erected them at Chiswick in 1837. They resemble Bakewell's gates at Okeover Hall, between piers which are identical with the gate piers at Devonshire House. A very lofty wicket gate, of precisely the same make and sketched by Ebbetts when at Stoke Newington, is now at Inwood, near Templecombe. This gate is plain with the twist and button spikes and scrolls over the lock rail and plain arrow-pointed dog-bars. The piers are lyre pattern and resemble those of the Clandon gates, while the overthrow rests on a gadroon base, and by a coincidence comprises a monogram T.G. in a circle of the initials of the present owner Lady Theodora Guest.

Some gates removed from Sunbury a few years since and advertised for sale at the time as "the earliest example of iron gateways in England," and now at Culford Hall, Bury St. Edmunds, are probably by the same hand. The gates are high, elliptically arched in the centre, and of plain vertical bars above the lock-rail, which forms a band of foliated scrolls fringed with moulded spikes and scrolls, and with arrow-pointed dog-bars below. The pilasters are tall and well proportioned, filled by a rich scroll and partly geometric design, with finely moulded and solid looking caps and bases. Over these are cone-shaped pyramids breaking into scrolls below and with solid caps and turned finials above, resting on three balls. Only the border to the base of the overthrow remains, following the contour of the gate top, and this is filled with scrolled panels alternating with ovals. Beyond the piers on either side are important fixed panels, each with two large squares containing quatrefoils of four enriched C scrolls round a circle, connected by vertical bars. Beyond these again are

FIG. 33. OVERTHROW TO CENTRE OF GATES, OAKLEY PARK, CIRENCESTER.

lesser panels with slender lyre filling, a geometric and scroll border passing over the whole.

The beautiful arched top gate to the garden terrace at Norton Conyers, near Melmerby, Yorks, is set between pilasters of lyre design with pyramid top, a graceful overthrow between supporting the monogram M.G. in a rectangular panel and surmounted by the pair of wings addorsed, the crest of the Grahams.

The gates to Lord Bathurst's park, Oakley, Cirencester, somewhat reconstructed, are plain with scrolled lock-rail and characteristic dog-bars and fringe. The overthrow (Fig. 33) rests on a horizontal base of scrolls with water-leaves and a small central mask, above which is a semicircle with radiating design of scrolls and water-leaves supporting larger scrolls of acanthus, laurel and water leaves. The coronet, garter, and monogram, two cast finials, and the light honeysuckle finials over the pilasters are nineteenth century additions by the third Earl.

To Warren may also be attributed the gates made for Lord Stawel of Midgeham House, Berks, whose coronet is now replaced by the falcon crest of Mr. William Congreve, who removed them to Aldermaston House, eight miles from Newbury. The gates, set between massive H plan pilasters under a rich pyramidal overthrow, form a very imposing entrance to the park. Long spikes with button bases and heads with twisted points and lateral leaves and scrolls, fringe the horizontals, and the dog-bars are short and arrow pointed, with the barbs scrolled. In the centre of each gate is an elegant vertical panel of scrolls and water-leaves. The lock-rail and the base of the overthrow are of scroll-design with horizontal breaks. The overthrow is a fine pyramid of scrolls and acanthus, sprays of laurel and tendrils, water-leaves, and an embossed drapery. The four heavy verticals of each pilaster terminate in flask-shaped vases, and their panels are of an attenuated lyre design with high pyramids above.

Gates at Barlborough, near Eckington in Derbyshire, are on similar lines, but less rich in detail. They are plain, with leaf and button-pointed spikes over the horizontally treated lock-rail and slender arrow-headed dog-bars to match. The pilasters consist of vertical bars interrupted by scrolls and water-leaves, and the handsome pyramidal overthrow oversails them. This is formed of two finely flourished C scrolls, with embossed rosettes and acanthus leaves supporting a flèche expanding into an open shield-shape design of scrolls and bent bars surmounted by the crest, a hand holding an olive-branch, which may account for two rather large sprays of laurel or olive below. Another large gate with fixed pilasters and wickets between stone-piers at Kirklees, near Dewsbury, Yorkshire, may also be by the same smith, the pilasters being like those of Aldermaston, but wider, with a twice-repeated lyre shape in each. The overthrow centres in a large tasselled and embossed drapery with acanthus leaves and eagle heads on either side. The gates to Arbury Hall, near Nuneaton, have the characteristically slender and enriched dog-bars, scrolled lock-rail, lyre pilasters and fine overthrow, recalling that to the Barlborough gates, but with an oval shield of arms for centre and with acanthus leaves and two large sprays of laurel on either side, and fleur-de-lis crest. The single gate between stone piers with enormous fir-cones is very graceful, and, like the panels of the railings, is surmounted by the fleur-de-lis crest.

Work in Winchester and the neighbourhood presents affinities with the group already described. At Longwood, now in a wall by the roadside, is a fine gate, with pilasters and overthrow on an added base with dog-bars. It is plain with semicircular head and simple lock-rail with a fringe of C scrolls and curious spikes of twisted leaves and points. The rectangular panels on either side are of the same work, and there are also rich pilasters of a twice repeated lyre design, and an overthrow of arms and supporters, motto and coronet, encircled by broken scrolls, acanthus and finials. A pair of gates at Avington Park not far off, once the property of the Dukes of Buckingham and Chandos, are plain with scrolled lock-rail and the same very distinctive spikes and dog-bars. Their tall and slender pilasters have elongated lyre shapes and the overthrow consists of a richly scrolled base and a triple pyramid set with many small finials of the same twisted leaf spikes seen in the gates.

A small but very fine pair of gates of delicate workmanship by

Warren forms the entrance to Eagle House, Clapton. They have been drawn and published by Ebbetts. They have the slender dog-bars with two lateral scrolls and button-twist points, and fringes, the upper one of two bars converging from the base and swaged into a button and twisted point. The slender pilasters have the rich and attenuated lyre-filling seen in Warren's work at Cambridge and Newmarket, with acanthus capitals and solid bases. The overthrow rests on a panel with scrolls, and comprises a fine monogram of E.S. and M. in a rectangular panel between a double set of supporting scrolls, laurel sprays, and six heavy beaded finials. Many of the scrolls have the ends produced spirally in the manner of Warren's gates at Trinity College, Cambridge, and elsewhere.

The plain semicircular-headed gate at Queen's House, No. 17, Cheyne Walk, built in 1717 (Plate xxxvi) may be by Warren. Its single lock-rail is fringed with arrow points above and C scrolls below, while the barbs of the arrow-pointed dog-bars are incurved and scrolled. Four stout verticals, surmounted by flask-shaped vases, form with a lyre panel the pilasters, a favourite construction used at Clandon and Aldermaston. Some of the bars and terminals are beaded, with bent-over bars below. Over the gate is an oval monogram, R.C., for Richard Chapman, between two G scrolls with water-leaves and tendrils and laurel sprays, and two bent-over bar supports; it rests on a simple panel. On either side are plain panels with scrolled buttress tops and lamp-holders, and beyond these plain leaf-headed railings with lyre panels on a low wall. The gate to the Little Cloister by Westminster Abbey is of the same work, and one to Abney House, Stoke Newington, with square pilasters and flask-shaped finials, also recalls that at Cheyne Walk.

The house built for John Sheffield, Duke of Buckingham, about 1703, had a forecourt "encompassed by an iron palisade," in the midst of which was a great basin with statues and fountains, to

Plate XXXVI.

GATE TO 17 CHEYNE WALK, CHELSEA, KNOWN AS THE QUEEN'S HOUSE.

Attributed to Warren.

Plate XXXVII.

GATES TO BURLEIGH HOUSE, CHURCH STREET, ENFIELD.
Possibly by Warren.

which the existing Mall with its old avenues of limes formed one of the approaches. The design of the gates is well shown in contemporary engravings, from one of which the annexed figure (Fig. 34) is taken. It presents several peculiarities, notably the eight square panels of scrolled quatrefoils. These with other features are repeated in the existing gates to the forecourt of Lower Lypiatt House at Stroud, which still comprises handsome stone piers and iron railings. The name of the artificer of these gates, which have a wide lock-rail of richly interlacing work in the German taste, was unknown, but it is related that Judge Coxe, for whom Lypiatt was built, reprieved the blacksmith for two years while he was completing the ironwork.

This is probably an idle tale, as an examination of the still existing pair of gates at Burleigh House at Enfield (Plate xxxvii) leaves little doubt as to the work being by Warren. In these we find the same four small square panels, each filled in with four scrolls proceeding from a circle and united by vertical bars, occupying precisely the same positions in each gate, with central panel between formed of scrolls and water-leaves, connected to the horizontal rails above and below by short vertical bars. The horizontals also are similarly fringed with C scrolls holding waved spikes and the dog-bars are arrow-pointed. The pilasters are of heavier work, with low pyramid tops surmounted by solid vases of a form used by Warren. The overthrow rests on a horizontal base and consists of two magnificent buttress scrolls, some of the ends produced spirally, with acanthus leaves and rosettes, and waving laurel sprays with berries and tendrils, in the manner of the Horseheath gates, but the centre is merely a small panel containing a circle and scrolls, under a flame-tuft finial.

Except as to the lock-rail and the region below and the ducal coronet and collar of Buckingham, the designs of all three gates are almost identical, and are evidently by the same smith. Buckingham House, it is well known, was purchased for George III in 1761

108 English Ironwork of the XVIIth and XVIIIth Centuries

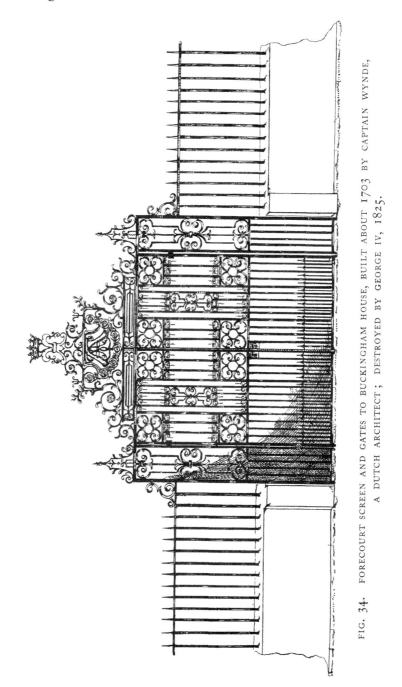

FIG. 34. FORECOURT SCREEN AND GATES TO BUCKINGHAM HOUSE, BUILT ABOUT 1703 BY CAPTAIN WYNDE, A DUTCH ARCHITECT; DESTROYED BY GEORGE IV, 1825.

Plate XXXVIII.

GATES TO DULWICH COLLEGE.
By George Buncker, 1728.

Plate XXXIX.

GATES IN DULWICH VILLAGE.
By George Buncker.

and taken down by George IV in 1825, who caused the present building by Nash to be erected.

Work by George Buncker.

Through the courtesy of Mr. S. W. Bickell we learn that the stately gates to Dulwich College (Plate xxxviii) were completed in 1728, by George Buncker, smith, for the modest price of £25. Narrow and massively framed between fixed panels of corresponding design, and octagonal stone piers surmounted by vases, they appear worthy to rank with the College gates at Oxford or Cambridge. They are massively framed, narrow, the width being but one-fifth of the height, each comprising a scrolled lyre panel between vertical bars, continued below the lock-rail, which is also panelled and scrolled. The fixed panels at the side each contain two lyre panels of similar but not identical design, with plain and heavy vertical bars below the lock-rail. Over the panels are pyramids of G scrolls supporting solid flask-shaped finials with twisted points, seated on a massive horizontal bar. Under the central overthrow is a small semicircle bearing the words "God's Gift," and curiously filled in by small laurel leaves and tendrils with the large oval above, bearing the arms, and a crest of Edward Alleyne the Founder of the College; and on either side are scrolls and leaves, stepped and bearing finials of water-leaves and spikes ending in buttons and twisted points. The details, comprising leaves and seed-spikes, are practically identical with those used by Thomas Robinson, with whom presumably Buncker may have worked. The general effect of the design is, however, wholly different. The gates closed the Inner Court, but were removed to the Outer in 1847, when both were thrown into one by Sir Charles Barry.

In the village not far distant is a simpler pair of gates similar

110 English Ironwork of the XVIIth and XVIIIth Centuries

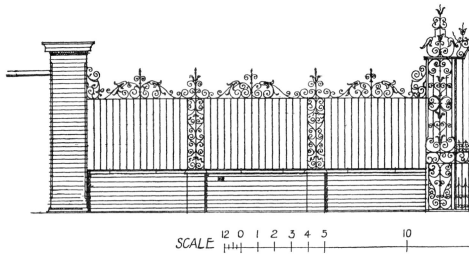

FIG. 35. SCREEN TO ORMELEY HOUSE

as to details, but lighter (Plate XXXIX). The scrolled panels do not pass below the simple lock-rail, and those of the narrow pilasters resemble them, though differing in design. The overthrow on a plain horizontal bar comprises two pyramids of scrolls with water-leaves over the pilasters, and a large central pyramid, raised over a horizontal panel, under a small semicircle enclosing two small and naturalesque branches of laurel. The scrolls and water-leaves once culminated in a flame-tuft finial, now replaced by a button and twist, like those over the pilasters. Pendant from the top-rail and erect over the lock-rail are balls on spikes with twisted points emerging from scrolls and leaves, and the dog-bars are arrow-headed with button and twisted points, like those frequently used by Robinson.

Ormeley House, Lord Sudely's place on Ham Common, is screened by a lofty gate, with semicircular top, rich pilasters and overthrow, and six panels of railing with scrolled pilasters,

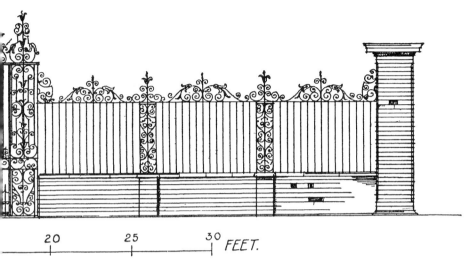

M COMMON, BY GEORGE BUNCKER. *Drawn by* HEATON COMYN.

all with high pyramid tops (Fig. 35). The dog-bars, enriched with side scrolls, the fringe over the scrolled lock-rail, and the finials, etc., are as at Dulwich College. The scroll-work of the handsome pilasters reaches to the ground below high pyramid tops. The arching overthrow has a monogram, perhaps P.H., and a wolf's head crest in a pyramid of scrolls, leaves and beaded tendrils. Scrolled brackets connect the pilasters with the railings, which are on a dwarf wall (Fig. 36).

A gate with railings much like that at Ormeley House is at Bridesfoot House, Iver, 2½ miles south-west of Uxbridge. The gate is formed of a central panel of scrolls, with tendrils and leaves, between plain bars, and the pilasters on either side are similarly scrolled, with the typical dog-bars below. The overthrow is lofty and oversails the pilasters, with a lyre-shaped pyramid and scrolls clothed with water-leaves, tendrils, and seed-spike drops. The railings, on a dwarf wall, are divided into panels by wide

112 English Ironwork of the XVIIth and XVIIIth Centuries

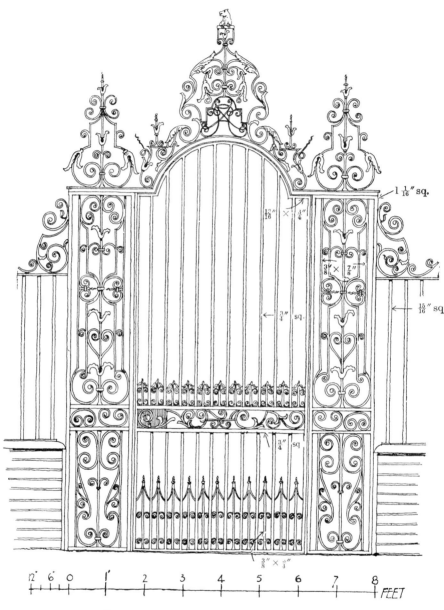

FIG. 36. THE GATES AT ORMELEY HOUSE, HAM COMMON.
HEATON COMYN, *del*.

Plate XL.

GATE NOW AT TOTTENHAM VICARAGE.
Ascribed to George Buncker.

Plate XLI.

ENTRANCE TO GOUGH'S PARK, FORTY HILL, ENFIELD.
Ascribed to George Buncker.

pilasters with pyramid tops, and the vertical bars all end in spikes between scrolls, each alternate one carried higher than the next.

A gate brought to Tottenham Vicarage from a neighbouring house (Plate XL) recalls the work of those at Dulwich in its general effect. The gate has an arching top with radiating design and a long central vertical panel, continued below the scrolled lock-rail. On either side are four vertical bars with a small oval and scrolls between them and handsome drops of leaves and scrolls. The dog-bars are arrow-pointed with scrolled and incurving barbs and scrolls and buttons to the shafts. The pilasters match the central panel and their scrolled panels extend to the ground. The arching overthrow rests on a border following the contour of the gate top and filled with peculiar bell flowers and scrolls. The central pyramid is of scrolls with tendrils and water-leaves, and the usual button and twist-pointed finials, comprising R.N. in monogram.

The entrance to Goughs' Park, Forty Hill, Enfield (Plate XLI), consists of a single gate of plain vertical bars, the centre bar bearing a pair of water-leaves, and all with single light scrolls above. Over the lock-rail are twisted spikes with scrolls, and the dog-bars are arrow-pointed with a button half-way up the shaft. It opens under a deep horizontal panel of scrolls and water-leaves, repeating four ways from an oval centre. The panel is between two wide and handsome pilasters, more decorated than the gates, finishing above in light pyramids with three water-leaf finials ending in twisted points over buttons. Between these is the small central pyramid with the monogram C.J. in a rectangle between scrolls and under a large flame-twist finial. A plain railing with arrow points and handsome pilasters extends on either side, and connects to the pilasters with buttress brackets. At Old Park, also in Enfield, is an entrance with plain gates with characteristic fringes and dog-bars, between pilasters of scrolled bars and water-leaves, with pyramids ending in button and twist-point

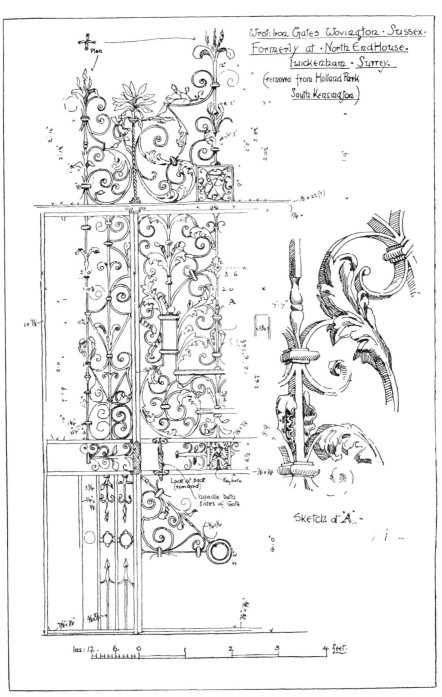

FIG. 37. AT WOVINGTON, SUSSEX. *Drawn by* F. LISHMAN.

finials between water-leaves. The central pyramid, on a border of scrolls and water-leaves in pairs, has three flame-tuft finials.

A more usual gate is drawn by Ebbetts from Baker Street, Enfield, comprising a narrow and vertical central panel of arabesque design extending below the scrolled lock-rail. The dog-bars are arrow-pointed with a button in the shaft, and every horizontal is fringed with button points emerging from leaves seated in **C** scrolls. The pilasters are wide, of richly scrolled and arabesqued design, extending to the ground and with unusually large water-leaves. The overthrow consists of two pyramids of **G** scrolls over the pilasters, over inverted **U**'s with flame-tuft finials; and a centre raised over a horizontal border of scrolls with laurel sprays and acanthus bearing a heater shaped shield of arms. These are between handsome railings with pilasters bearing flame-tufts. The gate is now much dilapidated.

A small but singularly rich gate, made for Holland House (Fig. 37), though recalling the work of Tijou, may be by Buncker. It found its way to North End House at Twickenham, and thence still farther afield to Wovington, Sussex. A single but very elaborate panel of rich acanthus work occupies the space above the lock-rail, which is scrolled with an embossed mask as centre, while below a square panel of scrolled geometric design repeats round a circle, as in the gate to New College. The richly worked vertical panels of the pilasters repeat on each side of a decorative centre bar, with a trellis effect, and are completed by the usual arrow-pointed dog-bars, with long drops and circles below. Over the pilasters are **G** scrolls reversed, and over the gate a higher pyramid boldly scrolled with acanthus and laurel sprays above a small rectangular panel containing a delicately interlaced monogram. All the pyramids finish in flame-tuft finials, and between them are two high twisted bars bearing remarkable fanlike tufts of laurel.

FORECOURT SCREENS.

We have now seen that the grandest gates produced in England were once the central features of the screens to forecourts in front of the house. They recall the magnificence of those to the outer court of Versailles, and to many great châteaux of the French nobility. A fine though not entirely characteristic French example forms a screen to Elvaston, near Derby (Fig. 38), known as the Golden Gates, though now painted blue. It consists of high carriage gates, with

FIG. 38. THE GOLDEN GATES, ELVASTON.

rich overthrow, lofty square or rectangular piers, plain wickets, and a long range of very tall halberd-like railings with tassels. It was erected by the 4th Earl of Harrington, and is said, probably erroneously, to have been brought from the Château of Madrid, near Paris, now destroyed.

When fully developed the forecourt screen consists of somewhat severe entrance gates, with their richness concentrated in the pyramidal overthrows of scrolls, foliage, cyphers, or armorial bearings; two wickets to correspond; four lofty piers of iron also surmounted by scrolled pyramids; and beyond these extensive bays of railings divided by decorative pilasters, all with pyramidal tops, and attached to the piers by buttresses of richly worked scrolls. The whole screen is set between massive stone piers, usually moulded and carved, and surmounted by vases or figures. Such screens remained fashionable under Queen Anne and most of them date from about 1710 to 1720. It is doubtful whether any typical forecourt screen by Tijou exists, unless at Drayton House, though several of those remaining are the work of the remarkably skilled artists and craftsmen who carried on his traditions. The more important are illustrated here, except a few well-known examples, which are only described, having already been amply illustrated by Baily Scott Murphy and D. J. Ebbetts, whose folio works should be consulted. A few forecourt screens owe their preservation to some fortunate chance, but far more were swept away, and for all record of them we are indebted to three or four county histories, and engravings of English seats by Kip. Though gates and screens necessarily appear in these to a minute scale, their arrangement and characteristics are perfectly clear. In the 1708 edition of Kip, Tijou's work at Hampton Court and Wimpole is well shown; and in the bow-fronted forecourt to Dawley in Middlesex, with railings and richly worked gate and overthrow, comprising arms and coronet, we probably have a record of another of Tijou's works, all trace of which has disappeared. Other less elaborate examples are not so identified with Tijou's manner. Atkyn's *Gloucestershire*, 1712, and a later Kip show a bow-fronted court to Fairford with iron railings, and gates with an overthrow comprising a fine coat of arms and crown-like pyramid. Rendcomb has gates with lofty overthrow, wickets, and iron piers designed as richly as Tijou's at Hampton Court and possibly by him, but more probably by the Roberts. Dyrham possessed a

FIG. 39. SKETCH OF IRONWORK AT CHEVENING, FROM KIP.

gate of uncommon design with an extremely bold spread eagle in the centre, perhaps by Edney. The overthrow to a pair of gates at Cirencester Abbey bears a large shield and palm branches, and the Hatherop gates are on the same lines. Harris' *Kent*, 1719, represents a handsome forecourt at Chevening (Fig. 39), with richly worked iron piers and gates, having decorative panels and lock-rail, and pyramidal overthrow, with plain railings on a dwarf wall on each side. The house was built by Inigo Jones in 1630, and modernized in 1700, soon after which the screen may have been erected, perhaps by Robinson; but no trace of it exists at present. The screen to Squerries, not far distant, had similar gates, with six bays of loftier railing on either side separated by rich pilasters, no trace of which now exists. Waldershare possessed an extensive screen to the forecourt with bowed-out gates and pilasters, apparently of rich work. High Street House (Fig. 40) is represented with a screen to the forecourt, having a gate and

FIG. 40. SKETCH OF GATES AND RAILS AT HIGH STREET HOUSE, KENT, FROM KIP'S " THÉÂTRE DE LA GRANDE BRETAGNE."

Forecourt Screens

four richly worked square piers, two with pyramid tops, and two supporting a high pyramidal overthrow, under which is the very plain wicket gate; the railings on either side are lofty, plain, and in three bays, divided by pilasters matching the piers, on a stone base, and returned at right angles, when the railing is in panels between stone piers, surmounted by lead statuary, in a grand manner. There was a plainer screen to Lees Court, and gates to Knowlton Court, with eagles surmounting the stone piers. The gates to Umberslade in Warwickshire must have been very remarkable, with wide stone piers supporting unusually tall and slender steeple-shaped obelisks, and correspondingly high scrolled overthrow, comprising shield, crest, and coronet over severe gates. A second pair almost as fine is seen in the same engraving, with piers surmounted by large vases, probably of lead.

The number of fine screens represented in the few county histories published during the brief period when iron screens to forecourts were in fashion, bring home to us very forcibly how numerous these must have been throughout the country, and

FIG. 41. GATES TO THE FORECOURT OF WENTWORTH CASTLE, NEAR BARNSLEY, BUILT IN 1708, FROM THE ENGRAVING BY BADESLADE, 1730.

120 English Ironwork of the XVIIth and XVIIIth Centuries

how very few have escaped total destruction. The houses engraved by Kip were the stateliest in the land, most under Court influence, and built in the latest prevailing fashions of their day. The later editions of Kip, those of 1716 and 1724, show increasingly stately and lofty screens with plainer gates, and more concentrated richness in the overthrows. The grand forecourt to Wentworth Castle, built between 1708 and 1715, with its wide and slightly bowed front, presented like that of Versailles a magnificent sweep of railings with lofty gates and wickets

FIG. 42. FORECOURT SCREEN TO POWIS HOUSE, GREAT ORMOND STREET, BUILT ABOUT
EMBASSY, WHEN THE PIERS AND SIDE

in the French taste. The gates shown in Fig. 41 were constructed of long vertical bars, with the lock-rail low down, under a rich overthrow horizontally treated, with pyramid top comprising the fully displayed arms and supporters of Thomas Wentworth, Earl of Strafford. The wickets corresponded, their overthrows bearing crests. The arms were repeated on the lofty stone piers and again on the escutcheons born by the spirited lion and griffin supporters which surmounted them. An unusual feature was the piercing of the piers to receive vertical panels of iron with semi-

Forecourt Screens

circular tops in the same taste as the gates. Only one example of this treatment now exists, at Chester-le-Street (illustrated in Fig. 69). Another fine screen in the 1724 edition of Kip was at Fragnall, Kent, and good gates at Highgate, near Hawkhurst.

The screen to the town mansions of the nobility were no less magnificent, that to Powis House in Great Ormond Street, built in 1700, being undoubtedly the finest. This house was burnt in 1712, while in the occupation of the French Ambassador, and rebuilt in a sumptuous manner by Louis XIV, who defrayed

>, BURNT AND REBUILT IN 1712, WHILE IN THE OCCUPATION OF THE FRENCH
ELS WERE PROBABLY ALTERED. *Engraved for Stow's Survey.*

the cost, though the building was insured. The screen, however, is not so distinctly in the French taste as that to Wentworth, but the piers are as lofty and surmounted by similar supporters holding escutcheons. The striking feature is the richness of the long length of railing on either side, divided into panels by open work pilasters, both panels and pilasters surmounted by high pyramids of scrolls finishing in fleur-de-lis (Fig. 42). Noticeable features are the unusually large and handsome scroll-work buttresses on either side of the gate-piers. The fleur-de-lis of the railings and

122 English Ironwork of the XVIIth and XVIIIth Centuries

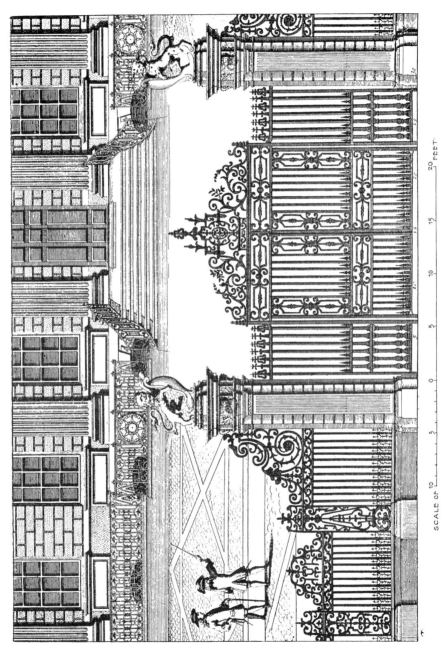

FIG. 43. THE GATES AND RAILINGS AT POWIS HOUSE, GREAT ORMOND STREET, TO A LARGER SCALE. *From an Engraving by* BOWLES AND CARRINGTON.

Forecourt Screens

the fixed panels of vertical spear-headed bars on either side of the gates are convincing evidence that this closure was either erected or altered for the new building by Louis XIV. A low balustrade of rich design (Fig. 43) was seen immediately in front of the house and continuing up the steps to the front entrance, like that still existing at Chesterfield House. Powis House was taken down in 1777, when the site was built over and the ironwork disappeared. Monmouth House in Soho Square was built for the unfortunate Duke in 1683, by a Mr. Ford, a joiner, who acted as architect; and also for a brief time

FIG. 44. SCREEN TO THE DUKE OF MONMOUTH'S HOUSE, SOHO SQUARE, BUILT IN 1683 AND TAKEN DOWN IN 1783.

became the French Embassy; it was pulled down in 1783. The gates or screen (Fig. 44) may be of late date and consist of three panels of almost equal dimensions between stone piers, the centre pair surmounted by swans with outspread wings and the others by vases. The ironwork is of vertical bars, crossed by lock-rails with geometric border, fringed above and below, and with horizontal top bars also fringed. The overthrow repeats the geometric border with a semicircle of radiating ornament and scrolled pyramid above. A house in Covent Garden belonging to Lord Orford had plain railings and gates, the latter each with high and rather elaborate pyramidal tops. There was a screen of high railings and gates to the house in Lincoln's Inn Fields, built by Lord Powis in 1686, and sold to the Duke of Newcastle in 1700. These gates were also essentially French in design, plain, with elliptical tops and overthrow with scrolled border and pyramids of scrolls and acanthus, comprising an oval escutcheon and ducal coronet. This and Buckingham House were built by the same architect, Captain Wynde, a Dutch settler patronized by the Earl of Burlington. A rare example of a raised forecourt with panelled railings and handsome gates is shown in the curious drawing of Crowley House, Greenwich (Plate LXXVI).

Time has dealt quite as hardly with the gates to the forecourts of mansions in town as with those in the country. Indeed they have fared worse for all are demolished, the ever increasing building values of open spaces being fatal to their preservation. Those to the halls of wealthy City companies have been among the last to disappear. Remnants of a few may still be seen in the City and about Whitehall, Piccadilly, Mayfair, Kensington and Marylebone. Some of the older hospitals retain them, and scant vestiges are still traceable in Lincoln's Inn Fields. The acquisition by Government of Buckingham, Marlborough, Burlington, Montague, Somerset, and Hertford Houses has been the means of preserving their courts, at least in part, while many others, like Gloucester, Harcourt and Cumberland Houses, the Old War Office, have recently fallen a prey to the speculator. When building over the large London estates began, square gardens were left, around which the houses were built, a sort of forecourt in common to several houses, but more lately almost every inch has been built over.

In the country the destruction of forecourts with their screens and gates seems to have been due to mere caprice and changes of fashion. The Italian style, said by Aubrey to have been brought in by " Sir John Danvers of Chelsey who first taught us the way of Italian gardens," whose mansion was on the site of Paulton

Square, came in under James I. In the reigns of Charles II and his brother James, houses were built in the midst of parks and gardens, which were laid out in the French taste under the influence of Lenôtre, who first extended the formality of the garden to the park by planting great radiating avenues and rectangular groups of trees, all spaced at equal intervals; and necessitating the expenditure of vast sums in levelling the natural undulations of the ground. William and Mary brought with them, and rendered fashionable, a less dignified and more definitely Dutch style of gardening, which carried to excess became later a subject for ridicule. To quote a little known writer on gardening of the eighteenth century.* " The mournful family of yews came over with the House of Orange, the sombre taste of Holland grew into vogue; and straight canals, rectilineal walks, and rows of clipt evergreens were all the mode. It was the compliment which England paid her new sovereign, to wear the dress of the Dutch morass. The royal gardens of Kensington, Hampton Court and Richmond, set the same example, and good Whigs distinguished their loyalty by fetching their plans from the same country which had the honour of producing their king." . . . Gardens were " filled with yews in the shape of giants, Noah's ark cut in holly, St. George and the dragon in box, cypress lovers, laurustine bears, and all that race of rootbound monsters, which flourished so long and looked so tremendous round the edges of every grass-plat." The King's gardeners, London and Wise, set up as nurserymen in Chelsea, and supplied the demand for yew and box trees clipped into these extravagant and fantastic forms. The absurdity of much of the topiary work brought on it the ridicule of Horace Walpole, Chesterfield, Pope, and Addison. Walpole professed to see nothing in Kip's views of the seats of the nobility and gentry, but tiresome and returning uniformity; every house approached by two or

* *The World*, No. 15, vol. i, 1794. Adam Fitz-Adam.

three gardens, consisting perhaps of a gravel walk and two grass plats and borders of flowers, each rising above the other by two or three steps, and as many walks and terraces, having so many iron gates that he was reminded of those ancient romances in which every entrance was guarded by nymphs or dragons. The persistent attacks on formal gardens by the celebrated wits opened the way to the landscape gardeners.

Bridgeman, gardener to George I, led the way by forsaking rigid formality and symmetry, almost discarding topiary work, and introducing the sunk fence or "ha-ha." Kent, patronized by the Earl of Burlington and applauded by Walpole, went much farther, striving to banish everything artificial and to reproduce the pictorial effects of the Italian landscape painter. According to Kent nothing could excel the beauties of Nature when arranged and distributed to the taste of the landscape gardener, and Nature's supposed abhorrence of a straight line became his guiding principle, and until his death in 1748 his time was occupied in destroying courts, terraces, avenues, canals, walls, hedges and statuary. A beautiful undulating sward, accidented by trees, grouped or single, with ornamental waters if practicable, were to replace them. His ideals left no place for iron gates or railings. Fitz-Adam considered Kent to be " truly the disciple of Nature, imitating her in the agreeable wildness and beautiful irregularity of her plans, of which there are some noble examples remaining, that abundantly show the power of his creative genius." Brown, known as " Capability," though ignorant and untrained, became the royal gardener at Hampton Court, and thence dictated his crude theories of naturalistic design, and until his death in 1783 continued the indiscriminate destruction of pleasure grounds commenced by Kent. Repton, the first to call himself " landscape gardener," published a book in 1795, and followed on and completed the work so effectually that Sir William Chambers declared, " our virtuosi have scarce left an acre of shade or trees three in a line from Lands End to Tweed." The plans of all equally demanded that undulations should be levelled, hollows created, hillocks transposed, ponds extended into lakes, avenues should disappear and the trees be transplanted. The garden disappeared from sight and the park extended unbroken to the front door. The house had to stand in the midst of the most delightful natural scenery without intervening artificialities of any kind—terraces, steps, walls, hedges, even flower-beds and garden walks disappeared, and the grounds arranged by Kent or Repton are seen to have an unbroken sweep of sward right up to the house itself. To again quote Fitz-Adam: "Gardens were new created once in twenty or thirty years and no traces left of their former condition; paradise itself would have no charm for a modern gardener, unless its walks be disposed into labyrinth and mœander." Repton, however, frequently regretted the destruction of those majestic terraces which marked the precise line between nature and art; and later even the removal of the courtyard and lofty garden walls. Entrance gates, however, were not to be seen from the mansion unless opening into a courtyard. Hogarth, who loved an iron gate, satirized the relatively harmless Bridgeman in the *Rake's Progress*, believing that the extravagances of gardening had brought many to ruin.

Thus the beautiful courts, walled gardens, bowling greens, hedges and terraces, reservoirs and fountains, statuary, vases, and sundials, quaint mounts with their quainter banqueting houses, all vanished as completely as the baseless fabrics of dreams. We have to deplore that with them went the iron gates and screens, not only to the courts and gardens, but to the plantations and avenues often miles from the house. The latest of the county histories to represent an iron screen is Dugdale's *Warwickshire*, 1730, and then but one, that to Four Oaks Hall. Thenceforth no house apparently was thought worthy of illustration where any vestige of formal grounds remained. Stately houses, once surrounded by acres of costly and delightful gardens and lawns were left forlorn in the midst of coarse meadow grass dotted with occasional trees and reaching to the house doors. The lament of Sir Uvedale Price, who destroyed his walled-in garden with summer houses and rich wrought iron gates, has been handed down. He did this with no pleasure to himself, and no motive except that of being in the fashion, and succeeded at much expense to himself in making his garden like everybody else's, and the fields outside. This exaggerated cult of the naturalesque is a first and striking proof of the steady degeneration of our national taste.

Under Louis XV, when the stability of England was envied and great Frenchmen came here to reside, a taste for the new and costly English landscape gardening was introduced into France by Montesquieu. It spread widely and rapidly, conferring new charms, it was thought, on the domains of princes and magnates, whose surroundings under its influence presented lovely and reposeful retreats for rest and meditation. The once fatuous and dissipated spent large sums in order to appear lovers of solitude and of the serious thoughts which this engenders. The Abbé Delille in his poem on gardens desired to save the art of landscape gardening from the false taste which sought to crowd pitiful parodies of the wonders and happy accidents of nature into restricted spaces. In the reign of Louis XVI, still more untold expenses were incurred by the great nobles of the Court in imitating the wastefulness of wealthy English nobles, and the Duke of Chartres and the Count of Artois were among the foremost to destroy their old French parks and convert them into "*jardins anglais*" of most costly and pedantic irregularity.

Fortunately the park itself could not be abolished, and its existence preserved some of the few iron gates that remain. As an institution it is of the most venerable antiquity, for the Anglo-Saxon possessed his deer reserves and Canute's law allowed freeholders to sport on their own lands. Entries in *Domesday Book* show many owners of "*parcus bestium sylvaticarum.*" Parks adjoined royal palaces in the Middle Ages, as at Woodstock and Windsor, and the castles of the nobility, and even wealthy ecclesiastical establishments, as Peterborough, possessed them. Leland, writing in the reign of Henry VIII, describes them as pleasantly wooded, enclosed by ditches and banks, or with rough walls of stone following the contours of the land to keep in the deer. Later they contained plantations for game and reserves of timber, grown both for home use and for profit. During the last century rights of way became closed or diverted where possible, and lodges, built at the entrances for privacy and protection, at last caused the reintroduction of the iron entrance gates.

THE INFLUENCE OF ARCHITECTS.

So far designing the gates had been as essential a part of the smith's work as making them. The architect and builder concerned themselves with stone, brick and timber, materials with which they were conversant. The carving, the decorative painting, the plaster enrichments, the glazing and the metal working were within the province of their respective craftsmen, who may have been instructed by the architect, but more often dealt with the owner direct. Very gradually architecture crystallized into a profession, and centuries elapsed before any definite distinction was drawn between the amateur and the professional. Any person of taste and leisure, or student travelling abroad, could take notes of buildings and use them when opportunity occurred. If he scored a success he might be consulted by others intending to build, but his real calling in life, sculptor, painter, scholar, author, soldier, prelate, gentleman, or politician, would remain unaffected. We generalized then, and a man's avocations were only limited by the versatility of his genius. The architect patronized, and was in turn assisted by, designers practising the various crafts. Even when professional architecture became established with Mansard in France and Wren in England, that is to say when so much professional work was thrust *ex officio* on them as Crown surveyors, that their whole time became absorbed in it, they did not break with custom, but continued an almost free hand to the skilled artists and craftsmen who were their contemporaries and assistants. During Wren's career the designs for the ironwork were left wholly to the executants. We have seen the work Tijou produced, and it has never since been surpassed. Bakewell possessed an innate knowledge of constructive design and sense of proportion, the value of light and shade and the balance of plain vertical bars in juxta-position with rich acanthus and scroll work, which is apparent in every gate he produced. If the Roberts and Edney in their more daring flights occasionally lay themselves open to criticism, their work is always grand and impressive, and as expressive of the best English art as contemporary architecture or painting. The essentially English treatments of Robinson are most refined and never approach the commonplace or vulgar in design. His school was developing rapidly along the best lines, when the architects, headed by Gibbs, arrested it and banished craftsmen's designs from architecture.

Gibbs' *Book of Architecture*, published in 1728, is the first work by an architect comprising designs for wrought iron work. In it are two plates of designs of forecourt screens, and one of gates. Even before it appeared, however, the forecourt for country mansions was practically a thing of the past, and it does not appear that any of Gibbs' designs were actually executed. The wide stone piers are the most interesting features, three of the four having recessed niches as if for statuary, while the fourth is recessed for a trophy of arms. One finishes in a pediment and vase, the others are surmounted respectively by Roman warriors, horses, obelisks. Three are here reproduced (Figs. 45, 46, 47), but for want of space the obelisks, etc., are omitted. The designs for the ironwork appear to be directly adapted from the grilles and gates to

THREE DESIGNS FOR FORECOURT SCR

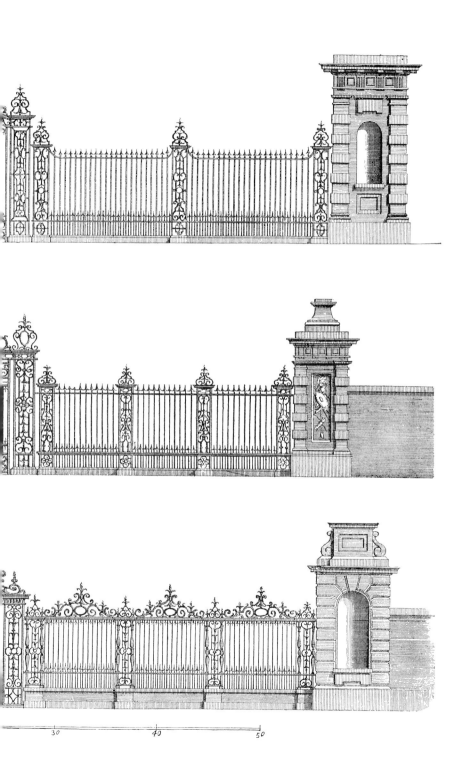

GIBB'S "BOOK OF ARCHITECTURE."

The Influence of Architects

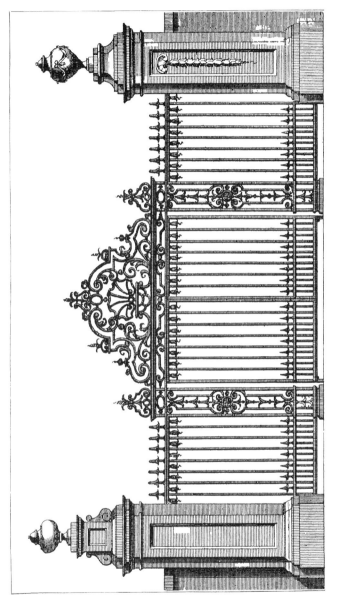

FIG. 48. DESIGN FOR IRON GATE, FROM PLATE 88 OF GIBBS' "BOOK OF ARCHITECTURE," 1728.

the front of Versailles. Viewing these plates one feels for the first time the trammels of definite rules of proportion, the doom of smithcraft as a fine art. Though variety is obviously aimed at, either design might be chosen indifferently, for all produce the same effect. Otherwise the details of the ornament are not very original or different from those in current use by the smith. Of the gates in Gibbs' book three have elliptically curved tops and overthrows with large and empty ovals for centres. Two are illustrated; in one (Fig. 45) the overthrow is confined between the pilasters, which have pyramid tops, and in the other it rests upon and oversails them (Fig. 47). One has a scrolled lock-rail, and the other scrolled panels below it. In another design, illustrated in Fig. 46, the gates have horizontal panels of scrolls at the top and bottom, and an empty shield in the overthrow. This presents a plain railing on a stone coping, with three pilasters on either side; and Fig. 47 a railing on a dwarf wall with four pilasters, each between massive cast balusters like those forming the railings to St. Martin's Church. There are pyramid tops to these as well as to the railings between them. A fourth, not illustrated, has verticals finishing in pike-heads with tassels, and borders of small circles, the essentially French treatment.

Equal monotony is seen in the three smaller gates of Plate 88 of Gibbs, all of them plain, with dropping husks and arrow-pointed dog-bars between the verticals, and heavily moulded top bars. They hang between decorative pilasters with pyramid tops, and have pyramid overthrows. The one reproduced here has a shell centre, the rest have empty ovals, with buttress scrolls and finials. Between the gates and their stone piers are fixed panels designed like the gates, but with the vertical bars carried up into arrow-points (Fig. 48).

In 1747 Gibbs published the *Bibliotheca Radcliviana* with the severe and heavy gates and window grilles to the ground floor (Fig. 49), and the iron stair balustrade. The former are all of one design exactly alike with closely set bars, the verticals alternately 1 inch and $\frac{3}{4}$ inch in section, and the horizontals $1\frac{1}{4}$ inches square laboriously blocked out for the passage of every vertical in the mediaeval manner. Grilles of radiating bars to match fill the semicircular heads of the doors and windows. The gates and grilles to the Bank of England are still more forbidding and prison-like, heavy and almost destitute of ornament. Some of the Mansion House grilles may be designed by Dance (see Fig. 107, p. 269). The four square pillars with rich panels and angle bars carried up into globular finials and solid pyramid covers finishing in a large cone, and the plain gates and high grilles seen in old engravings

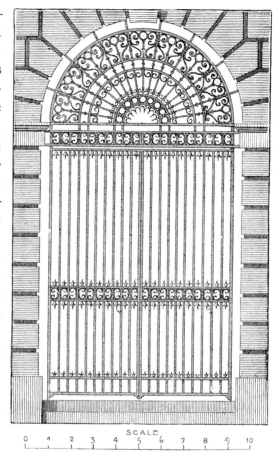

FIG. 49. IRON GATES FROM GIBBS' "BIBLIOTHECA RADCLIVIANA," 1747.

to have shut in the porch of St. George's Church, Bloomsbury, were perhaps designed by Hawksmoor about 1731. The ironwork of the screen (Fig. 50) to the forecourt of the Horse Guards, not completed by Vardy till after 1748, was probably designed by him, and is here reproduced from Ware's *Body of Architecture*, Plate 10, published in 1756, the existing massive four-sided piers, however, being shown as flat pilasters. The

134 English Ironwork of the XVIIth and XVIIIth Centuries

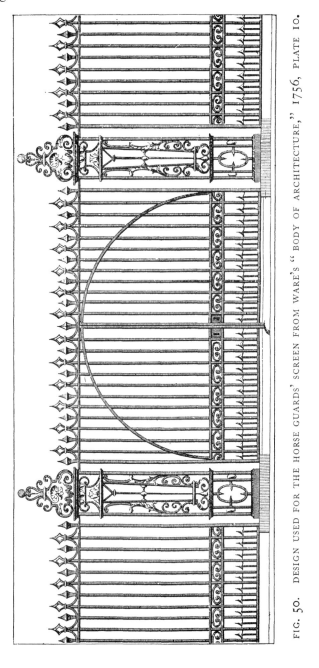

FIG. 50. DESIGN USED FOR THE HORSE GUARDS' SCREEN FROM WARE'S "BODY OF ARCHITECTURE," 1756, PLATE 10.

gates are plain, and, like the railings, about 10 feet high, with open welded spikes, a border of C scrolls and arrow-pointed dog-bars between the verticals. Gibbs' lead was, however, not generally followed and ironwork fills a very unimportant place, if any, in architectural books of the eighteenth century. The traditional designs of the smiths were little influenced by them, for some at least among our best craftsmen had been familiar with French styles for quite fifty years. Jores published his *New Book of Iron Work* in 1759, "containing a great variety of designs, useful for painters, cabinet makers, carvers, smiths, fillegre piercers," etc. It contains twenty copper plates " designed by J. Jores," but twelve of them are simply copies of Huquier's designs, as pointed out by Guilmard in the *Maitres Ornamentistes*. Welldon's *Smith's Right Hand*, 1765, was a smaller book with the majority of the plates also taken from French originals, but presumably the rest may be his own designs described as " modern, new, new Italian, Chinese, Venetian, or Gothic," all in the Chippendale manner. Among those who tempted the smith to abandon his traditions was Batty Langley, who illustrated in 1736 in *Ancient Masonry*, the different " orders " in twelve plates with " curious designs for iron gates of which we have none so noble yet executed in England." These he had taken bodily from the work of J. J. Schübler, a German designer then living. Three years later a fresh series of eight plates of designs for iron-work appeared " of the most exquisite Taste, from which many curious Enrichments may be composed, for the Embellishments of Cabinet Works, Ceilings, etc.," taken with very slight modifications direct from Tijou's book, then fifty years old, without in either case any acknowledgment of the original designer. If these had any influence at all, it was ephemeral and in the direction of a passing revival of Tijou's style as seen in the gates to Hawksmoor's screen to All Souls' College, Oxford, of about this date, drawn by Murphy. There are other gates at Oxford, in the vicinity, of late date. Still later gates in a different but yet florid style were erected as an entrance to the Botanic Garden, Cambridge, in the third quarter of the eighteenth century. All these, however, were exceptional, and in a way archaistic.

Ironwork not designed by themselves was henceforth rigorously excluded from the stately buildings that architects were erecting for the nobility, as it had been through the influence of Kent from the royal parks and palaces, and the gardens of the wealthy. Thus ironwork became unfashionable, and the great smiths who succeeded Tijou left no equally important successors. The tendency of the architect to monopolize all the designing, not only of the structure, but of its decoration and contents increased progressively, culminating in the brothers Adam, who would not permit so much as a picture or piece of furniture to be posed without their advice and consent. By them the "*maître ornamentiste,*" or professional craftsman and designer, the very originators of all applied design, were finally suppressed and squeezed out of existence, the result being within a few decades the utter collapse of all art in the country in the early Victorian days.

An architectural training can do no more than teach the science and art of building on the best and most generally approved lines of the day. It can no more create a designer in the applied arts than it can produce a painter or sculptor. There are so many purely practical sides to architecture of vital consequence to the client, in which art hardly enters, the selection of sites, surveys, planning, foundations, drainage, water supply, fitness and strength of materials, construction, offices, contracts, heating, lighting, ventilation, flues, laying out of roads and grounds, that the first essential to a modern architect is to be a sound man of business. If in addition his training and natural ability enable him to design beautiful elevations and devise skilful plans, and he has a correct sense of proportion and balance he is equipped with all the essential and masterful qualifications required by his profession.

The extraordinary advances made in every branch of science within recent years put art to shame, and these, it is well known, have only been possible by specializing. The architect alone, among professional men, seeks to become all-embracing and would monopolise every branch of design even to the knife and fork used at his client's table. Yet no profession has perhaps ever had less cause to boast its progress than modern architecture, for it has not yet surpassed the art of Mediaeval, or even equalled that of Renaissance days—the results achieved by Inigo Jones and Wren, master minds in association with capable and zealous craftsmen. Whenever and wherever Art reached its noblest expression in the past, there were the master craftsmen and *maîtres ornamentistes* held in honour and esteem. The modern view, almost confined to England, which still so largely ignores, and thus discourages, all the minor arts outside the vision of the Royal Academy, does not make for any general revival of art appreciation in the country. The names of carvers, glass painters, enamellers, potters, metal-workers, founders, jewellers, designers of textiles, have been household words in the past—but in these days for a craftsman to become known may too often debar him from architects' work on which, as things are, he must mainly depend. Not every born designer now, or in the past, can practise architecture. On general principles it would be conceded that no one should be *ipse facto* more qualified to design for the applied arts than the masters of the crafts concerned in them; but this elementary fact is too often ignored by the powers that be.

Gates by Undiscovered Smiths

THOUGH the blacksmith found himself practically banished from the houses of the great, the value of well designed ironwork, whether in gardens or in houses, was too generally recognized for his work to be immediately overlooked, and for another thirty years he continued to find employment. The middle-class dwellings, in city or suburb throughout the country were frequently designed by the builders, and their elevations were usually plain but substantial. Few were without their quaintly designed iron gates and grilles, since the value of the well-knitted, restrained and graceful lines, which had become traditional to the English smith were still widely appreciated, forming as they do the best foil to masonry and brick. To appreciate their peculiar merit they only need to be contrasted with the prettily flimsy contemporary work of Italy, the tormented work of Germany, or the measured magnificence of that of France. In short the simple dignity and fitness of the English ironwork harmonized admirably with the national temperament and physical conditions, and testify eloquently to the ever widening base of wealth and freedom throughout the days of Queen Anne and her immediate successors. Houses being built back from the highway, iron gates and rails were in requisition to close the front approaches, and as the smiths continued to make them on the old lines, they are rarely other than quaint and charming. The only progressive modification seen in them is towards severity, and this chiefly in the larger works for public buildings, a tendency which deprived smithing of its vigorous characteristics before the middle of the eighteenth century was passed.

Gates by Undiscovered Smiths

Dated Gates.

Since considerable misconceptions as to the dates of these gates have existed, it appears best to first briefly consider the few dated examples we have left to us. Unfortunately it at no time became the fashion to include dates as part of the decoration of gates, though the arms and especially the monograms of the owners are not unusual features and sometimes enable dates to be fixed. The date 1719 appears on the Chirk Castle gates by the brothers Roberts (Plate xiv).

In London only two of the many important gates erected in the time of George I and the early days of George II that remain are dated. Those closing the gardens of Gray's Inn are severe and heavy, the verticals $1\frac{1}{4}$ inch in section, only relieved by a slight central panel. The date 1723 and initials $\frac{T.}{W.I.G.}$ are rectangularly framed in the overthrow. The gates are set between stone piers surmounted by eagles, with railings on either side.

The similar screen to the Temple Gardens, dated 1730, consists of three panels, the centre forming a wicket, and all perfectly plain under a deep overthrow of five panels, four with scrolls and the centre bearing the date. The screen to Guy's Hospital, not erected until after the death of the benefactor in 1724, also exists, with plain gates and rich and handsome overthrow and pilasters. The original gates to Chelsea Hospital are severe and quaint and relatively plain.

Gates to Dacre's Almshouses in Tuthill Street were taken down only some twelve years since, and were probably earlier than either of the dated examples. Of similar kind may have been the "stately iron gates and piers" to St. Thomas' Hospital, presented by Mr. Guy in 1707 at a cost of £3,000. Gates resembling those still at Gray's Inn have disappeared from St. Andrew's Church, Holborn, to which they formed a handsome approach.

Dated gates are so rare that the old and interesting entrance gates to Sandringham, (Plate xlii) with the monogram of one of the

Henleys, and date 1724 in the overthrow, cannot be passed over. Their design is unusually good.

Other dated gates are at St. Nicholas' Church at Lynn, sketched by E. G. Dawber, and bear the date 1742. They are almost on the lines of those at Sandringham but without the pilasters, which are replaced by two narrow fixed panels of ironwork between brick and stone piers. The overthrow comprises, besides the date, two circles with interlaced letters and a pyramid of scrolls with high finial. The similarity of these dated gates, whether in London or in Norfolk, renders it at least possible that they are by the same makers. A pair of plainer gates at Lynn, with high overthrow has a circle with letters over the date 1798. Except a small gate to the Richmond Almshouses, erected by the Misses Houblon in the Sheen road, dated 1757, these comprise all the eighteenth-century gates yet met with bearing iron numerals as an integral part of the design. A beautiful gate between wide pilasters, to the College at Bromley in Kent, with an overthrow of three pyramids and five finials, bears a tablet recording the date of the will of John Warner, Bishop of Rochester, who, in 1666, bequeathed funds and directions for the foundation of the College. The building was not commenced till 1670, but the date has for long been accepted as that of the ironwork, which is probably not earlier than 1720. This gate is almost repeated in one that was until lately in Cheyne Walk, with an overthrow sketched and published by Ebbetts. The design is preserved in some modern gates there in which the old one may possibly have been worked up.

LONDON GATES

Before proceeding further to describe the existing London gates, the makers of which are still unknown, it should be mentioned that besides those to fore-courts and gardens, iron gates were also used in London, as in most of the cities of Europe,

Plate XLII.

THE OLD ENTRANCE GATES TO SANDRINGHAM,
NOW IN THE GARDENS, DATED 1724.

to close the inner courts or quadrangles of important public buildings and private mansions. Of these Halton wrote in 1708 (*New View of London*, p. 627) : " Those especially about half a mile in compass round the Royal Exchange, particularly eastward therefrom, are so numerous and magnificent, with Courts, Offices, and all other necessary apartments, inclosed to themselves, and noble gates and frontispieces of some towards the street, but chiefly so ornamental and richly furnished within, that it would require too much room to give the names and situations." Shaftesbury House in Aldersgate Street was no doubt one of the houses referred to. A few still remain, as the great but very plain gates to the Bank of England, and Saint Bartholomew's Hospital. The last existing example in London of iron gates closing the inner court of a private building was swept away when the fine mansion, No. 102, Leadenhall Street, was demolished in 1875, '76. The view of these (Fig. 51) is by J. W. Archer. They were large and massive, of plain vertical bars, with lateral borders of scrolled and geometric design. Though comparatively late they are of interest as survivals of the many of earlier date and finer workmanship referred to by Halton.

When in the eighteenth century it became the fashion for merchants and others to live away from their places of business, numbers of substantial houses were built for them in the villages and hamlets near town, now incorporated in the suburbs. These were mostly detached, and nearly always set back from the road with a courtyard in front, affording endless opportunities for iron gates and railings of moderate dimensions ; and many blacksmiths must have set up to meet the demand in a business which requires so small a capital. As the entrances were as a rule only to admit pedestrians, single gates sufficed, of simple design ; their importance depended on the fixed side panels, tall pilasters and overthrows. Iron railings on low walls with stone copings formed the screen, not infrequently completed by brick or stone

142 English Ironwork of the XVIIth and XVIIIth Centuries

FIG. 51. GATES TO THE INNER COURT OF THE FINE MANSION, NO. 102, LEADEN-
HALL STREET, DEMOLISHED IN 1876. *From a Watercolour Drawing by*
J. W. ARCHER, *about* 1850.

piers surmounted by balls, pine-apples, vases or crests. Suburban gates were no doubt produced by great smiths like Robinson, but probably they were more often the work of smaller men. It is difficult to discover their makers and to group them, as in the case of the more important earlier gates; for smiths in becoming numerous became individually less important and less distinctive in their styles. Their traditions must have been largely based on work executed for masters to whom all alike in those days had to serve apprenticeship. It is obvious that, as already mentioned, in London every smith's work so soon as fixed becomes open to the inspection of rivals, so that ideas and designs very soon merge into common property. Itinerant and temporary assistants carry all novel ideas and trade secrets from shop to shop. Throughout the half-century or more in which these charming gates and railings were produced, though traditional lines were not departed from, a general but not universal tendency towards a more severe and geometric treatment may be observed. During a career of even average length, as with artists, most craftsmen's standards of taste become modified. They change with the times, more abruptly perhaps when successors carry on the business. The trend of fashion gradually passed from the magnificent richness of Tijou and his contemporaries to greater reticence, and eventually the cheaper process of casting was substituted for the costly elaboration of handicraft. When the paved courts became suburban front gardens, cast iron finally gained ascendancy over wrought, giving place in turn to brick walls and to stucco and cement balustrades.

A natural and easy grouping would be the lighter and richer work contrasted with the sedate and severe, to which the dated and other gates just described belong, but any useful classification must be based on the characteristics of individual craftsmen, their ideas of proportion and balance, technical skill and general idiosyncrasies. In short it is the contributions by individual smiths to the development of the art and design of smithcraft that we seek to discover and appreciate, for these make its true history. Nothing short of an exhaustive and critical comparison, gate by gate, will enable any certain pronouncements to be made, so similar are the London gates in general design, and for this extensive co-operation is obviously necessary. Roughly, however, certain groups may at least provisionally already be detached.

The most important craftsmen must have carried on an extensive business in and around London. Their work, as we group it, is characteristically solid, and their designs, always restrained, seem exactly suited to the sedate but handsome brick and stone dwellings of wealthy London merchants. Their gates are usually plain, of vertical and horizontal bars, with rather heavy scrolls and water-leaves, always well tenoned and riveted together, and either barbed arrow-points or plain spikes to the dog-bars. The pyramidal overthrow usually comprises a pair of more or less elaborated and enriched G scrolls. The pilasters may comprise one of the many conventional "lyre-designs," or be formed of scroll-ended bars with water-leaves. Bent over bars, like inverted U's, are of frequent occurrence.

No. 4, Cheyne Walk, occupied for a time by George Eliot, possesses a plain gate with elliptical top, a drawing of which, made by J. W. Archer in 1851, is here reproduced (Fig. 52). The gate was even then in need of repair, and the lower part of the pilasters have since been buried in cement and a poor overthrow added. The filling of the pilasters is one of those complicated and varied forms briefly designated as "lyre," all partaking more or less of some one or other of the fanciful renderings of that classic instrument. The design is not remarkable but good, and not one of those in general use, perhaps suggesting the similar awl-like central figure, not curved, which seems to pierce the lock-rail, and is quite peculiar to the lyre pilasters of three or four gates in the West End.

FIG. 52. 4, CHEYNE WALK.
From a Watercolour Drawing by J. W. ARCHER, *about* 1851.

One of these at Clapham, Mr. John Norton's sketch of which was published many years ago, is conspicuous by a shield surmounted by a helmet and crest, one of the few instances in London gates. The design of the pilasters is repeated with variations in a less interesting gate formerly near the church at Hammersmith, also published from one of Norton's sketches, and again in those to a third sketch by him, the finials, fringes and dog-bars being alike in all three. A curious gate at Acton, also sketched by Norton and now demolished, had the pilaster panels of direct converging bars, their upper terminations concealed by a large acanthus-leaf capital.

A drawing (Fig. 53) by Maurice S. Adams, of the gate to Latimer House in Church Lane, Chiswick, is reproduced. The gate is plain and not remarkable, with simple lock-rail, fringes, and short arrow-headed dog-bars. The overthrow comprises a monogram, J.E.M., in a stepped rectangle. A gate at Walpole House, Chiswick Mall, presents the same arrangement of panels. A drawing of this with the fine side railing, by Maurice S. Adams, has been made since the disappearance of the finials, shown in the earlier drawing by Norton. The house is named from the Walpole family, and is said by Walford to have been the residence of Barbara, Duchess of Cleveland, who died in 1709 and was buried in the chancel of Chiswick Church. A lamp disfigures the overthrow. Another gate formerly at Chiswick, with a central lyre-pattern panel, repeated in a somewhat simpler and narrower form in the pilasters, had also the whole of the overthrow removed to make way for a lamp holder.

Another gate has a much richer panel in the centre than those of the pilasters. The pyramids in this case have been destroyed to form a lamp holder, and in a further example, where the central panel is richer than those of the pilasters, the overthrows are replaced by plain spikes and cast vases. The decorative value of gates is frequently enhanced by the substitution of a

FIG. 53. LATIMER HOUSE, CHURCH LANE, CHISWICK.
Drawn by MAURICE S. ADAMS.

central panel of scrolls for plain bars, as those just described. For our knowledge of these, and of two others without localities, we are indebted to Norton's sketches. All appear to be by the smith who made the gate for Walpole House. A last example by a different smith has the three panels identical, the pilasters or side panels being wider than usual. They are chiefly formed of scrolls, the salient feature being a stepped rectangular figure presenting an unusual effect over an equally unusual lock-rail, with five panels below, apparently cut down to fit the gate to its present position between piers, and under a lean-to covered way, on the Twickenham Road. The pyramids of the pilasters merge in the overthrow, on a base of horizontal scroll-ended bars, and are still tolerably complete, except as to the finials, and the probable removal of a monogram from the stepped rectangle to make way for a street lamp. It is curious to find the identical pattern of the pilasters used for the very decorative gate to Fenton House at Hampstead (Fig. 54). Here they are continued to the ground by vertical bars, scrolled at the base, with two crescents, finishing above in a large trefoil of acanthus, now lost. Below the lock-rail of the gate are panels as at Twickenham but with unusual dog-bars. The pyramid has G.C.S. in monogram in a stepped rectangle, with outer scrolls and bay leaves in acanthus.

A pair of gates to Twickenham House with horizontal tops have pilasters of the Greek-wave pattern, without pyramids, and the scrolled overthrow is imperfect. The lock-rail is of C scrolls placed horizontally in pairs, and above and below are vertical bars in pairs with ends scrolled next the lock-rail as in the Fenton House gate.

A small but beautifully designed garden gate at Inwood, near Templecombe, has the tapering spikes with the spherical swelling below the apex for dog-bars, and twisted spikes between thrown-over leaves as a fringe to the horizontal, and also as finials to

FIG. 54   FENTON HOUSE, HAMPSTEAD.   *Drawn by* ARTHUR STRATTON.

the lyre pilasters. The gate consists of a boldly scrolled central panel and an overthrow, its enrichments ending in arrow points and in acorns.

A gate to Kent House, Chiswick Mall is plain, with pilasters of vertical bars, scrolled over the lock-rail and cut obliquely at the top by the ascending horizontal bar of the railings, a weak and happily uncommon treatment. The overthrow consists of a large pair of G scrolls with water leaves, etc., including two bold tendrils with barbed ends.

The same smith was much employed in Essex, where he made frequent use of a peculiarly mannered border between the lock-rails of his gates, by which many of them can be identified. Such repetition is rare and the more remarkable since other telling and important features are constantly varied, as usual in smithcraft. The design is continued through the pilasters or panels, and as this border involves much intricate welding it was reserved for the more costly gates. Our illustration shows it in a gate at 6, Forest Lane, Stratford (Fig. 55), with arrow-point dog-bars below and button points between scrolls above. The top is in this case a low arch over the gate but horizontal over the side panels. In the centre is the monogram E.J. or E.J.F. in a stepped rectangle with arched top. The illustration (Fig. 55) is from a reproduction of a drawing by Mr. G. G. Poston when the gate was more perfect than at present. The well-known entrance gate to Sydenham House, Devon, is practically a replica except as to a central panel, which almost repeats the design of the pilasters to 15, Cheyne Walk. At Easton, Lord Warwick's place in Essex, is another replica of the gate and panels, but they are between heavy H-plan piers, with wide solid moulded bases and caps. The gate has been restored, and some of its existing features may not be original. The well-known house at Rainham, illustrated on Pl. 111 of Belcher's "Later Renaissance," has also a gate of nearly the same design, without the border to the overthrow or the acanthus

London Gates

FIG. 55. 6, FOREST LANE, STRATFORD. *Drawn by* G. G. POSTON.

leaves. A similar but simpler gate is at Whalebone Hall, Chadwell Heath (Plate XLIII), where the pilasters are of lyre design and the overthrow low, of recurved scrolls with water-leaves, berries and tendrils. In contrast to these, but with the same lock-rail, fringe and arrow-pointed dog-bars, are the pair of low and plain gates with wickets at Raphael Park, Romford (Plate XLIV). A much more lofty and imposing gate at Battersea, with side panels, recalls the Forest Lane gate, and is between high piers somewhat like those of Easton. The wide overthrow is partly a repeat of that at Forest Lane, without the border at the base or the acanthus leaves and monogram, and there are fine railings with pilasters on either side. A gate to Grove Hall, Woodford, (Plate XLV), resembles this, except that the intricate and typical lock-rail gives place to an extremely simple one of scroll-ended bars placed horizontally. This repeats in the overthrow, but with two oblong panels with diagonal attachments over the low arching top of the gate, and a high pyramid of scrolls with horizontal breaks and finials with the U supports introduced. Another gate with side panels, pilasters and horizontal top is at Abney House, Church Street, Stoke Newington, the lock-rail of typical design slightly modified. A fine pair of gates at West Drayton, are by the same hands, but with many peculiarities; and there is a good gate at Inwood, Templecombe, which must have been produced in the same works. Other handsome gates with pilasters and overthrow, still in good preservation, are in Romford Road, Stratford; the Grove, Stratford; at Elm Hall, Snaresbrook, and Church Place, Stoke Newington, of all of which illustrations have been published. That in Romford Road (Fig. 56) is interesting as one of the few with perfectly plain tapering spikes for dog-bars and over the scrolled lock-rail. Its pilasters are of lyre design, one lyre within the other and handsomely scrolled with leaves.

The gate at Elm House, Snaresbrook (Plate XLVI), has the typical fringe to its single lock-rail, and dog-bars. The overthrow,

Plate XLIII.

GATE TO WHALEBONE HALL, CHADWELL HEATH, ESSEX.

Plate XLIV.

ENTRANCE TO RAPHAEL PARK, ROMFORD.

Plate XLV

GATE TO GROVE HALL, WOODFORD.

Plate XLVI.

GATE AT ELM HALL, SNARESBROOK.

FIG. 56. ROMFORD ROAD, STRATFORD. *Drawn by* G. G. POSTON.

on a moulded bar comprises A.G. in monogram within a circle, possibly intended for the letter O, in a stepped rectangle. Another at Eagle House, Ponders End has pilasters with conical scrolled tops and flask-shape vases, and the lyre panels. Fore Street, Edmonton, still rich in gates, presents one with lyre pilasters and G scroll pyramids of the usual type, and a rich scrolled overthrow, with tendrils and two good sprays of laurel and berries. A gate to Elm House, Chase Side, Enfield, with lyre pilasters, has been spoilt, like very many others, by injudicious restoration. The fine entrance gates, with scrolled overthrow and flame-tuft finials, to Old Park, Enfield, are important.

A good effect is given to some of the overthrows with rectangular panels by prolonging and finishing the verticals with swaged and twisted ends, or duplicating and suspending them like reversed torches. A gate at Eltham, sketched by Norton, with J.S. in monogram, has the external bars of its low stepped rectangle carried high with flask-shaped finials united by leaves and scrolls, which also support the central higher rod, with its leaves and a heavier finial. A gate in the High Street, Walthamstow, has a similar but higher centre, on a horizontal base of scroll-ended bars with the finial, about 3 feet high, ending in a small flask-shaped terminal and twisted point; other finials rise from two large side scrolls. Both gates have button fringes over the lock-rail, the latter with C scrolls below it and arrow-pointed dog-bars. A sketch made by Ebbetts, at Stoke Newington, shows a similar overthrow, in which the stepped panel with scrolls and leaves has the centre finial passing through. This overthrow rests on a horizontal panel of scrolls with a centre which perhaps once carried a date or initials. The pilasters are similar to but simpler than those already noted. A gate at Woodbridge has a top very like this but richer, with a monogram in the stepped panel. Another sketched by Norton almost repeats this, but the stepped panel has an arched top and scrolls and no horizontal panel below; the pilasters are of much the same design, with handsome scrolled pyramid tops and large finials of scrolls and leaves.

In a somewhat different class must be placed a few less original and attractive gates. Some beaten and thrown-over leaves are introduced, while all have the swaged and beaded finials which terminate in buttons with short twisted points, these peculiarities preserving a connexion with the preceding group.

Among the most interesting are the gate and railing to Church House in Church Street, Stoke Newington, once the residence of Isaac Disraeli. The gate is plain with a fringe of twisted points between scrolls over the lock-rail, arrow-pointed dog-bars, and lyre pattern pilasters. The overthrow contains an oval with intricate monogram, over a panel of scrolls between branching stems, from which proceed scrolls, leaves, and tendrils, uniting above in a scrolled finial ending in a button point and twist. Beyond the brick piers with stone caps and bases are handsome railings, with scrolled pyramids and pilasters on a low wall.

At Elm House, Fore Street, Lower Edmonton, is a gate with a central panel of scrolled bars, with leaves in pairs, almost repeated in the pilasters. The overthrow rests on a short horizontal panel formed of a swaged flèche passing through an inverted U. Gates with scrolled centre panels are rarer in Essex than to the north and west of London.

Returning to the West End we meet with a small group of gates which present peculiarities demanding notice. One of these at Argyll House in the King's Road, Chelsea, has a rich overthrow of scrolls and water-leaves, with a very small central rosette; below being a stepped rectangle with P.J.V. in monogram, and scrolls beneath. The very attenuated and refined pilasters are striking features, with their low simple caps of a U between concave sides. This top recurs in a gate formerly near to Holland House, but the pilasters differ somewhat in design.

The small pilaster top is met with again in a gate on Richmond Green, but here the pilasters are much wider and of lyre pattern, richly worked. An overthrow of scrolls with acanthus, laurel and water-leaves, bears the small distinctive rosette of the Argyll House gate and below is a stepped rectangle containing G.L. in monogram, with a circle on either side and horizontal bars below. The buttons of the fringe are squared and pointed, and there are C scrolls below and arrow-pointed dog-bars.

Again the pilaster top is seen at 23, the Old Town, Clapham (Plate XLVII), also over a rich lyre-pattern. The gate has an elliptical top with an overthrow of the same general design as the last. A curious feature common to the Clapham and Richmond gates is the repetition of the design of the upper part of the pilaster below the lock-rail, but cut off and ending abruptly in vertical bars, with a by no means pleasing effect, looking as if part of the design had been buried. This feature is not accidental; it is shared by a gate in Seymour Place, Chelsea, formerly at Grove House, now restored and refixed at a cottage, a curious cluster of leaves being recently added as an appropriate finial (Plate XLVIII). Here the pilasters are disproportionately wide and coarse. All these gates have alike the same plain arrow-pointed dog-bars, fringes of twisted points and scrolls over the lock-rail, in three cases with an additional pair of leaves, and in four out of the five with the not very common fringe of C scrolls below it.

The gate, formerly at the Old Manor House, Church Street, Stoke Newington, of which a complete drawing has been published, was undoubtedly by the same maker. In this case the gate itself is of two twin panels of scrolls with water leaves separated by a centre bar with husks and scrolls. The panels are continued below the lock rail, but truncated, and the pilasters are wide like those to Grove House.

Probably in inverted order, each of these gates was an improvement in design on the other, with perhaps many an inter-

Plate XLVII.

GATE IN THE OLD TOWN, CLAPHAM.

Plate XLVIII.

GATE IN SEYMOUR PLACE, FULHAM ROAD,
FORMERLY AT GROVE HOUSE.

London Gates

mediate link now destroyed. One such, sketched by Norton in Queen's Road, Chelsea, had pilasters as sedate as those to Argyll House in the King's Road. Another, sketched by Norton without definite locality, has pilasters of scrolled bars with an oval for centre and a charming overthrow.

A gate at Kensington without pilasters, sketched by Norton and published, shows the peculiar small rosette in the centre of the overthrow, as well as the same finials, a fringe of twisted spikes between double thrown-over leaves over the lock-rail, and C scrolls below it, a combination conclusive as to its having belonged to the group. A sketch taken more recently, but with no note as to locality, shows that one even finer than the Clapham or Richmond examples existed somewhere in the west of London. Here the gate top is elliptical, the pilaster panels of two vertical scroll-ended bars, while the overthrow comprises P.B.A. in monogram in a stepped rectangle.

A sketch made at Chiswick by Norton shows a gate with lyre pilasters, a small rosette in the middle, and the simple concave top scrolled on each side with button-twist finial. The overthrow is of large scrolls and tendrils, with an open pear-shaped finial. In another gate with similar pilasters the monogram J.W. in ogee frame, scrolls and a laurel-tuft finial, rest upon a horizontal panel of leaves in pairs, and form the overthrow. The short dog-bars are barbed with button-twist points suggesting the hand of Buncker for the whole group. The presence of the low top with inverted U beneath, over lyre pilasters in a gate to Cedar Villa, Enfield, requires noting here.

A coarsely designed gate at Clapham, several times sketched and published, has wide-scrolled pilasters, with horizontal panels under the overthrow, consisting of scrolls which form a large heart shape, with tufts of leaves for finials. There is a small vertical panel in the centre of the gate, which attaches to this group through the truncated panel at the base of the pilasters.

158 English Ironwork of the XVIIth and XVIIIth Centuries

Other West End gates mostly of refined and excellent design might be placed with these. Of such may be mentioned a sketch published by Norton of a narrow lodge gate at North End, Fulham, with dolphin scrolls rich with waterleaves and tendrils. Another sketch shows a gate, probably at Chiswick, of plain vertical bars, with scrolled lock-rail carried through plain pilasters, and an overthrow of scrolls diverging with characteristic drops between, finishing in button twists like the three pyramids. This gate is connected immediately with the group by its small central rosette. A beautiful example at Ravenscourt Park presents a tall plain gate with scrolled lock-rail, C scrolls above it and dog-bars below enriched with scrolls and buttons. There is a monogram C.J. in stepped rectangle in the overthrow, with branching G scrolls, leaves, and tendrils; and the pilasters are finely and delicately worked. A simpler treatment with B.B. in the stepped rectangle was sketched at Brook Green by Norton, where the panels of the pilasters had leaves welded in pairs. Vertical C's over the lock-rail occur in a gate with wide scrolled pilasters formerly in Chiswick Mall. Another sketch has them vertically under the top-rail, and arranged diagonally in fours above and below the lock-rail. A plain gate with scrolled overthrow, sketched by Norton at Fulham, was remarkable for waved points on flattened spheres over the lock-rail. It was supported by the lyre pilasters of the railing set upon a low wall.

A gate with semicircular top in Chiswick Mall, sketched and published by Norton, but now removed had a usual and well-designed arrangement of scrolls with leaves and tendrils, horizontal breaks, finials of leaves and twisted spikes for the overthrow. A second pair of gates in the Mall, sketched in 1885, of much the same design, bore a shield and two small laurel sprays in the overthrow and had a scrolled lock-rail with fringe, and fine pilasters of lyre design. A gate at Hampstead has a similar top but plain pilasters, and another at Romford a bolder and less well-proportioned overthrow of two large scrolls with acanthus and laurel sprays and open vase-shaped centre.

One of the finest of the gates in this group, and indeed in the vicinity of London, is in Sheen Road, Richmond (Frontispiece) The work is unusually rich, the ends of the principal scrolls spirally produced, with secondary scrolls and bars, beaded and almost hidden by water-leaves. The overthrow bears a most intricate monogram in a circle supported by dolphin scrolls with clusters of leaves and berries on waved stems, with a crest as finial. Much of the gate is taken up by a central panel of lyre design, repeated in the pilasters over the scrolled lock-rail. A fringe to the upper horizontal bears button and twist points on diverging stems, and to the lock-rail fringes of button points between scrolls, and the dog-bars are arrow pointed and scrolled.

Hampshire Hog Lane contained a gate with J.A.C. in monogram in a square frame, and finials each of three twisted laurel leaves; and Wandsworth another, now lost, with one central vertical panel to the gate, and a wide horizontal panel above between the pilasters, both of scroll-work and leaves, while dog-bars and the finials to the overthrow are of plain spikes with button and twist points; this is broadly scrolled and contains D.P. in monogram in a rectangle, while the pilaster panels are of simple lyre design. It is remarkable how the London smiths clung to these. A noteworthy gate at Merstham, has a moulded broken pediment and scrolled finial for overthrow, over a massively moulded circle between two supporting scrolls with vertical breaks. The gate below is lofty with scrolled lock-rail, and the pilasters of five verticals are capped by a reversed U between scrolls and an arrow point.

While most of the gate tops noticed are designed on convex lines, a very beautiful variety is produced by reversing these and making the overthrow of a tent-shaped outline. Comparatively few were so treated, however, and those in the neighbourhood of London must almost all be regarded as practically the work of a single smith. One of their most beautiful features, common to several, is a drooping festoon of long sinuous interlacing stems, sparsely set with waved lanceolate leaves in groups of two or three, and occasional berries and tendrils. This feature recalls the work assigned to Warren on earlier pages, and no other gate-smith yet identified seems so likely to have produced them.

One still, sketched by Norton, remains at Elmsdale, on the green at Newington (Plate XLIX). The pyramid consists constructively of only two graceful wide-spreading scrolls and branches, recurved above and brought together on each side of a finial, to form a sort of heart-shape centre, repeated lower down. This pyramid rests on a simple horizontal panel, low down between the pilasters. The high pilasters have lyres with beaded centre bars, and finish above in scrolls, tendrils and a spike. A gracefully drooping bracket connects the pilaster with a railing.

A simpler rendering of this was sketched by Ebbetts, without the horizontal base to the pyramid and with lower and less imposing pilasters. A far more important example, sketched by Norton, has two side panels beyond the pilasters. The base to the overthrow extends over the pilasters and side panels, interrupted only by three small looped centres. The pyramid is also precisely like that described, but more extended, and finishes over the side panel beyond the pilasters in reversed scrolls with finials and tendrils.

Another sketch by Norton shows an overthrow of similar outline carried up in converging lines. A fourth sketch, unfinished, represents a gate on the old road to Newington, with rich and unusual pilasters; waved and barbed dog-bars, with buttons and twist points. Scrolls, diverging at the base and meeting to hold two dropping husks and a finial, are under the top horizontal, and waved spikes between leaves over the scrolled lockrail. The drawing of the overthrow shows scrolls and tendrils, but is unfinished. These gates are very remarkable. Two further sketches

Plate XLIX.

GATE AT NEWINGTON GREEN, STOKE NEWINGTON.

London Gates

the one taken in the Grove, Highgate, and the other at 42, Newington Green, afford simpler examples of overthrows of tent-shaped outline. The fine gate on Stratford Green is by the same artist.

A great group may be distinguished by the use of a lanceo-

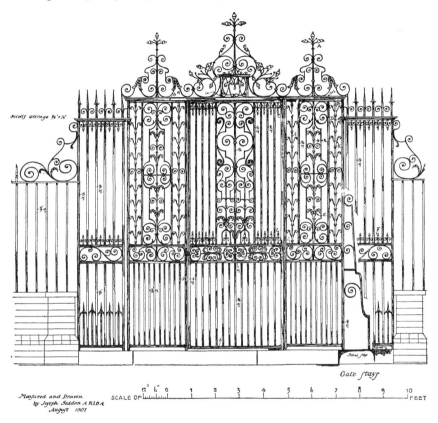

FIG. 57.   EAGLE HOUSE, MITCHAM.

late leaf form thinned down and beaten out from the end of a rectangular bar, not welded to it, and thrown over with a half-twist, generally with the point downwards. Though an obviously simple form to smithcraft, its introduction seems to have been late, but after a time to have passed into general use. It forms a principal feature in the gate to Eagle House at Mitcham (Fig. 57), once the property of Sir Walter Raleigh, and rebuilt, Mr. Garraway Rice believes, after the death of Sir Walter Plumer its then owner in 1697. Though in effect this gate with its rich panels is imposing, in point of design it is not comparable to those of earlier date. It consists of a gate between wide pilasters, each with scrolled panels, the latter bordered vertically with thrown-over leaves disposed symmetrically in pairs on a beaded stem. The lock-rail is scrolled, and the space below is wholly occupied by plain vertical bars. The overthrow, on a moulded bar, comprises three pyramids, the centre with J.M.D. in monogram in a square frame between two G scrolls and large laurel sprays with berries and tendrils; the others simpler, but all with finials of three leaves and berries. Mr. Garraway Rice believes these to be the initials of James and Mary Dolliffe. James Dolliffe was a director of the South Sea Company and was knighted in 1714 when the gates were perhaps put up. His death a very few months later fixes the date of the gates as, at the latest, the beginning of 1715. His widow removed shortly afterwards. Much of the ornament, including acanthus rosettes to the panels, has been lost in restorations. On each side are two added panels, of vertical bars with scrolls, alternating with others which formerly finished with leafy arrow points.

A beautiful gate with monogram to Barons House, Mitcham, was removed in 1906.

An earlier example of this work exists at Eagle House, Fore Street, Edmonton (Plate L), in which the lock-rail has a fringe of twisted points between leaves and two pairs of scrolls, and the dog-bars are arrow-pointed. The pilasters recall the centre of the Mitcham gate, but repeated below the lock-rail. The overthrow comprises an elaborate monogram, E.S.R., in a stepped rectangle supported by G scrolls with acanthus and other leafage, and a finial terminating in a flame tuft. The piers are surmounted by eagles supporting Italian-shaped shields of arms.

Plate L.

GATE TO EAGLE HOUSE, FORE STREET, EDMONTON.

Plate LI.

GATE TO NO. 15 CHEYNE WALK, CHELSEA.

London Gates 163

The same leaves characterise a gate at Percy House, in the High Road, Tottenham. A high overthrow with H.S. in monogram in a stepped rectangle, set with a tall flèche of beaten leaves and twisted point, between scrolls bearing acanthus leaves, completes the design. A second gate in Fore Street, Edmonton, has identical fringe and dog-bars, but with scrolled lock-rail. Its pilasters are lyre pattern, with thrown-over leaves and beads to the central bar, and G scroll pyramids above. An overthrow bears thrown-over leaves, tendrils and two handsome sprays of laurel.

No. 15, Cheyne Walk (Plate LI) presents an interesting gate of this group, surmounted by the gilt dolphin crest and monogram, L.K.C., of a Lord Courtney. It is high with a large central panel of scroll-work between vertical bars, a single lock-rail and arrow-pointed dog-bars. The pilasters comprise a simpler panel with dog-bars below and finials of S scrolls above. The overthrow is a pyramid chiefly of two enriched G scrolls with horizontal breaks carrying leafy finials. The top is stated to be new by Mr. Walter Godfrey in the *Survey of the Parish of Chelsea*, Part I., and that the scrolls connecting the pilasters with a plain railing fixed on a dwarf wall, served for the design of the new top.

The gate at No. 5 Cheyne Walk, is fixed between massive brick and stone piers spaced for large entrance gates, two plain panels of five vertical bars with lamp-holders occupying part of the space. The gate has a button and scroll fringe over the lock-rail, and arrow-pointed dog-bars. The pilasters are high with an oval centre and pyramid of recurved scrolls and laurel sprays. The overthrow rests on a frame of parallel bars and a C scroll, and is of scrolls with acanthus supporting an oval with E.L. in monogram. Two side gates match with overthrows of dolphin scrolls. Mr. Godfrey notes that a drawing of Lindsay House, Chelsea, in 1750, has been published in England's account of the Moravian Settlements, showing fine iron gates on the river front, the piers and ironwork coinciding with that of No. 5 except that there were double gates between the piers. Should the ironwork have been altered to adapt it for its new position, the initials would be those of Erasmus Lewis, who lived at No. 5 from 1748 to 1751.

Some forty years since Mr. Norton published a sketch of a gate near the old church at Fulham which still remains. The overthrow is now a rectangular frame with delicately worked monogram R.L. on a horizontal base, remarkable because supported on five U's or semicircles, all above being lost. The pilasters are almost perfect, of rich design and with unusual pyramid tops and thrown-over leaves. In a cross lane near Merton Abbey, out of the road to Morden, he happened on a fine pair of gates and fixed panels matching them, with unusually wide lock-rail, the design of which practically repeats that of the Fulham pilasters. The high pyramid overthrow of scrolls rests on a horizontally treated stepped base with tall flèche finishing in a flame twist, bordered and supported by scrolls closely set with beaten leaves, tendrils, etc., and continued as a low cresting across the gates and panels. These gates were removed three or four years ago and disposed of. He also found close by a second and no less interesting gate which still exists near a wooden bridge, by the same hand, with peculiar bulbous, almost flask-shaped spikes with short twisted points over the lock-rail, particularly good pilasters of unusual design, and rich overthrow. A large monogram in a square panel seems to comprise the letter S repeated four times, and E.R. smaller repeated twice, and the buttressing scrolls and pyramid are rich with acanthus and laurel, beaten and water-leaves. A sketch on Stepney Green shows a gate between fixed panels and handsome pilasters, with fine pyramids and buttressing scrolls over plain railing, and a well-designed overthrow with J.M. in a stepped rectangle between dolphin scrolls. This and the fine gate at Cranford should be included in the group, for these and the Merton gates are far superior in design to those at Mitcham.

A rather simple gate with pilasters and overthrow, sketched

by Norton at Fulham, belongs to this group and having for monogram an M in a circle between two J's reversed. A sketch made many years since shows one of a remarkable group of gates at Brentford, of very delicate and unusual workmanship. It no longer exists, but consisted of an almost plain gate and fixed panels. A deep frieze divided into panels is well filled by bold dolphin scrolls, and acanthus, represented in outline, amid graceful leaves and tendrils. A central pyramid above is formed of two dolphin scrolls with solid acanthus and tendrils, over a stepped rectangle and a narrow horzontal base of scrolls. There are lesser pyramids over the pilasters connected by a cresting; and the finials are of clustered leaves and berries.

A second richly worked gate is in Marlborough Park, at Brentford. Neither the gate nor the pilasters of lyre design, though of rich work, present any striking originality of design, except that the latter rise high above the gates. Between the pilasters is a semicircular overthrow, with scroll filling, and a narrow border of great taste and simplicity, and the cresting of usual but good design, the scrolls mounting with the arch, with horizontal breaks bearing finials, G scrolls with a mask and acanthus leaves for centre completing the pyramid. Another of the same delicate workmanship remains to Beaufort House, the Butts, Brentford. The pilasters are slender, their panels of scroll ended bars, and centre set with thrown-over leaves in pairs. The overthrow is simply of horizontal lines and a circle with three simple scrolls above. There are gates of more usual type by the Richmond smith to the Convent in the Butts, and to the Cedars in the Upper Butts at Brentford.

The only English gate in the Victoria and Albert Museum (Fig. 58) is of similar workmanship to that of Beaufort House, with the characteristic fringes and dog-bars. The pilasters are wide, of slender vertical bars bent and scrolled, and enriched with scrolls, thrown-over leaves and buttons. The overthrow is a stepped

166 English Ironwork of the XVIIth and XVIIIth Centuries

FIG. 58.   GATE NOW IN THE VICTORIA AND ALBERT MUSEUM.

pyramid, resting on C scrolls and inverted U's upholding finials. Over the pilasters also are high finials buttressed by scrolls, with tendrils.

A gate to the Barnes District Office also finds its place here. It is plain with side panels to match, each alternate vertical with pairs of scrolls above, a wide scrolled lock-rail and dog-bars with arrow points. A frieze, divided centrally, of two scroll-ended horizontal bars and cross-ties, has a refined effect immediately below three well-proportioned pyramids of scrolls and leaves.

An old sketch of a gate still existing at West Drayton shows laurel-leaf finials to the overthrow and pilasters, with R.G.B. in monogram in a square panel. Three vertical panels of ornament are shown with beaten leaves, and it thus appears to be among the most decorative in the vicinity of London. A good typical example is in front of Harold House, at Waltham Cross built in 1757, but the gate can hardly be so recent. The lock-rail is handsomely scrolled with turned-over leaves, which pass through the pilasters. Over this the pilasters are of stiff lyre design. An overthrow of recurving scrolls oversails the pilasters, and comprises a small circle with a most delicate monogram between two ovals in rectangular frames. A simple gate at Stratford Green, with plain spikes over the lock-rail and for dog-bars, has very narrow pilasters filled by a centre bar with leaves and scrolls, and an overthrow of a small circle with J.W. in monogram between dolphin scrolls with beaten leaves. A sketch at Eltham shows the same pilaster and fixed panels beyond, matching the gate, the overthrow comprising an indistinct monogram in a stepped rectangle between vertical bars, with solid turned finials. There is a drawing, published and lithographed by George D. Stevenson, of the only still existing gate at West Hill, Wandsworth, its overthrow of recurving scrolls with thrown-over water-leaves and a stepped rectangular panel with J.E. in monogram.

Panels of converging bars are the characteristics of several pairs of gates in central London. Those of Christchurch, Newgate Street, illustrations of which have been published, are unique in design, the most striking of several peculiarities being the two central panels of each gate, one above and one below the scrolled lock-rail. These consist of a cone formed of two bars scrolled at the ends, and a third between them passing vertically through both panels and the scrolled lock-rail, clothed with beaten leaves in pairs, points upward. Each gate is completed by two pairs of vertical bars with scrolled ends, above and below the lock-rail. The overthrow consists of an oval with L.S.C. in monogram, under a smaller cone with scrolled base, between G scrolls, and with a finial of minute leaves, and large scrolls below with short vertical instead of the usual horizontal breaks.

A similar cone or obelisk more richly treated made an artistic filling to the pilasters of a gate at Whitelands, Chelsea, also sketched and published some years since. The lower panels are as interesting. Pilasters comprising centre bars with leaf points in pairs turned upward are often seen, as in gates sketched by Norton at Brook Green, and Queen's Road, Chelsea, all now destroyed.

A small and rather local group united to this by the presence of thrown-over leaves is chiefly represented at Richmond. A gate to Forbes House on Ham Common is distinguished by a row of plain tapering spikes with a spherical ball under the apex. Its pilasters are of two vertical bars, bent into scrolls at the ends, with a third bar between, clothed with leaves and scrolls and bearing a heavily moulded oval for centre. A second gate with the same spikes at 143, London Road, Richmond, has lyre pilasters with long welded centres. A gate to Sudbrooke Lodge on Ham Common has the short bulbous points and scrolls over the lock-rail, and twisted points between leaves fringing the top-rail. The pilaster panels are of two verticals brought together and scrolled at both ends and in the middle, with scrolls and thrown-over leaves, repeated below. The Park belonged to the Duke of Argyll about 1717. The overthrows to the Ham Common gates are of dolphin scrolls with loose water-leaves and coarse tendrils, larger in the Sudbrooke Lodge gate, where they oversail the pilasters, and rest on a short horizontal panel with two C scrolls, and shortened up in the Forbes House gate to make space for two G-scroll tops to the pilasters. Over the Richmond gate are scrolls with moulded horizontal breaks and finials, with R.S. in a moulded circle between, over a short panel with a C scroll; between two pyramids over the pilasters of G scrolls, with a beaded centre bar finishing in an arrow point. Many different ends to the scrolls are intentionally introduced by the smith, but in all the dog-bars are alike, being seldom varied in a workshop unless by special instructions. On the west side of Richmond Green is a gate with an overthrow of dolphin scrolls and loose water leaves, oversailing the pilasters, which are mainly of scrolled vertical bars with thrown-over leaves. The three tall and massive gates in Honor Row, next the Palace, have similar scroll overthrows with horizontal breaks, and lyre pilasters with scroll pyramids. They date from about 1710, but one has been "restored." A gate to Petersham House, now in the garden, has very fine pilasters, somewhat on the lines of those in the London Road but much richer, with cone-shaped pyramids on a base of three ovals. The gate head is semicircular. There is said to be a fine pair of gates leading from the garden to the meadow behind the house. The gate to the adjoining Rutland Lodge is severe, but a coat of arms is said to be concealed by ivy. A gate on Ham Common near Forbes House, with semicircular top, should be included in the group. The pilasters are of lyre design, resting at the height of the scrolled lock-rail on two heavy moulded ovals, and the scrolled overthrow with pyramid centre oversails them.

A gate on the High Road, Tottenham, repeating the Forbes House gate overthrow, with lyre pilasters, sketched by Norton, should also be included in this group. The gate in Seymour Place,

Chelsea, with a rectangle in the overthrow, moulded at the top, and divided by two vertical and one horizontal crossing bars with heavy moulded oval centre, has the same massive scrolls above with long water-leaves and large tendrils. The pilasters are of scroll-ended verticals, with pyramid tops, concave and scrolled, horizontal moulding, and cast vases as finials.

Pilasters repeating those of Greek-wave pattern by Tijou are rare, but a sketch of one at Hampstead is by Ebbetts. The pilasters are low and wide and comprise several repeats of the Greek wave with water-leaves, on a beaded centre bar. The gate top rises in a curve to the centre pyramid of recurving scrolls, with two drooping button twists. The lock-rail is of dolphin scrolls with a circle for centre. A gate at Twickenham repeats the pilasters with two flame-tuft finals and a fan-shaped spray of laurels.

A published sketch of a gate at Clapham shows pilasters of a series of semicircles on both sides of a centre bar welded and forming a series of open lozenges, the centres marked by a bead. The overthrow is of two dolphin scrolls with long water-leaves and a high finial like the spike of an aloe.

Probably a gate sketched by Norton on the Great North Road at Highgate, with scrolled lock-rail having a circle for centre, may be by the same hand. The pilaster panels are of vertical bars ending above in a pear-shaped pyramid of scrolls. The overthrow is a pyramid of two recurved scrolls supporting an oval, on a scrolled horizontal base with flask-shaped finial. Another gate at Hampstead has the pilaster filling in the outline of a vase, with scrolls and a centre bar which opens into a vesica, while the gate top rises in an ellipse under a scrolled pyramid.

Two gates with semicircular heads have been sketched by Norton and also published by Ebbetts. That at Bolton House Fulham Road, the remains of part of the mansion of Lord Tregunter, and said to have been the Royal Military Academy, since at Woolwich, had the pilasters finished in low concave tops and

Plate LII.

GATE IN KENSINGTON GORE.

vases, now lost, and overthrow finishing above in a platform for a crest and two small leaf sprays. Only fragments of the scrolls which supported the centre remained when the sketches were made, and still less exists now. The second gate is at Stoke Newington, by the same smith. The pilasters have high pinnacles of G scrolls with tall flask-shaped finials, and leaves; their long lyre panels comprising scrolls and a bodkin-like centre, point upwards, with an oval and leaves below it. The overthrow centres in a small arch ending in leaf and button-twist finials between two open pilasters.

For want of a more appropriate place, the large pair of gates to Hampstead Church are included here. They present a certain resemblance to those just described and are of rich design. They are believed to date from 1745, but possibly brought from somewhere else. They have centre panels with arching tops and acanthus, over recurving scrolls, and arrow-pointed dogs between incurving scrolls. The overthrow is of two large recurving scrolls with heavy acanthus leaves, thrown-over leaves and high finial. The pilasters are designed in the manner of the centre panel.

The group is completed by the small but rich gate at No. 24, Kensington Gore, sketched both by Ebbetts and Norton (Plate LII). It has a semicircular top, the region above the lock-rail filled, except as to two vertical spaces, with a panel of scroll design, much like that at Hampstead, with two heavy compressed moulded ovals. The pilasters correspond, and their scrolled pyramids also recall those to Hampstead Church. The overthrow is like that to the Brentford gate on a smaller scale with high finial. All below the single lock-rail is plain vertical bar, with ordinary arrow-pointed dog-bars. These have certain affinities with the work of Warren; at least the Little Cloister gates at Westminster and some others of richer work are by the same hand.

A gate with intercrossing ornaments in the Chippendale manner is illustrated (Plate LIII) from Baker Street, Enfield, dating from about 1760.

The later eighteenth century gates are usually of plain horizontal and vertical bars, spiked, and required the support of stretchers or bars crossing the gate diagonally, through which the verticals passed. These usually curve either upward or downward completing a semicircle when the gates are closed; but they also frequently cross diagonally in a direct line. There are interesting gates and railings to the Jermyn Street front of St. James' Church, of verticals with moulded spikes and lozenges between the duplicated horizontals. The massive octagonal piers enclose a high rectangular panel of alternately larger and smaller intersecting diagonals.

The garden entrance to Lansdowne House, perhaps designed by Robert Adam soon after 1765 (Plate LIV) for Lord Shelburne, afterwards Marquis of Lansdowne, is of spear-headed verticals with three duplicated horizontals enclosing circles, and with two large ovals below the lock-rail of bars radiating from rosette centres. The piers are massive and four-sided with scroll and honeysuckle panels, surmounted by the Lansdowne beehive. The purely decorative parts are of cast iron. The entrance to Sion Park is a noble architectural structure by the Adams, in which the metal work is subordinate. The gates, some 12 feet high, fall to the centre like a reflected arch. They are of wrought iron except the enrichments below the lock-rail, which are bronze. Richness is gained by intermediate bars, scrolled at the ends, with water leaves, and opening centrally into a lozenge.

This is, however, not a very characteristic example of Robert Adam's work. A number of his designs are preserved in the Soane Museum, and show an extraordinary mastery of details within the lines he had laid down, for frequently there are three or four rough alternative sketches for the treatment of even a simple gate of small cost. His designs for entrances are sometimes majestic, but rely for their effect either entirely, or chiefly, on the masonry.

Plate LIII.

HOUSE AT BAKER STREET, ENFIELD.

Plate LIV.

GARDEN ENTRANCE TO LANSDOWNE HOUSE, BERKELEY SQUARE.

Robert Adam was engaged in 1778 in making designs for the entrance to Hyde Park, which was not erected until 1828 by Decimus Burton, on lines that are hardly superior. In one of these the gates beneath the main arch are large panels of treillage, or bars crossing diagonally with rosettes at the intersections, between borders designed as pilasters and filled in with repetitions of vesicas, supporting a pyramid with arms, garter and crown, a vesica frieze over the panel, and vertical work under the lock-rail. On either side are three lesser arches with simpler pairs of gates or railings to correspond. In a second design the principal gates are treated vertically with enrichments something like those at Sion. Among the entrances is a design for Lord Coventry at Croome, 1791, in which the centre gates under a triumphal arch have horizontal tops supporting an oval coat of arms, coronet, crest, and supporters, placed centrally, with horizontal borders of Greek wave pattern. No less important gates beneath arches of masonry are for the Rt. Hon. Charles Loftus, 1785, and for Lord Wemyss at Gosford. The horizontal tops are in one case surmounted by a shield and crest and in the other by a monogram W.M. under a coronet, a unique example. Both are divided by horizontals, filled with circles or lozenges with geometric treatments below the lock-rail. Lord Dumfries' gate, 1784, has arms and coronet, but is otherwise plainer, though the wickets are occupied above the lock-rail by great circles of radiating ornament, as gates were sixty years before. Gates for the Hon. Richard Rigby, designed in 1781 and delivered in 1782, are remarkable for the large fixed grille of radiating design above them, but otherwise resemble those for Mr. Loftus described above. Of other designs for high gates, two of 1776 are of plain verticals above the lock-rail and treillage below, kept from the ground by a base of short verticals. Other sketches seem imperfectly worked out but show at least that Robert Adam had no inclination to repeat himself; though he was indifferent as to whether the designs could be executed in wrought iron or needed to be cast. In the case of his noble Admiralty screen he seems to have permitted the old railings to be used. Gates between piers were usually plainer, of vertical bars without lock-rail, often with duplicated horizontals, usually with semi-circular stretchers rising towards the centre. A richer treatment is produced by doubling the stretchers and filling in between these, with lozenges, scales, circles, etc. In the lodge gates designed for Osterly Park, 1777, a set of decorative intermediate verticals stop on the single stretcher, a series of arches, between the alternate verticals that pass through, appearing to support it, the larger part of the gates below the stretcher thus appearing more open than the rest. An even more unsatisfactory treatment is that in which all the verticals are cut off abruptly by the semi-circular stretcher and the region below occupied by a fanlike design. Three or four designs share this treatment and appear to date from 1790. It is however abandoned in the latest design, made in 1794 for Dalkeith, in which there is a lock-rail on which the stretchers stop, below being borders and waved bars. A singular effect is given by a compressed fan-shaped design below the lock-rail, stretching across the whole width of each of the pair of gates intended for Findlater Castle. Among the rest is a "Gothic iron gate" for the porch of the Church at Croome, by Robert Adam, 1763.

Gates designed by William Thomas are extremely like those by Robert Adam, and of the same dates, while those designed later by Sir John Soane are more severe.

Carter presents one especially rich in the *Builders' Magazine* for 1774, of segments of intersecting semicircles, with the spaces filled in with elaborate scroll-work. Another is of plain vertical bars crossed by circles and segments of ellipses.

Plainer gates to the public garden at Bromley have a border of lozenges to the lock-rail and cast iron piers similar to those of Lansdowne House, but of richer and more delicate design, brought from the Bishop's Palace at Farnborough.

Notes on Country Gates by Undiscovered Designers

THERE remain the vast majority of gates outside London, the names of whose artificers have yet to be discovered. Some may have formed the centres of fore-court screens, others were gates to gardens, avenues, pleasure-grounds, porches, and the like.

Numbers have been transported from long distances to be set up amidst new surroundings, and perhaps at the same time restored or reconstructed to suit altered conditions: comparatively few remain in the original sites, as contemplated by their designers. This part of the subject must necessarily be incomplete, and additions and corrections may probably be numerous and are earnestly invited.

The South-Eastern Counties

Kent.—Parts of Kent and Surrey fall within the London area, and gates situated within these limits are described under the London section. These counties also comprise with part of Sussex the "Weald" or ancient "Black Country" of the Tudors and Stuarts, then the greatest seat of the Iron industry. Kent as we know from its fine County Histories, once abounded in magnificent gates and fore-court screens, such as those represented in the views of Chevening, Squerries, Waldershare Park, High Street and Highgate Houses, Lees Court near Faversham, etc., all of which have disappeared without leaving a vestige behind. Penshurst and Knole are among the very few historic houses that have preserved even some of their gates.

The gates at Knole (Fig. 59) are not visible in the 1707 view by Kip, but in a later one five gates are seen in nearly their present positions. The principal gates are distinguished by a horizontal base to the overthrow, two feet deep, like those frequently seen in Robinson's work, of scroll-ended bars converging towards a central quatrefoil. Over this, on a narrow border of scrolls, is the central pyramid, bearing the monogram and coronet of the Earl of Middlesex and Dorset, and lateral pyramids of scrolls and flowers The pilasters are tall and attenuated, with lyre panels recalling those at Exning, and between these are the gates, with each alternate vertical bar finishing above in a pair of scrolls, a scrolled lock-rail fringed on both sides, and short arrow-pointed dog-bars. On either side are fixed panels of scroll-ended bars forming a pattern twice repeated, and beyond the pilasters other panels of vertical bars with scrolled cresting rising towards the stone piers. Some other garden gates also bear monograms and coronets, and a small pair in an arched opening reproduce the M and D in the lock-rail.

These gates differ from all others in the southern counties, but reproduce the peculiar horizontal panels of scrolled bars converging to a central circle seen in the gates to Jesmond Hall, Newcastle, Chester-le-Street, and Tanfield to the north of Durham.

In the garden gates at Penshurst the space above the lock-rail is mainly occupied by a panel of repeating scrolls with numerous lily leaves in pairs forming the centre, and the overthrow is a pyramid of scrolls with acanthus leaves centring in a diapered drapery bearing a fleur-de-lis and baron's coronet. There are curious gates at Chiddingfold, of plain bars with four lightly scrolled vertical borders, and a lock-rail to match, while below are scrolled panels. Fixed panels of plain bars with loosely

Country Gates

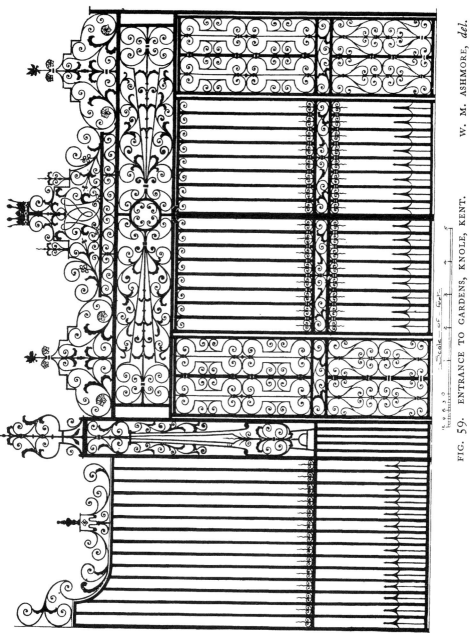

FIG. 59. ENTRANCE TO GARDENS, KNOLE, KENT. W. M. ASHMORE, del.

scrolled pyramid tops are on either side, and between them an important overthrow comprising two rectangular panels, one above the other, the lower with a filling of scrolls, and the upper with monogram P.M., supported by scrolls bearing acanthus and laurel leaves.

The gate at North Cray Church (Plate LV) recalls somewhat that to Dulwich College, by George Buncker. It is fixed between two wide panels, which match the gate, but have centres of scrolls between bars, with arrow-pointed dog-bars and fringes of twisted spikes and leaves. The lofty pyramid overthrow rests on a narrow horizontal base with small mask, its bold centre formed of an oval enclosing five arrows saltire between the initials H. H., of the Hetherington family, supported by large scrolls with horizontal breaks, acanthus, laurel, water-leaves and tendrils, and handsomely scrolled finial. At Foot's Cray Place a gate, now without an overthrow, consists of a panel of scroll-ended bars with moulded ovals as centres and arrow-pointed dog-bars below, with lyre pattern pilasters. At Frognal, Foot's Cray, a gate between wide panels and lyre pilasters, with pyramid overthrow, is probably also the work of Buncker. The fine entrance gate between fixed pilasters and stone piers to the not far distant college of Bromley is plain with C scrolls below the top rail, a fringe of button and twist points and scrolls, a scrolled lock-rail centring in an oval and arrow-pointed dog-bars. The pilasters are of scrolled bars, some converging; and the overthrow is scrolled with tendrils and leaves, in three pyramids, surmounted by five pinnacles with cast finials. It resembles gates at St. John's and Jesus Colleges, Cambridge, and also an overthrow with three cast vase finials formerly in Cheyne Walk. At Lewisham (Plate LVI) there is a late but interesting wicket gate with a pyramid overthrow of scrolls with tendrils and a high centre of two lozenge-shape panels one above the other of intersecting curves, and cast vase finials. The pilasters are of scroll-ended

Plate LV.

GATE TO THE CHURCH YARD, NORTH CRAY, KENT.

Plate LVI.

GATE AT LEWISHAM.

Plate LVII

GATE AT ELTHAM, KENT

Plate LVIII.

GATE TO ASHBURNHAM HOUSE, SUSSEX.
Said to have been brought from Wales.

bars held in place by three ovals with twisted spikes; and the lock-rail is panelled with arrow-pointed dog-bars below.

Eltham (Plate LVII) possesses a plain gate with coarsely moulded spikes and scrolls over the lock-rail, between fixed panels to match comprising a scrolled pilaster-like decoration; the pyramid overthrow with an oval monogram and two open lozenge shape and two flame tuft finials rests upon a wide border of scrolls and thrown-over leaves. This is a local production, but other gates at Eltham are described on pp. 154 and 167. A semicircular-headed wicket between lyre pilasters with overthrow of scrolls and laurel branches, forms an entrance to Restoration House, Rochester. Some rather late gates and railings to the Clock House, Beckenham, were removed twelve or fifteen years since and are in the possession of Mr. Garraway Rice, F.S.A. The gates to Hall Place, Bexley, are described page 91 (Plate XXIX).

FIG. 60. THE PRIORY GATEWAY, REIGATE.

Surrey.—The numerous gates along the Surrey banks of the Thames and in the vicinity of the metropolis are treated with those of the London district. The superb gates at Beddington (Plate XXVIII) and Carshalton (Plates XXX-XXXI) have already been noticed.

The Priory screen at Reigate (Figs. 60 and 61) comprises a conspicuous and elegant example of plain gates, each with a semicircular head, and scrolled spandrels and cresting; and opening under a finely designed overthrow. These are in Bell Street, and in West Street is another fine gate with fixed side panels, under a pyramidal overthrow.

At Leatherhead is a small gate with pilasters and overthrow, probably by the same hand. The gates to the Durdans, near Epsom, are described on page 78, Plate XXIV, and there are others at Tadworth House. The gate to Colston's House, Mortlake, is interesting in connection with Bristol.

FIG. 61. DETAILS OF THE PRIORY GATEWAY AT REIGATE.

FIG. 62. THE GRANGE, FARNHAM. *Drawn by* HAROLD FALKNER.

Hardly less important are the two gates at Farnham by the same smith drawn and described by Mr. Harold Falkner. The Grange (Fig. 62) formerly occupied by the Bishop of Winchester's Secretary, has a handsome brick screen with a fine central gate between fixed panels and two small wickets in arched openings some distance away. The second gate (illustrated in Davie and Green's *Old Surrey Cottages*) is in Castle Street.

The ancient gates at Ham House have been illustrated (Plates I and II); but perhaps those described as existing in the time of Charles I in the Royal Park of Wimbledon would be of even greater interest. According to the Survey made for the Commonwealth a flight of seventy steps led from the park to a pair of railed gates set between large pillars of brick in the middle of the wall on the north side of the lower court. Eight other steps landed on a pavement where stood a pair of iron gates, in a turned stone baluster railing, while a third ascent led to a pair of iron gates railed and a fountain with a lead cistern. Decorative gates certainly existed in England before the reign of William and Mary, but their designs and treatment are but obscurely known.

Sussex, though once containing the great majority of iron furnaces and mills, is almost destitute of fine old gates. Iron founders, puddlers, mill-hands and smelters do not meddle with smithing, and a " black country " is the district in which finely wrought and artistic ironwork need not be looked for. It seems that no wrought-iron work was produced in the Weald until the smelters were deserting it, when some few workers in iron, clinging to their rural homes, eked out a livelihood for a time by forging simple objects, such as candlesticks and other articles of general utility, which could be disposed of locally, or producing small decorative works in cast iron, such as vases or fire-backs. The ancient gates at Groombridge and Cowdray (Figs. 5, 8 and 9) have been noticed. At Ashburnham House (Plate LVIII) is an eighteenth century wicket, possibly brought from Pembrey, Carmarthenshire, with a central vertical panel, wide pilasters and overthrow, in which great use is made of thrown-over leaves. At Newhouse, Buxted, near Uckfield, is a wicket with semicircular top between narrow fixed panels and stone piers. Over it is a scrolled overthrow with leaves and a high central finial with branches of olive, a rebus on the family name. Another example occurs at Lewes.

An entrance to Parham Park, near Littlehampton, is plain and restrained, and consists of a wicket between two decorative pilasters and side panels, with scrolled overthrow rising to a pyramid. It is probably of London make. Several very fine gates are shown in old views of Stanstead Park, near Chichester. In this town is an overthrow without wicket-gate to North Pallant House. The gates at Chichester to the Deanery were formerly the chancel gates in the Cathedral, and are handsomely worked with large central panels of scrolls and leaves, a wide scrolled lock-rail centring in a quatre-foil, and scrolled top in place of overthrow. Between the verticals on each side of the central panel are leafy drops with twisted ends, and C scrolls above and below the lock-rail, the dog-bars with incurved scrolls to the barbs. A pointed gate in the cloisters is chiefly occupied by a large scrolled panel, and there is a low gate to the Close with two scrolled panels in the centre, resting on a border of circles with leafy arrow points above and without lock-rail. One of two gates at Wovington in Sussex is illustrated in Fig. 37, and described page 115.

Hampshire.—Work in Winchester Cathedral and its neighbourhood may point to a masterful smith in the south, though it presents certain affinities with a group already described. At Longwood and at Avington Park are gates described on page 105. In the town itself is a high gate with vertical panels of lyre design between fixed panels to match, and three scrolled pyramids. The

184 English Ironwork of the XVIIth and XVIIIth Centuries

railing is plain except as to very large buttress brackets at either end with clustered spikes and acanthus leaves.

At Alton are three curious overthrows of spikes with scrolls, etc., over the entrance to the Churchyard, which may possibly be of the seventeenth century.

COUNTIES WEST OF LONDON

Oxfordshire.—We have seen that the most imposing of the gates at Oxford are by Robinson, but there are many excellent specimens, probably by other makers.

The iron gate in the garden front of St. John's College at Oxford is charming though of quiet design. The verticals are inch square in section, but an unusual effect is given by the unequal section of the arrow-pointed dog-bars, $\frac{3}{4} \times \frac{3}{8}$, and the blocking out of the horizontal bars for their passage. A row of shorter arrow-points reversed depends from the lower side of the lock-rail. Four concentric semicircles, penetrated by five pointed and scrolled bars converging towards a centre, form the top over a delicate horizontal border of wavy intersecting bars, producing a series of elliptical and lozenge shaped spaces. The gate opens within a framework formed of one complete segment of the design. A very pretty and unusual effect is seen in a garden gate at Wadham College, where all the $\frac{7}{8}$ vertical bars are bent inwards towards the centre and intersect, producing two semi-ellipses filled in with scrolls and water-leaves. A very successful Italian effect is produced in a garden gate at Corpus College by using bars only half an inch square in section with rich fringes of scrolls to all the horizontals. The gates closing the old Divinity School are of plain vertical and scrolled dog-bars between richly worked pilasters, under a semicircular grille of fine radiating design with scrolled borders. The Sheldonian doorways are seen in old prints to have been closed by gates of great richness, if of somewhat confused design, their varied ornament arranged in four vertical bands divided horizontally into three panels. In marked contrast to all these are the gates designed by Gibbs for the Ratcliffe Library, where all the doors and windows on the ground floor are severely plain and identically treated. The low gates and railings separating the schools from the Sheldonian Theatre are apparently those seen in old prints, each gate, about 5 feet 7 inches high, being formed of a four-centred panel, with plain border and short diagonal connections at the angles, and rich tops in Tijou's manner.

The gates to the Clarendon Press by Tijou, pp. 52-54, probably suggested the design of those for All Souls'. These fill an arched opening to the cloisters, and are thirty years later. The pilasters are of restrained design, the embossed square caps of coarsely executed cherub's heads with rays, this chief feature being, perhaps, placed over the scroll-work at a later time. A panel over the scrolled lock-rail is in Tijou's manner, and below are bent over verticals with elaborately scrolled dog-bars. Over them is a deep frieze of scrolls with embossed shell centre and large rosettes, and the arch above is filled by scrolls with acanthus and water-leaves, a large shield of the college arms forming the centre. The gates cannot be of much earlier date than the completion of the College by Hawksmoor in 1734. They have been carefully drawn and detailed by Mr. Bailey Murphy, who has also detailed the much finer gates to St. Mary's Church, Fig. 63, p. 187. In the vicinity are three or four other light gates, dating from about 1730 to 1740. Somewhat in the same archaistic manner are the gates to the President's Garden at Magdalen College, which have bold fringes with leafy husks, lock-rail of ovals, and scrolls in place of dog-bars. The pilasters are restrained and good, but the overthrow is depressed, with large circular monogram and crest supported by heavily moulded zig-zagged bars, light scrolls, and a profusion of acanthus and branches apparently of holly. An engraving by Burghers, about 1700, shows a Renaissance forecourt, never executed, to Wadham College, with plain high railings between the massive piers, the only relief being a fleur-de-lis in the centre. The gates are plain above the lock-rails, but below is the well-known arrangement of scrolls set diagonally and radiating from a centre, here a shield, adopted by Tijou. Apart from the University town, the Oxfordshire gates are not numerous. A wicket at Burford, shown in Plate LIX, has wide "lyre" pilasters, an arching top and central pyramid, with acanthus and water leaves, tendrils and finials; the pyramids over the pilasters are of G scrolls with finials, and simple buttress scrolls connect the railings. The gates to Mapledurham House, seen in a picture dated 1732, and removed towards the end of the eighteenth century to face the churchyard may perhaps belong to the Berkshire group. They have short thickset dog-bars and fleur-de-lis spikes with twisted centres over the scrolled lock-rail, and an overthrow of scrolls, water-leaves and tendrils, without acanthus, enclosing a shield. The pilasters have a scroll filling but with an unusual entasis; and their pyramids with three closely set vertical bars for centre, environed by scrolls and water-leaves, are also quite unusual. A much more charming gate is that leading to Addison's Walk, with elliptical head, artistic pilasters and graceful overthrow.

Another remarkable example closes the porch of St. Mary's Church (Fig. 63). The long vertical bars over the scrolled lock-rail are bent into scrolls at both ends and coupled together in pairs by moulded collars, producing a pilastered effect; with arrow-pointed dog-bars below, each bearing a pair of scrolls and leaves. The over-throw has a wide scrolled border and a narrow one of husks and water-leaves, over which is a tasselled drapery with the University arms worked in front, under a large fluted vase in outline with scrolled handles, from which fall on each side garlands of lilies and tulips arranged rather stiffly. The handsome pilasters widen towards the base as those at Carshalton

Plate LIX.

A GATE AT BURFORD, OXFORDSHIRE.

Plate LX.

ENTRANCE TO "REMNANTS," GREAT MARLOW.

FIG. 63. PORCH OF ST. MARY'S CHURCH, OXFORD.

Park and finish in high pyramid tops with sprays of flowers. There are fine scrolled ramps to the railings. It is interesting to note that this coupling of the bars is first seen in England in the design by Tijou (Pl. 15 of his pattern book), 1693, and was adopted by Bakewell in his screens for All Saints', Derby. It also occurs in a few tomb rails erected towards the close of the seventeenth century.

Berkshire.—A few interesting gates are met with along the Berkshire banks of the Thames. The gate to Hadleigh House, at Windsor, has a central panel and lock-rail of scroll-work, a low pyramid overthrow of scrolls with a shield outlined, and a spreading tuft of laurel leaves as finial, on a panel of scrolls over-sailing pilasters of scroll-ended bars. A small gate at Cookham near the church has good pilasters, and an overthrow with embossed drapery, laurel leaves, and tendrils. Both may be by the same local smith.

Elsewhere Berkshire remains especially rich in gates, though few are as yet assignable to particular smiths. Many of them appear to have been removed from one park to be set up in another. Few are of first-rate importance, though all are interesting. Those at Aldermaston have been described (p. 104) as possibly by George Buncker. Two fine pairs are at West Woodhay House, near Newbury, between pilasters, charmingly quiet, with restrained overthrow. Also two pairs somewhat more decorative, between stone piers and with wickets, are at Welford Park, not far distant, erected some time before 1736 by an Eyre of Derbyshire, whose crest surmounts the high overthrow, while the monogram below, W.S.A., is composed of his own and his wife's initials after assuming the name of Archer. The pair of gates at Woolly Park, near Wantage, with massive pilasters, high overthrow, and rich filling, are probably by the same smith. At Wolverton Park, near Kingsclere, is a very fine pair of gates, formerly an entrance to Freemantle House, built by Lord Cottingham. According to William Hewitt in his *History of Compton, Berks*, the "Splendid iron gates" of Langley

Lodge, now known as Compton Beauchamp, six miles from Newbury on the Oxford road, were brought from Hodcott, West Ilsley, pulled down in 1824. The gate is imposing, between pilasters and wide fixed panels, all with separate pyramids and a flowing border below. The monogram in a stepped rectangular frame forming part of the pyramid over the gate, is that of one of the Southeys who held Hodcott till 1813.

Buckinghamshire.—The gates to Wootton (Plates XXVI–VII, p. 89) are the glory of the county, which otherwise does not appear to be rich in ironwork. The house named Remnants at Great Marlow, Bucks (Plate LX), interesting as having been the precursor of Sandhurst, has a low and wide wicket without lock-rail, separated by two handsome lyre pilasters from two exactly similar fixed panels, all with scrolled pyramid crestings and beaded finials. The dog-bars are arrow-pointed with the barbs incurved and scrolled, as at Queen's House, Cleyne Walk; the work being evidently by Buncker. In the beautiful grounds of Huntercombe Manor, near Taplow, are two garden gates with central panels of scroll-ended bars, with water-leaves and scrolls alternately, above the lock-rail, and with thrown-over leaves in pairs below; on either side are plain bars, with twist points and thrown-over leaves between them, and arrow-pointed dog-bars. The pyramid overthrow over a horizontal border is of broken scrolls, with laurel sprays and tendrils and flame tuft finial. A finely embossed mask still forms a centre to one of these. Other gates have been brought from elsewhere, notably a rich pair from Tiverton. There is an unimportant entrance gate to Aylesbury Churchyard.

Wiltshire.—There are no very striking or interesting gates in Wiltshire, though apparently it was intended to have some on a grand scale at Ramsbury, where the gates to the richly worked piers of the double lodges are insignificant. The best in the county are at Littlecote House, with an extensive range of railings. The pilasters are narrow and of scroll-ended beaded bars, with U-shaped bars and scrolled pyramids. The gates are simple, fringed with horizontal panelled lock-rails, a lofty and stepped overthrow with a thick cluster of leaves and arrow-pointed finials, acanthus, water-leaves and tendrils, clearly by a London smith. Two good and restrained wickets with overthrows and pilasters are at the Moot, Downton. A local group is seen in the Close, Salisbury, the most decorative bearing the Mompesson crest and monogram; and another is at Netherhampton House, not far off, with a large shield of arms and crest in the overthrow. There are one or two plain gates at Trowbridge and also at Chippenham, and some good railings at Wylye illustrated in the *Art Journal*.

Gloucestershire.—The city of Gloucester seems now to possess but one eighteenth century gate, in Northgate Street. The severe pilasters, with ovals and acanthus leaves for the caps, and an open-work shell within a semicircle for the overthrow, supported by scrolls and laurel leaves with three heavy turned vase finials, are its chief features. The county was formerly rich in gates and screens,

FIG. 64. AT MISSENDEN PARK, GLOUCESTERSHIRE.

which are seen at Rendcomb, Fairford, Dyrham, and Hatherip, in Atkyn's History of the County. Gates at Lypiatt, near Stroud, and at Tewkesbury Abbey remain (Pl. xxi, p. 73), and though those to old Cirencester Abbey have disappeared, others to the entrance of Lord Bathurst's Park, of Oakley, take their place (p. 103). At Sandywell is a pair with monogram, supporters, and crest, illustrated in Ditchfield's *Manor Houses of England*. Great Missenden Park, near Cirencester, possesses a fine pair of entrance gates (Fig. 64), the lock-rail of scroll-ended vertical bars, united in pairs by scrolls, giving the effect of caps and bases, as at St. Mary's Church, Oxford. The overthrow is stately, resting on circles and compressed ellipses, with larger branches of laurel. There is an equally fine wicket with semicircular top, between lyre pilasters and an overthrow with acanthus and drapery, said to have been brought from Holland House.

South Western Counties

Dorsetshire.—The county of Dorset can boast of few gates, those to the entrance and in the gardens of Ven, the seat of the Medlicotts, at Milbourne Port, being amongst the best remaining in their original sites, and no doubt contemporary with the house and of London make. The entrance gates dip towards the centre, supporting a handsome scrolled cresting, with water-leaves and finials. In the gardens are two pairs of plainer gates, and a pair with pyramid top, pilasters, fringes and scrolled lock-rail, now partly buried. Near by, at Inwood, Templecombe, the extensive pleasure grounds contain seven remarkably fine specimens of English gates by London smiths, besides numerous panels, balustrades, finials, etc. The grounds are celebrated for their Italian and other antique ironwork, lead statues, etc., and the fine modern entrance gates to the three lodges. The gates to Sherborne Abbey are relatively late and of provincial make, chiefly noticeable for their large radiating shell designs in the overthrow. There are gates dating from about 1760 at Charmouth with curiously scrolled spikes and richly worked heads to the standards.

Somersetshire and Devonshire.—The fine work by Edney in Bristol (p. 72) confers distinction on the county of Somerset in regard to its ironwork, and there were perhaps good smiths at Frome and at Bruton, but, if so, little of their work now exists. The gates to the Colt House at Bristol are remarkable, with every alternate bar carrying scrolls and some with rosettes, perhaps of early eighteenth century date. In Devonshire little ironwork seems to have been used, and the gates now to be found there, as at Sydenham, have perhaps been acquired in more or less recent years and from London. There are imposing gates at Bradfield, which may be modern.

THE MIDLAND COUNTIES

Warwickshire.—The ironwork in Warwickshire, by the great Bristol smith Edney, has already been noticed (p. 73). Mr. Hart has also given an account of the ironwork of the county, illustrating the gates to Maxstoke Castle (Fig. 2, p. 12), and mentioning others at the Manor House, Studley, which have a rich overthrow, and at Middleton House, near Tamworth, as well as gates at Solihull and Castle Bromwich Churches, all perhaps by a local smith. The west entrance gates to Arbury Hall, near Nuneaton (illustrated in Belcher's *Later Renaissance*) have scrolled lock-rail, fringes and arrow-headed dog-bars with button points and leaves, scrolled pilasters, and overthrow with arms, crest, acanthus and tendrils. These correspond in some details with Edney's work, like the not altogether dissimilar gates to Shobdon Court in Herefordshire. Low gates to Sutton Coldfield Church are without lock-rail, and have a lyre panel in the centre and simple pilasters of ovals and water-leaves with pyramids above. There are fine gates at Studleigh, but the handsome forecourt gates in Kip's View of Umberslade, not far off, disappeared no doubt long ago. Good gates are shown in Dugdale's history at Four Oaks Hall, then the seat of Lord Folliott.

Undoubtedly the most important gates in the county by a yet unidentified smith, were at Ragley Hall, Alcester, which formerly possessed a forecourt with bowed front and screen comprising a plain pair of gates, rich overthrow and two fixed panels, between high stone piers, with about 200 feet of railing beyond. Four additional gates in the front wall and six gates on the garden side are also seen in an engraving, all of which have disappeared, to be replaced by a new pair of gates and screen to the drive. There is also a gate to the kitchen garden much restored, with fixed panels and an overthrow bearing the arms of the first Lord Conway. Photographs taken over twenty-five years ago show that three fine pairs of gates then existed, though falling into decay, all between lofty stone piers with large moulded caps and carved fluted vases. Two are set in high walls of undressed stone built without mortar—a lost art; and the third between plain iron railings with aroïd dog-bars and decorative pilasters, on a low wall of dressed stone. The overthrow has a scrolled horizontal base and a pyramid bearing a small circle with P. C. interlaced, and coronet and crest, for Popham Conway, supported by boys which are encircled by scrolls, short acanthus leaves and rosettes. Another more perfectly preserved gate is plainer. The overthrow has a base formed of scrolls with tufted acanthus, water leaves and rosettes, and a pyramid with interlaced C's, and small dense branches of laurel leaves. The third pair were imperfect, with scrolled lock-rail and a vertical panel in each gate. Scrolls, water-leaves, and tendrils form a base for an overthrow, of which only two cornucopiae remained, with rich foliage and flowers. There are handsome gates to the front and in the gardens of Packwood House.

Some magnificent work in the grounds of Stoneleigh Abbey is traditionally believed to have been brought from Watergate beyond Southam. Excellent gates have been made during the past century for Lord Leigh by the Fardons, local smiths who have worked at the Abbey since 1814. A gate with pilasters and overthrow, perhaps by Edney, was brought from the Hall or ancient manor house of Preston-on-Stour, and is now at the church.

Northamptonshire.—The ironwork of this county is of interest, comprising the gates, etc., to Drayton House, Burleigh, Harrowden, Bulwick Hall, and to the front of Peterborough Cathedral. Several

194 English Ironwork of the XVIIth and XVIIIth Centuries

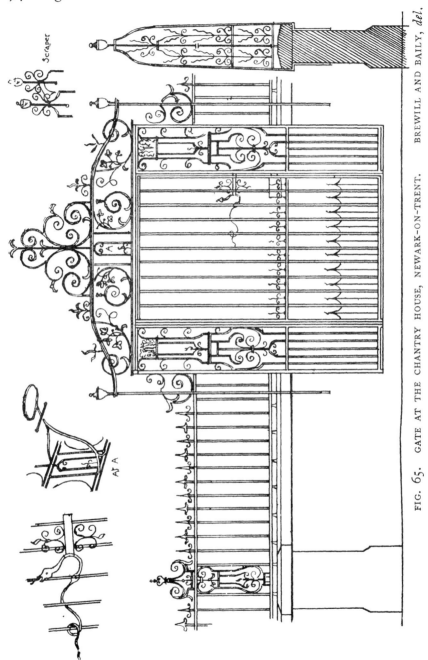

FIG. 65. GATE AT THE CHANTRY HOUSE, NEWARK-ON-TRENT. BREWILL AND BAILY, *del.*

have already been described, one of the most interesting being that to Bulwick Hall (p. 80), remarkable for the dog-bars, each of which is opened twice into ellipses, with barbed arrow points. The entrance gates to the grounds of Burleigh House are curious and appear to be of light and local work, executed possibly between 1730-40, but certainly before the close of the century. The overthrow is of scrolls with acanthus enclosing a shell design. A charming garden gate is at Finedon formed almost entirely of scroll-work. The gates to the north front of Thorpe Hall, near Peterborough, between finely proportioned stone piers carved with eagles, are remarkably good and designed by an accomplished smith. The centre vertical is continued up to support a drapery and scrolls with acanthus. The lateral scrolls bear tendrils, rosettes, and branches of laurel with berries, the leaves disposed in clusters of three.

At Milton House, near Peterborough, is a remarkably fine gate in the walled garden, between pilasters and fixed panels, with a rich overthrow and pyramid comprising the arms, supporters, and coronet of the first Earl Fitzwilliam, created 1716. It recalls the work of Warren.

Nottinghamshire.—Messrs. Brewill & Baily have drawn our illustration of the gates to the Chantry House at Newark-on-Trent (Fig. 65). The trefoil leaves of the overthrow, the duplicated stays with their connecting work and the serpent latch, are peculiar features; while a gate nearer the castle is hardly less interesting in the design of the pilasters and overthrow. For the drawing of the imposing screen to Newdigate House, Nottingham, illustrated in Figs. 66 and 67 (p. 200), we are indebted to Mr. F. E. Collington. The work here also is unusual, owing to the void spaces in the design of the pilasters and termination of the overthrow in a cluster of trefoils as at Newark. The effect of the whole is greatly enriched by the pyramidal crestings to the railings. The gates to Willoughby House have been noted (p. 62), as by Bakewell. A rich example on the Low Pavement is practically a *replica* of one at Lincoln, with an

FIG. 66. THE GATE AT NEWDIGATE HOUSE, NOTTINGHAM.
Drawn by F. E. COLLINGTON.

Plate LXI.

GATES FROM COLWICK HALL, NOTTS,
NOW IN THE NOTTINGHAM MUSEUM.

Plate LXII.

GATES AT CHATSWORTH.

elliptical top, central lyre panel, and lyre pilasters, with the overthrow resting on them, comprising laurel sprays, acanthus, and shield of arms. In Houndsgate is another gate with overthrow and elaborate pilasters and crested railing, all by the same hand. A pair of gates from Colwick Hall (Plate LXI), now in the Museum, and supposed to date from 1776, are remarkable for dog-bars opening into an ellipse, as at Bulwick, and the four rectangular panels above the lock-rail with light G scroll filling. The pilasters are of lyre design above the lock-rail, richly worked with acanthus and water-leaves, and high pyramids above. The overthrow has two large clusters of laurel with berries and tendrils. They can hardly be in their original state. Nothing is known or can be traced as to Huntington Shaw having lived at Nottingham.

Staffordshire.—The gates to Sandon Hall, Lord Harrowby's seat near Stone, closing the forecourt are important. Each has scrolls between the verticals and a central panel of scroll-ended bars and scrolled lock-rail. Over the elliptical top is a pyramid of moulded scrolls and acanthus, very richly worked, supporting a garter with interlaced B's under an earl's coronet and laurel sprays. It rests on a scrolled border centring in a large mask. The piers are four-sided with massive bases and moulded caps of acanthus, somewhat vertically treated and surmounted by converging acanthus scrolls upholding a massive turned finial. Beyond are wickets and smaller piers. These were presented by Lord Harrowby to the third Earl Bathurst, who returned them after adding his garter and coronet, which are also inserted in the overthrow to his gates of Oakley Park, Cirencester (Fig. 33). Gates at Cannock Chase are by Bakewell.

Derbyshire.—Derbyshire abounds with works by Bakewell to the exclusion almost of every other, except at Chatsworth. Tijou's work there is confined to the stair balustrade and balconies, but the gates and balustrades in the gardens are probably by " Richard Oddy, the gatesmith at Chatsworth, when it was building," who is thus commemorated on a monument in Baslow Church. The very fine gates in the arched entrances of the north front (Plate LXII) recall the work of Bakewell, but are stated in old guides not to have been erected until after 1829. The forecourt gates of Barlborough Hall, near Eckington (p. 104), are perhaps by a London smith.

Leicestershire.—The splendid Berwick gates now at Newnham Paddox (Plate XIX and XX and Fig. 25, p. 71) attributed to the brothers Roberts and partly by Bakewell are famous through the county, which otherwise is by no means rich in ironwork. The gates to Scraptoft Hall have been illustrated (Plate XXIII and Figs. 27-8, p. 77), and those formerly at Quenby Hall, now at the Leicester Museum, are described on pp. 78 and 79.

West Midland Counties

Shropshire.—With the removal of the Berwick gates (Plates XIX–XX) Shrewsbury lost one of the finest specimens of ironwork in England, and retains now but a single example, and this may also be assigned to the brothers Roberts. The gates to the Abbey House (Plate LXIII) present a large panel of scrolls of original design, with verticals on each side bearing fleur-de-lis of open work. Beyond are wing pieces to correspond with vertical panels of scrolls, the rest below the scrolled lock-rail being plain with the scroll and leaf javelin-headed dog-bars, so characteristic of the Roberts' work. The wide overthrow of broken scrolls with acanthus rests on a border like that of the lock-rail, and centres in a large oval below a *flèche* surmounted by a vase. Fine gates are said to exist at Chillington Hall, which the owner proposes to re-erect very shortly.

Herefordshire.—Iron gates are not now, and perhaps never were, numerous either in this or the adjoining counties. The old gates in front of the cathedral have been noticed (p. 22). A forecourt screen remains at Shobdon Court, near Leominster, with gates

Plate LXIII.

ENTRANCE TO THE ABBEY HOUSE, SHREWSBURY.

Plate LXIV.

GATE AT EVESHAM, WORCESTERSHIRE.

noticeable for the large overthrow with acanthus and laurel round a monogram of J.B. (p. 79).

Worcestershire.—Apart from the fine screen with gates in front of the Guildhall, Worcester, by Bakewell, (p. 63) which has been ruined by reconstruction and the renewal of the foliage some thirty years ago, there are no interesting eighteenth century gates in the city; and indeed, apparently but few anywhere in the county, except at Severn End, where there is a pleasing wicket with pilasters and overthrow. In Plate LXIV is illustrated a gate at Merston Green, Evesham, on the Gloucestershire border, of curious local design. The overthrow with its high obelisks, and the dog-bars are especially remarkable.

THE COUNTIES IMMEDIATELY NORTH OF LONDON

Bedfordshire.—That few gates exist in the county of Bedford, so near London, is remarkable. There are good gates in Church Street, Ampthill, with overthrow, pilasters, and railings; and a small Georgian house in that town has a pair of plain forecourt gates between fine piers. There is a good garden gate at Sir Edgar Sebright's Mansion, Beechwood, near Luton, between scrolled pilasters with scrolled lock-rail, an overthrow with shield of arms and acanthus, and one or two pecular features. Others are at Hinwick Hall, Poddington.

Huntingdonshire.—In the town of Huntingdon is a wide wicket gate without lock-rail between duplicated pilasters, surmounted by three pyramids of scroll design with water-leaves. There are noble gates to Kimbolton Castle with scrolled borders and magnificent pyramids surmounted by the ducal arms.

Essex.—The county abounds with fine gates but most of them are described with those of the London district. The relative wealth of the east side of town being probably far less than of the west, has no doubt led to their preservation. At Raphael Park (Plate XLIV) and Romford House are good gates, and another is to be seen in

200 English Ironwork of the XVIIth and XVIIIth Centuries

the town of Romford. At Easton Hall, near Dunmow, and at Grove Hall, near Woodford (Plate XLV) are fine gates. Braintree, Snaresbrook, Chadwell Heath (Plate XLIII), Walthamstow, Waltham Cross, and Woodford Road all possess typical examples. Those to old Loughton Hall are among the best and have been illustrated by Ebbetts. In Duke Street Chelmsford are gates remarkable for their very tall pilasters and overthrow of radiating design under

FIG. 67. THE GATE AND SCRE

a pyramid, with monogram, acanthus, and water leaves. There is a space of 2 ft. 6 in. between the overthrow and top of the gate. According to Defoe, Audley End was formerly entered through a large and wide pair of iron gates to a spacious courtyard.

Hertfordshire.—A fair amount of good ironwork remains in the county. The original gates to the old Bluecoat School, with pyramid crestings, fringes and scrolled lock-rail are at Hertford. The old gates at Hatfield House are plain with single lock-rail and fringe of fleurs-de-lis and arrow-pointed dog-bars, opening under a graceful triple arch, with a light overthrow composed of a pyra-

Country Gates

mid centre and two buttress scrolls. The six saltire arrows with a viscount's coronet, form the principal feature in a rectangular frame. The pilasters though less elaborate than those at Reigate have finer pyramid tops, and the work appears to be by the same smith. Gates to the private garden are somewhat older and of great interest.

A pair of low gates at the Lordships, Much Hadham (Plate

NEWDIGATE HOUSE, NOTTINGHAM.   F. E. COLLINGTON, *del*.

LXV) shut the stable off from the drive. They are well designed with panels next the piers, and scrolled pyramids over the centres of the gates, comprising draperies and crests. A second pair without lock rail and with plain spikes as dog-bars and three flask-shaped vases over the pilasters, is in front of the house (Plate LXVI). High Street, Hoddesdon, presents a plain wicket with broad lyre pattern pilasters and pyramid overthrow. There are gates at Harpenden with scrolled panel and border between fixed panels, the whole set with leaf spikes as cresting; at Stansted Abbotts near Ware, with shield of arms, motto and crest; and at St. Peter's,

St. Albans, with central panel repeated in the pilasters and scrolled pyramids above surmounted by fleur-de-lis (Plate LXVII). Another excellent gate with pilasters and overthrow is at Hall Place, St. Albans. Gates at the Priory Barnet have now disappeared.

THE EASTERN COUNTIES

Cambridgeshire.—The Gates at Exning and Cheveley are described (pp. 98–100, Plates XXXII and XXXIII) together with some of the finest gates to the University (Figs. 30, 31, pp. 96–100).

The avenue gates at St. John's are believed to have been erected in 1712 when the bridge was completed, and stand between massive stone piers by Grumbold, carved with the portcullis and surmounted by the Johnian eagles, with curves of plain railing on dwarf stone walls beyond. The gates are high and plain in the centre, with panels of scrolls next the piers, narrow lock-rail with rings and fringed horizontals, and short arrow-pointed dog-bars. Part of each gate now opens independently as a wicket, but whether this was always so may be doubted. The pyramid overthrow rests on a single horizontal bar, with a scrolled step above, and contains a large oval shield of the College arms, supported by high buttress scrolls, with a single pair of acanthus leaves. These scrolls also form the finial above and carry a drapery with the Tudor rose on either side, with a peculiar turned knob between two short scrolls for finials. Gates to the bridge between fixed pilasters are plainer, under an overthrow of three pyramids, the centre one enclosing a monogram in a circle with drapery. A less important gate leads to the kitchen garden.

An entrance to Jesus College is believed to date from 1703, but has been re-arranged, and now consists of two gates at present fixtures, with a short fixed panel between, leaving an empty space for a wicket below. The overthrow has a scrolled base under a square medallion of arms with tasselled drapery and several small

Plate LXV.

STABLE GATES, "THE LORDSHIPS," MUCH HADHAM, HERTFORDSHIRE.

Plate LXVI.

FRONT GATES, "THE LORDSHIPS," MUCH HADHAM.

Plate LXVII

GATE AT ST. PETER'S, ST. ALBANS.

Plate LXVIII.

GATE ON STAIRCASE, NORWICH TOWN HALL.

finials like those at St. John's. In the garden is another small gate with a circle of radiating scrolls above, and vertical bars with arched tops below and open arrow-pointed dog-bars of spindled outline, like some in the gardens of Clare. St. Catherine's College has plain gates and fixed side panels, with scrolled lock-rails and plain spikes for dog-bars. The overthrow is a narrow scrolled border and three low pyramids enclosing a gilded wheel for St. Catherine. It is said to have been erected in 1757, but may be somewhat older and perhaps re-arranged for its present position.

The gates to the Botanic Garden have handsomely scrolled lock-rail and fringes, with semicircular head of scrolls and laurel leaves arranged concentrically; opening under an arch of scrolls with a cresting, supported by severe geometric pilasters. The gardens were not purchased until 1760 by Richard Walker, who conveyed them to Trinity College in 1762, and were originally entered by a gate since walled up. The present gates cannot be of much earlier date than 1775. There are fine gates in Trumpington Street of probably London make, with good pilasters and overthrow.

Neither *Norfolk* nor *Suffolk* are particularly rich in eighteenth century ironwork. The dated gates at Lynn and Sandringham are noticed on pages 139 and 140. Norwich Town Hall has a small gate at the head of the stairs massively framed with three panels of ornament and heavy bars between, with scrolled borders and slight pyramid top with finials in the form of old mace heads, apparently of late seventeenth century date (Plate LXVIII). There are richer and larger gates of the same peculiar type fixed in their present position about 1850 and said to be modern (Plate LXIX). Mr. Grahame Cotman recalls good gates in Colegate Street which were removed to Mr. Reginald Gurney's seat, Earlham Hall. These stood at the entrance to Messrs. Jewson & Sons' offices, originally the town house of a great Norwich family, the Harveys, and are plain with the lock-rail panelled horizontally, and the overthrow scrolled with water-leaves and tendrils. The piers are of plain vertical bars with low concave tops and flask-shaped finials, and the wicket gates and their overthrows match. He also calls attention to the Old Manor House gates, rather decayed, on the Beeston Park Estate, Coltishall Road. The Oxnead Hall gates are plain, and have been removed to the Old Hall, Aylsham. Kip's view of Melton Constable shows no less than eight pairs of iron gates, all of which have disappeared. North Runcton, near King's Lynn, the residence of Sir Somerville Gurney, has interesting garden gates, believed to be about 200 years old, with fine lyre pilasters and rich overthrow. These are said to have been made by a blacksmith named Robinson, and the design agrees with his work, but the local tradition adds that he was a baronet. Fine entrance gates and wickets, somewhat on the same lines, were made in 1839 by the village blacksmith named Jackson. The garden gate at Beechwood, Sir Edgar Sebright's place in Bedfordshire, is believed to have come from Norfolk.

The screen at Houghton (Fig. 68) is 52 feet in length and over 11 feet in height, consisting of four fixed panels and a pair of gates, all of vertical bars with an upper border of rings, and arrow-pointed dog-bars. A cresting of scrolls, laurel branches and javelin points extends over the whole, broken by the pyramids of the pilasters.

A gate on the North Quay at Great Yarmouth has been drawn and published by Norton, between fine lyre pilasters and with some loose scrolls forming an overthrow and supporting a dolphin.

In *Suffolk* there is a good gate to the churchyard, Woodbridge, with fringes and arrow-pointed dog-bars, between pilasters and fixed panels of somewhat geometric design, scrolls, and an overthrow with monogram—probably a gift. The old gates from Sunbury, p. 102, are now at Culford Hall, Bury St. Edmunds.

Lincolnshire.—The county boasts the fine display of gates at Belton (p. 90) and Bloxam Park (p. 94) now unfortunately removed, it is believed to Biel in Scotland. There is a fairly good gate to the Boston Grammar School with their arms of three

Country Gates

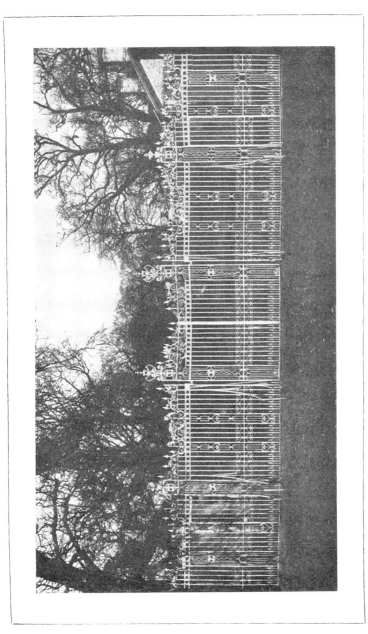

FIG. 68. THE SCREEN AT HOUGHTON HALL, NORFOLK.

crowns and the woolpack crest, and one of curious design to the church and Lindsay House near Stamford. The magnificent and lofty gates and railings, with their fine piers and heraldic overthrow at Grimsthorpe Castle are probably by Robinson.

In the city are gates and railings at the Gleestone stairs near the castle, with semicircular head and grotesque mask, almost repeating the design of those to Dr. Ransome's house, Low Pavement, Nottingham. Another is at the Market House near the Stonebow, date about 1737.

The Northern Counties

Yorkshire.—The excellent ironwork in the Cathedral at York induces the hope that other work by the same smith may be met with in the county. The beautiful gates at Kirklees, near Dewsbury, however, with double lyres in the pilasters and flask-shaped finials to the standards, forcibly recall those at Devonshire House and Clandon Park (Plates xxxiv and xxxv). The imposing screen at Kirkleatham, near Redcar, is of the same work. The arched overthrow to the gates comprises a table with drapery, crest, shield of arms, and large acanthus leaves with cocks-head finials, foliated scroll-work, with leaves, tendrils, and rosettes, arranged precisely as in the Clandon Park gate. The waved branches of laurel with tendrils are identical in spirit and execution, but the gadrooned border at the base is replaced by one of panelled design. The gates beneath are identical in all three both as to design and workmanship. The lofty piers are constructed on the same H plan as at Clandon, all the massive standards terminating similarly in flask-shaped finials. The extensive railings on either side are divided by lyre pilasters into eight bays, each with a wide and high scrolled pyramid top. Probably all are by Warren (see pp. 101 and 102). Mr. E. E. Bland has kindly noted that in Kip's view of 1714, the railings to the hospital were perfectly plain, and that tradition has it that the existing screen was erected elsewhere and

Plate LXIX.

ENTRANCE GATES NORWICH TOWN HALL.

Plate LXX.

ENTRANCE GATES TO STUDLEIGH ROYAL, RIPON.

sold to Chomley Turner, Esq., who utilized it for the improvements he made to the hospital in 1742. The arms are those granted to Sir William Turner. There is a heavier and ruder gate with arching top to the churchyard.

The gate at Norton Conyers (p. 103) is ascribed to Warren. A rich pair of gates at Studley Royal near Ripon (Plate LXX) have an elliptical top and overthrow with fine acanthus, laurel sprays and tendrils, comprising a shield of arms and crest and a delicate openwork finial, recalling the group of Berkshire gates, as at Aldermaston. There are simpler gates at Ledstone, near Pontefract. The screen and gates to Wentworth, which almost rivalled that to Versailles, is no more, and the fine forecourt screens to Ragley and Tong, engraved by Kip, have also long since disappeared. From the importance of the piers at Bramham Park near Tadcaster it was apparently intended to eclipse all these by erecting correspondingly magnificent gates, but if so the intention was never carried out and those existing are insignificant.

Lancashire.—There is an important group of local work in Lancaster, such as the gates to Castle Hill House, St. Leonards Gate, and Market Street, and this seems to extend north to Carlisle. The large gates to Kendal parish churchyard with unusually high pyramid overthrow are of the same make. A gate at Winchmore Hill has been removed from Lancaster and altered to suit its new position. These do not either in design or workmanship approach the London standard. In Liverpool the only gates of interest are those to Wavetree Hall, which are severe but have a fine pyramid overthrow, on a wide and richly worked base from which the arms except the helmet have disappeared. They are said to have been brought from an older mansion. A pair of gates without overthrow and with lyre pilasters and scrolled lockrail is at Hornby.

Durham and Northumberland.—The gates to the Deanery at Chester-le-Street (Fig. 69) are apparently not very early, each with a good centre panel, scrolled lock-rail with twisted leafy spikes above, and arrow-pointed dog-bars : the base of the overthrow is deep and of the same design as that to the gates at Knole, but over this is a semi-circle with a smaller circle above, enclosing a monogram under a pyramid top, and between side scrolls; all with the characteristic water leaves in pairs and absence of acanthus seen at Knole. They are now much rusted and no longer open, but have low wickets made practicable under the lock-rail. A curious feature, noticed in describing the now destroyed gates to Wentworth Castle, is only known to exist in these Deanery gates at Chester-le-Street, where arched niches in the stonework are pierced right through, perhaps owing originally to some flaw in the stone, and filled in with a high and narrow circular-headed panel of vertical scroll-ended bars and leaves.

A gate at Tanfield between wide pilasters, presenting the effect of triple gates, reproduces exactly the design of the Chester-le-Street gates with minor differences in the scrolled pyramid of the overthrow. The piers, however, are entirely of iron, plain, four-sided, a single central panel with heavy moulded cap, and pyramid of scrolls. These are reproduced, practically without variation, in gates to the Manor House, Jesmond, Newcastle-on-Tyne. Their resemblance to the gates at Knole Park, Kent, has already been pointed out, and all are obviously by the same hand, and may date from about 1730. Mr. Berkeley Cubey kindly calls attention to a gate with side panels at Clutterbuck Hall, Warkworth, and to those in the Armstrong College, taken from old houses in New-castle. The northern counties can, however, hardly be counted rich in eighteenth century ironwork.

Cheshire.—The fine ironwork in the county is by the Roberts (p. 67), as well as much of that across the Welsh border. Other work, as the larger entrance gates and the wickets between panels, with overthrows and the crest of the Egertons, is local work and of unusual character, like the gates at Malpas Church.

FIG. 69. ENTRANCE TO THE DEANERY, CHESTER-LE-STREET.
Drawn by F. LISHMAN.

Scotland.

Much of the ironwork of Scotland differs in its characteristics from that of England. The gates to Traquair House are illustrated (Fig. 10, p. 25), as perhaps presenting a complete example of a type which though once widely represented, has now almost disappeared from England. Mr. Baily Murphy states that the house was built by the Earl of Traquair at the end of the seventeenth century, and that the ironwork presents Flemish characteristics. Certainly the tulips and twisted spikes in the gate top, though mixed with roses, and the large clusters of tulips which surmount the standards of the railings seem to support this view, but flowers of this description are characteristic of the Scottish work of the first quarter of the eighteenth century. Mr. Murphy illustrates some similar gates formerly at Gogar House near Edinburgh which differ chiefly in their horizontal panels of scrolls above the lock-rail centring in ovals framing sprigs of thistle. At Craigie Hall is a gate much more English in design, of the early eighteenth century, but with it are very quaint and purely Scotch railings. The gates to Dunkeld Cathedral have pilasters of lyre design with solid caps and bases, and G scroll pyramids; while the overthrow is a handsome pyramid of scrolls and acanthus surmounted by a ducal coronet and circle with J.A. in monogram, all of essentially English type. Defoe notices iron gates between the park and garden at Yester, which are probably still there, and other ironwork at a not far distant seat which belonged at the time to the same owner. Hopetoun House possesses plain gates in the park with large Flemish looking flowers to the standards, and according to Murphy the Donibristle gates with their great semicircular overthrow were presented to the Earl of Moray by William III and brought from Flanders. They present unmistakeable affinities with English works of similar kind. There are low gates with scrolled panels and top of unique design at Worriston House, Inverness.

Wales.

The magnificent group of gates by the Roberts are treated of in pp. 63–67; and those to Tredegar Park, Monmouth on pp. 74 and 75. Gates closing the Porch to Llandaff Cathedral are noticed, p. 22.

RAILINGS

Railings

THE term "railing" as applied to iron fences of vertical bars is not strictly correct, since "rails" mean horizontal bars, as in "posts and rails," "railway" and so on, while vertical bars are properly "pales" from the Latin *palus*. In old days these were roughly shaped at the rolling mills and hammered to the required sections. Fences made from them were therefore called palings or palisades, but they are now generally known as railings, while paling is generally understood to be a fence of wood. Metal railings are used to inclose open spaces, parks, forecourts, gardens, squares, and cemeteries; to protect monuments; and to safeguard dangerous places, as bridges, terraces, and street areas.

Antiquity made slight use of metal for such purposes. The Romans may sometimes have used railings of bronze for sacred or official enclosures, and perhaps iron railings in amphitheatres, though no traces of such have been found. In England we first hear of iron railings as protecting shrines of famous saints, to close and screen off sanctuaries and chapels, when they were fashioned of scrolls of varied design in panels, or rectangular frames. Our peculiarly English type, of vertical bars spiked at the top and held together by horizontals, was no doubt first introduced for its practical defensive quality. Such railings appear around the monuments of the Black Prince, and of Henry IV in Canterbury Cathedral. Others, more or less elaborate, exist in cathedrals and abbeys, but numbers have been swept away, for old drawings frequently represent them in buildings where

Railings

no examples now exist. The standards at the angles of mediaeval tomb-rails were massive, often high, and richly worked with buttresses, and sometimes bore heraldic crests, banners, or prickets for candles. The massive standards give strength and support to the railings and their name may be derived from the fact that they surpass the rest of the vertical bars in height and often bear crests and banners, or the word may be derived from the Italian, and also be allied to the French " stanchion."

A notable departure is that by Edward IV who procured the superb rail of gilded iron, now in St. George's Chapel at Windsor, from the celebrated Jousse Massys of Louvain for his intended monument. This is probably the most elaborate and intricate railing ever produced in iron, and is not rivalled even by the fine interlacing grille to the Maximilian Cenotaph at Innsbrück. The stately gilt bronze railing, ordered by the will of Henry VII for his tomb in Westminster Abbey, and made by an Englishman, is more imposing, but less wonderful. Emulation induced Wolsey, and then Henry VIII, to desire to surpass in grandeur all previous monuments, but in the end their burial places were singularly unhonoured, and the black touchstone sarcophagus commanded by Wolsey, but appropriated by Henry, is worthily occupied by the remains of the immortal Nelson, while the four superb bronze candlesticks at Ghent, with Henry's arms and badges, are perhaps the sole remains of the sumptuous work upon which Torregiano and other artists were so long employed. No later sovereign has attempted to realize the ambitious and magnificent dreams of Henry, but interesting railings were erected round the tombs of royal persons. The rail to the Countess of Richmond's tomb, 1509, was plain with high standards and pennons at the angles. The rail to Elizabeth's monument, 1604, by Patrick the blacksmith, had a cresting of roses and prickets, richly gilt and decorated with her badges, and those to the monuments of Mary of Scotland, 1587, and the Countess of Hereford, 1598, had high standards bearing crests. These and others in Westminster Abbey have disappeared in England at the hands of the ubiquitous "restorer," hardly less completely and without any such edict for their destruction, as the decree in France in 1793.

Of mediaeval railings placed out of doors, no vestige exists, and in London nothing even of the Stuart days survives. The actual designs of the iron trellis to the gardens of Woodstock, the railings to the Eleanor Crosses, the iron palisades to Rochester and Bow Bridges, and of the iron "stakes" of Henry VIII, 6,000 of which (at 20s. per 1,000) railed in his Royal Pavilion, must be left to the imagination.

Our climate has joined issue and spared us no examples of outdoor iron railings such as those still existing in Italy, Spain, and Germany. We have no representations of the rails put round the Cross in Cheapside on the accession of James I, or those to Holbourne and the Fleet Bridges, which according to Stowe were "beautified with iron grates" after the Fire, even London Bridge having until then been paled with wood. The fine old iron railings at Cowdray (Figs. 8 and 9) may have been taken out of the dismantled Battle Abbey and re-erected at some more recent period, as in other cases, for the verticals are massive and the four still heavier iron standards have buttresses of ecclesiastical design (Fig. 9, p. 24). The railings at Traquair and other places in Scotland preserve their late mediaeval character. Seventeenth century illustrations, such as that of Sarsden (Fig. 6), a house built in 1641, make it clear how very gradually iron superseded wood for external railings and gates.

The ordinary railing is generally composed of vertical bars from $\frac{3}{4}$ to 1 inch square in section, rarely round, spiked above, spaced from about $4\frac{1}{2}$ to 5 inches apart, and held together by one or more connecting rails. At first the verticals were riveted between two rails on edge just below the spikes (Fig. 7, p. 21 and Fig. 9, p. 24). Later the rails were placed horizontally and the verticals passed through squared holes either cut clean out of the heated bar by punches, or drilled and filed out of the cold iron. Where the rails are too narrow for this a square punch or wedge was forced through the iron while hot, spreading it on either side; or wider squares of iron were welded in wherever a vertical had to pass, producing a series of rectangular projections. These methods are all seen in mediaeval work, and perhaps never entirely died out. In late seventeenth and eighteenth century work the rails and the verticals were frequently of the same section when they were morticed to intersect and riveted, or the verticals were tenoned through the rail and heads, or spikes screwed and riveted to them. As a rule there was but one rail, and each vertical and dog-bar was let separately into the stone and fixed by lead or cement. If a lower horizontal is present, as in balconies, the standards or a few of the verticals pass through it into the stone, or the lower rail is riveted to iron caulkings, which are leaded in. The upper rail is sometimes duplicated to form a border, and intermediate rails also occur, generally corresponding in height to the lock-rail of a gate, and at times also duplicated with scroll-work between.

The terminals of the vertical bars are plainly spiked or moulded, or assume the forms of the heads of weapons, such as spears, pikes, halberds, javelins, arrows, etc., or of fleur-de-lis. A most favoured form was the barbed arrow head, the points occasionally incurved, scrolled, or enveloped by leaves. Usually the latter alternate with plainer spikes. These, if not plain, rose from balls or spheres, but eventually a single type almost prevailed for nearly a century, tapering upwards in an ogee outline, blunted at the apex, becoming swelled towards the base, and finally constricted with deeply grooved V lines. The flattened lance or javelin-head was favoured in the seventeenth century, but used by few smiths except the Roberts in the eighteenth. On the other hand the barbed arrow-head first seen in dog-bars, became and remained exceedingly popular. Tijou shows a railing with the French lance-head and tassel in his frontispiece, and one of open-work among his published designs. Gibbs would have revived the former in 1728, and the open spear-head, without the tassel, is used in the screen to the Horse Guards, engraved by Ware in 1756 (Fig. 50). There is a magnificent range of tasselled spear-heads in the screen at Elvaston (Fig. 38), reputed to have been brought from the *château* of Madrid in Paris, and an early cast example in front of Dover House, Whitehall. The heads were sometimes forged separately to avoid passing the vertical bars through the horizontal and are tenoned and riveted, railings in Great Ormond Street and in Grosvenor Square presenting fine examples of this treatment.

Lighter and shorter intermediate bars are introduced to exclude dogs and rabbits, either short spikes fixed in the stone or arrow-points with the barbs riveted to, or inserted in the verticals.

The simplest railing is of plain spiked bars passed through one horizontal, but the spikes are generally moulded with a slight ogee outline. It is frequently relieved by " standards " which usually considerably exceed the rest of the verticals in diameter, and are higher, mostly of cast iron, and surmounted by a heavier spike, balls, pine-cones, vases or other conspicuous ornament. Their function is to strengthen and support the railing, and to receive the necessary struts. They are frequently seen in pairs, especially towards the middle of the eighteenth century, with a bar and sometimes a slight pryamid of scroll-work, or a decorative panel between them, when they take the place of the older pilaster. Possibly the idea of relieving the monotony of railings at intervals may have been suggested by the garden lattices of the sixteenth century, which were of wood between pilasters of stone or wood panelled or otherwise decorated and surmounted by some carved device such as a crown or fleur-de-lis.

Though seventeenth century railings of various dates are

well represented in churches, few early examples now exist in connexion with houses and gardens, except at Ham House. No specimen or even drawing seems to be preserved of an iron railing designed by Inigo Jones. There remain, however, several which if not designed by Wren were put up under his direction. Among the earliest produced, perhaps about 1668, are those which still occupy their original positions between the great stone terminals in front of the Sheldonian Theatre at Oxford—Wren's first great work (Fig. 12, p. 34). These are of plain vertical bars spiked at both ends and held together by two horizontal bars, one near the base and the other half way up, set with short intermediate spikes, and depending for their relief on a high central standard with fleur-de-lis head. An even loftier rail, also on a low wall, forms a *clairvoyé* to the front of Christchurch College, and is of spiked verticals, maintained in position by a single horizontal rather low down, and between imposing stone piers. In this railing the centre is marked by a short but rich lyre panel, not extending below the horizontal and a fleur-de-lis spike. This single spot of richness confers a remarkable dignity like a standard amidst a forest of pikes. An old print of Wadham shows a screen to the front of similar railing in short lengths between massive stone piers (see p. 36). Apparently this was an Oxford type. Even when the gates were richly worked, the railings continued for a long time to be severely plain, with standards at intervals and without dog-bars, as at Chevening in Kent (Fig. 39), Umberslade in Warwick, Stansted in Sussex.

Until Tijou's time railings were rarely interrupted except by standards, but in the eighteenth century pilasters formed of a pair of standards with decorative work between were quite usual. Generally a completely framed panel of decorative work is inserted between the standards, and below the horizontal bar of the railing. The pilaster was also carried with fine perpendicular effect high above the horizontal, interrupted for its passage. Above the pilaster is almost invariably a pyramid formed of scrolls, shaped like the letters C, G, or S, or of dolphin outline, frequently with vertical or horizontal breaks, and enriched with leaves, and a central *flèche* between them, rising either through or over an arch, circle, or border, and terminating in some form of moulded spike, button, twist, wave, arrow-head, tuft, pair of leaves, scrolls, or cast knob or vase. In outline the pyramid may be convex or concave, confined to the width of the panel below, or with scrolls oversailing it. In late work the standards are very frequently balustered, or otherwise moulded, and cast. The panel was occupied generally by a pattern of scrolled, foliated, or partly geometric design.

The most popular form for the pilaster panel was undoubtedly the "lyre." In its simplest form this assimilates to the original classic lyre fashioned of a pair of goats'-horns, or scrolls to represent them, with stretchers and strings, and is so found in balconies and stair-rails, but when adapted to the proportions of railing panels it required to be elongated. Thus was developed the well-known type in which the base is swelled out either abruptly or gradually, stilted, with the horns continued up in parallel or converging lines, more rarely diverging, and again swelling above, with the bar ends bent and scrolled. The place of the stretchers is taken by short horizontal bars or long moulded collars, and the strings by a single, or more rarely double centre bar. The lyre is sometimes reversed, swelled out and scrolled above, and the horns converging downwards and scrolled below. Richness was conferred in varying degrees by duplicating the same lyre outline in a modified form, one within the other, or making the inner one of contrasting lines, and also by beadlike swellings, husks, leaves, and scrolls in pairs. All designers of the English school used it, varying the relative proportions by the suppressions or enlargement of one of the parts at the expense of the rest, particularly by stilting up the base or diminishing the elongated centre, in any manner likely to occur to the craftsman in search of novelty. London examples of lyre designs abound and may be seen in Lincoln's Inn Fields, King's Bench Walk, some of the Squares, and in Westminster, Chelsea, and the suburbs. A great rival design is formed of three parallel bars· variously scrolled. The origin of this may have been the classic pilaster or tripod, the probability being rather suggested by early examples at Drayton House. A usual treatment was to bend and scroll the ends of the outer bars sharply in order to join the bars forming the panel with the outer standards. A third and central attachment resulted from again bending the same bars abruptly inward or outward and placing C scrolls in the spaces to connect them. Scrolls and water leaves, tendrils, etc., are introduced according to taste and price, but the richer treatments are obtained, as in the " lyre " panels, by duplicating the bars, placing them out of the perpendicular, and by beading or twisting. The " pilaster " origin was less lost sight of in France than with us, their panels being formed of several rather closely-set bars. These appear in the railings to the spacious fore-court of Wentworth House, 1726 (Fig. 41, p. 119), the panels having five closely set bars and simple pyramid tops. They occur in Grosvenor Square with acanthus caps and moulded bases (Plate LXXII), and in piers by Bakewell, and at Carshalton, Tadworth Court, etc. For some reason, however, the lyre pattern took precedence of all these and is found in the places of honour where the two designs are used conjointly. A form of pilaster panel entirely filled by a succession of reversing and broken scrolls and leaves on each side of a centre bar, with no definite rhythm, is perhaps based on the Renaissance pilaster with rich decoration. Combinations of all these are met with, produced by taking part of one and joining with another, and the introduction of an oval or geometric centre is common to all. Repeating designs like the Greek wave, favoured by Tijou, or of scrolls, are relatively uncommon. Four-sided pilasters and panels are present in several of the bastion railings at Hampton Court and at Great Missenden, and in works by the Roberts and Edney, and are seen in pictures of Gibbs' railing to St. Mary's Church in the Strand, 1719, and existing in a very plain form to St. Margaret's Church, Westminster. The dog-bars were often simple spikes, especially at first, but Tijou introduced a short form with barbed arrow-point in his gates for Wimpole. It is uncertain whether the ends of the barbs were fastened to the verticals of the railing, but the advisability of holding them by more than a single rivet at the base must have been apparent from the first. To effect this separate lateral scroll supports on each side of the barbed dog-bars were added at Ham (Plate II) and Drayton Houses, and there is a curious ogee arch with spike above accomplishing the purpose in the Orangery rail at Hampton Court (Fig. 90, p. 248), while in numbers of the early railings and gates scrolls and scrolled bars are used, as at Hampton Court (Fig. 17, p. 44) Clare College, Burleigh (Plate VI), Burley-on-the-Hill (Fig. 22, p. 57), and Drayton (Fig. 20, p. 53). But when smiths discovered that the barbs lent themsveles most readily to the purpose, providing the additional fixings at the best point, near the apex, aroïd dog-bars became general. The obvious embellishments are lateral scrolls and leaves and beadings to the shafts, and leaves and button and twist points to the apex. The shafts are split and opened out into flask shapes at Bulwick, Clare College Bridge (Fig. 30, p. 97), Colwick Hall in Nottingham (Plate LXI), etc. At Powis House (Fig. 43, p. 122) they not only opened into a heart-shape, but were waved and set with three pairs of leaves. Usually the flukes or barbs diverge outwards and their ends are either tenoned direct into the verticals or bent down and riveted, but in the gates or rails at Jesus College, Cambridge, Great Marlow, St. Mary's, Oxford, (Fig. 63, p. 187), the Durdans (Plate XXIV), Reigate Priory (Fig. 61, p. 180) and Hampstead Church, they curve inward towards the shaft and are scrolled.

In addition to the dog-bars the upper horizontals were frequently "fringed"; that is a moulded or barbed spike between one or

Railings

more pairs of leaves or scrolls was riveted to the under or upper side of the horizontal between each vertical bar. When a central horizontal was present at the height of the lock-rail of the gates, the fringe was erect above it and pendent below. Simpler scrolls occasionally replace the spikes. Horizontals were sometimes duplicated and filled in with a scrolled border, as at Raphael Park, Romford (Plate XLIV).

The richly wrought railings of Powis House in Great Ormond Street (Fig. 43, p. 122) must have presented a fine example of this treatment, and later Gibbs introduced borders of circles into his designs in the French manner.

When great richness was desired the entire bay of railing between pilasters was surmounted by a scrolled pyramid cresting, its centre frequently rising well above the pyramids of the pilasters. Fine examples exist at New College, Oxford (Fig. 29, p. 87), Ormeley House (Fig. 35, p.110), Drayton House, Belton, Leeswood (Plates XV, XVI), Chirk Castle (Plate XIV), Clandon Park (Plate XXXV), Kirkleatham Hospital Yorkshire, Newark-on-Trent, Newdigate House Nottingham (Fig. 67, p. 200), Bell Street Reigate (Fig. 72, p. 231), Carshalton (Plate XXX), etc.; but those to the screen at Powis House (Fig. 42, p. 120), no longer existing, must have eclipsed all. Gibbs introduced a crested railing among his designs in 1728 (Fig. 47, p. 130). Finally the horizontal nearly always terminated in a scrolled ramp next to stone or brick piers and walls, like a bracket reversed. Every smith made use of them, and some are finely proportioned and of the richest work.

The vast changes in the character of English ironwork which followed on the publication of Tijou's book of designs has been fully dealt with in preceding pages (pp. 37-58). The garden screen at Hampton Court (Plate III) is probably the richest iron-railing produced since mediaeval days, and in the strongest contrast to the then prevailing English taste. For the purpose required, an immediate screen and protection for the then newly planted Royal garden, it is admirably adapted. Nothing equalling the panels with the royal insignia have since been produced, but the pilasters have no doubt suggested many of the later treatments. As designed, these are massively framed, the filling of four vertical bars scrolled inward at either end and resting on a low-moulded table with concave supports; and the vertical centre is richly filled in with rosettes, festoons, and a mask above, all in embossed sheet iron. Over this is a moulded cap clothed with acanthus leaves, supporting the moulded base to a pyramid formed of two cornucopiæ of flowers. As actually executed these pilasters are little altered, except that the top is simply arched in the centre, plainly moulded, and surmounted by two **G** scrolls of the kind well known to smiths, in which short horizontals divide the scrolls, a vertical bar supporting a royal crown forming a centre. His gate pilasters are very varied, such as scrolls repeated like the Greek wave, with lily leaves in pairs; circles and husks; inverted cones with leaves, ovals, intertwined scrolls, and still more elaborate designs. A design for a remarkably rich railing is shown on Plate 7 of Tijou's book. This introduces a flower-like fringe with beaded points below the upper horizontal bar, a double lock-rail with ovals between, a fringe of horizontal **C** scrolls above supporting water husks with beaded spikes, and **G** scrolls in pairs with arrow-points between the verticals for dog-bars. This arrangement forms the basis of all the richer designs of railings which ensued, and must have originated with Tijou, before 1693. Another rich design for a railing (Plate 11 of Tijou's book) is of grouped vertical bars, bent sharply and scrolled at either end, separated by standards with open tasselled spear-heads. Between these over the upper horizontal is a rich cresting of pyramids of scrolls and flowers, the whole between massive and very rich pilasters. Spontoon-headed railings with tassels are seen in his frontispiece, but he scarcely favours the plain English type of railing, for a bare indication of them is seen in the design used at Wimpole (Fig. 19, p. 46). Perhaps neither of the rich designs were executed, and only those which now separate the Home Park from the Terrace Walk at Hampton Court, parallel with the river are known to be his. They are plain and were designed by Talman, and in all probability led to the loss by Tijou of all Royal patronage, giving rise to the family legend that he died of a broken heart through disappointment, which, like the authorship of Tijou's work at Hampton Court, became appropriated at a later date to Huntington Shaw. None of the railings or balustrades in St. Paul's Cathedral are by him; yet his last recorded commission, 1711–12, was for 77 feet of railing round the statue of Queen Anne in St. Paul's Churchyard, at nearly £5 per foot. A curiously-petticoated railing is seen surrounding this in Bowles' view. Possibly the low railing and gates to the Sheldonian Theatre, in close proximity to the rich gates of the Clarendon Press at Oxford, are his, since they are in his style and represented in engravings of his date. The railings are of spiked vertical bars with short dog-bars to match, riveted in a double horizontal and fixed into the stone coping by caulkings: the small wicket gates are of a scrolled design, repeated four times round a small circle within, in rectangular panes joined diagonally at the angles.

The River Terrace railing at Hampton Court is in panels of scroll-ended bars in pairs, and four-sided pilasters with solid caps, the panels each of two bent and scrolled bars, with an oval and husks for centre. An immense stretch of high vertical sharply-pointed bars set diagonally with plain arrow-pointed dog-bars separates the Fountain Garden from the Home Park, the gates only distinguished by two centre scrolls, though they are hung between four-sided pillars with rich scroll and husk filling, and spreading pyramids of scrolls, with vase finials and massive bases, almost repeating those to the East Avenue of Drayton House. The Bastion railing is lofty, of plain spikes and arrow-pointed dog-bars, with high and massive four-sided pillars capped by scrolls and vases, alternating with pilasters of the same design, and standards, with vase-shaped finials.

Next in interest to the railings of Hampton Court are those to Drayton House, at least two of which must have been erected for the Duchess of Norfolk soon after 1700. The most important, about 150 feet in length, is that to the fore-court, already seen in their present position in Buck's view of about 1710. They stand upon a low wall with pilasters of scrolls and closely beaded central bar, with water husks and two long beaded tendrils with whip-like ends, rising from a cluster of acanthus. The pyramids above are scrolled and have high-beaded finials spirally waved at the apex, and their massive standard bars terminate in spheres and buttons. The bars are plainly spiked, a C scroll between each, over a massive horizontal blocked out in the mediaeval manner but with a covering plate 2½ or 3 inches wide. The bars pass into the stone with S scrolls between each for dog-bars. The railing to the Bowling Green is contemporary and by the same hand. Pilasters at each end are quaint and original, of two scrolls with exaggerated horizontal breaks and a long-beaded spike between, which passes downward into a sort of scrolled parallelogram, split into loops with flowers, over reversed G's and acanthus. Their standards repeat those of the fore-court. The bars have high spikes, with necks, and the horizontal bar is moulded with swelled holes, and fringe of husks and balls with waved and beaded tongues. The verticals pass into the stone with G scrolls for dog-bars, and there are twisted standards at intervals.

The long railing to the more distant gates of the South Avenue are more recent and present a good example of the crested kind. The pilasters at the ends are of partly geometric design with an oval centre and water husks; and others are filled with repeats of a wave pattern with kite-shaped centres, all with high finials of scrolls and water-husks. Between are pyramid crestings of scrolls with high centres, of two alternating designs, clothed in water-husks, thrown over leaves and light moulded spikes.

Railings

The verticals 1 inch square are riveted above into a slight horizontal and pass into the stone with S scrolls between in place of dog-bars.

A garden railing has waved spikes over a wide horizontal, and pilasters of scroll-ended vertical bars united by moulded collars, with scrolled pyramids of concave outline and large finials of leafy twists. The East Avenue railing has the verticals set diagonally with moulded spikes, and plain spikes for dog-bars, transfixing short bent pieces, a local attempt to reproduce the arrow-pointed dog-bar of the South Avenue. The two fixed panels next the gates between lofty pilasters of scrolls and water-leaves repeat the border of ovals seen in the lock-rail.

It is perhaps worth noting here the early appearance of fringes of water-husks and beads over C scrolls, with waved and beaded tongues; and of plain C scrolls to the horizontal bars of the great forecourt gates, and of arrow-pointed dog-bars, in which the end of the barbs are bent down, though the actual attachments to the verticals are effected by scrolls lower down. There are similar fringes to the Bowling Green gates, in which G and E scrolls with water-husks and beaded centres serve the purpose of

FIG. 70. IN PACKERS ROW, CHESTERFIELD, BY BAKEWELL.

dog-bars. These are repeated in the gates to Burley-on-the-Hill.

Bakewell's railings are less remarkable. One of the most important, in front of the City Hall at Worcester (p. 63), is plain with moulded spikes, every alternate bar with scrolls and plain spiked dog-bars. The pilasters are of an unusual lyre design, and it finishes against the gate piers and walls in finely scrolled ramps with acanthus leaves. A Nottingham railing to Willoughby House has flattened spear-heads and scrolls to the bars and dog-bars. A curious railing in Chesterfield (Fig. 70) has lyre pilasters and pyramids, with peculiar barbed spikes to the bars and dog-bars, and fine ramped bracket as terminal; this and the pilasters almost duplicating those at Worcester. At Okeover is a railing with geometric border in a double horizontal, and spear-points above, a third horizontal receiving the plain dog-bars. A drawing in the Architectural Association Sketch Book of a railing at Norton, near Sheffield, presents bars with javelin-pointed heads on spheres between scrolls, and pilasters with arching tops rising high above the horizontal bar, in the manner of the Roberts'. It comprises flask-shaped finials over a lyre panel with embossed shell and Corinthian capital, and a scrolled pyramid centre with javelin finials and the beaded whip-like tendrils proceeding from husks, seen at Drayton.

The Roberts brothers, more fortunate than Bakewell, had several fore-court screens to carry out during their briefer career, and on the grandest scale. The screen at Leeswood rivalled the garden screen at Hampton Court, with rich pyramidal tops, taking the outlines of broken pediments, and handsome panels and pilasters (Plate xv). A second screen presents a splendid example of a lofty crested railing, with pilasters rising above the upper horizontal, finishing in arching pediments and flask-shaped vases. It has two intermediate horizontals with fringes, and flattened javelin-headed dog-bars with scrolls and leaves (Plate xvi).

The railings of the Chirk Castle screen (Plate xiv), seen in an old drawing by Buck, are also crested, and present the Leeswood dog-bars, and have been reproduced by their owner. An old print shows that the original railings to Eaton Hall were simple with moulded spear-heads and the typical dog-bars and somewhat plain pilasters with spreading pyramid tops. At Carden Hall the spear and waved points emerge alternately from leafy husks, and between the bars is a fringe of double husks and twisted points, while scrolls with barbed points form the dog-bars.

Edney, the Bristol smith, had no liking for plain vertical bars, and his railings to St. John's Hospital and St. Mary's Church at Warwick present no unusual features. Both have pilasters of scroll-ended bars and tapering spikes swelled at the base. The pilasters at Shobdon have oval centres and pyramid tops, and the railings have pyramid crestings, but are otherwise plain with arrow-pointed dog-bars. A railing to Sutton Coldfield Church has a central lyre pilaster and spreading pyramid of reversed G scrolls with water leaves in pairs, and narrower side pilasters with ovals and centre bars clothed with water-leaves and scrolls in pairs, and scrolled top, the verticals plain with moulded spikes. His most ambitious effort is at Scraptoft (Fig. 27, p. 76), where the pilasters are of unusual lyre design with finely scrolled spreading pyramids, the ends of the verticals tapered with small arrow-points, and the dog-bars scrolled at the base with arrow-points and incurving scrolled barbs. His richest rails and screens are in the interiors of Bristol Churches.

Few smiths can have excelled Thomas Robinson when in 1697 he had produced the beautiful railing to the Morning Prayer Chapel in St. Paul's Cathedral. The leaf-shaped spikes on hollow balls fashioned by the hammer, the latter from sheet iron, and the more massive standards between, are excellent work in the English spirit. Though the important commissions were given to Tijou, the whole of the wrought-iron railing and balustrade work, both inside and out, fell to Robinson, and he was kept employed till 1711 when Tijou, by quitting England left him without a serious rival. He was a Londoner with works at Hyde Park Corner, and his style, though undoubtedly influenced by Tijou's splendid works, remains completely distinct. In him they inspired emulation rather than imitation, and he clearly remained from the outset more Tijou's rival than pupil. He was a fine designer, with a real sense of proportion, balance, fitness and restraint, and should undoubtedly be honoured as the actual creator of the English style of smithing.

The railings to New College, Oxford (Fig. 29, p. 87), produced in 1711, and still occupying their original position, afford an excellent idea of the style Robinson had reached, when Tijou who had commenced his career here so brilliantly, left this country for ever, a broken and disappointed man. The strikingly lofty and perpendicular effect of the railings is aided by the absence of any intermediate horizontal bars, and still more by carrying the pilasters, of scroll-ended vertical bars and water-husks, not only high above the railings, but unbroken by the passage of any horizontal. They are capped by pyramids formed of C scrolls and leaves with solid turned vases as finials. The verticals are an inch square, and the dog-bars arrow-pointed, each with a pair of scrolls and a pair of thrown-over leaves. The upper horizontal is moulded with a very bold and finely scrolled pyramid cresting with dropping beads and water-husks. The most extensive screen or *clairvoyé* at Carshalton Park (Plates xxx and xxxi and pp. 92-93) is lofty, and without intermediate horizontals. The verticals rise from a low stone wall and are plainly spiked with arrow-pointed dog-bars between. The wide panels away from the gates have, to mark the centre, a standard and scrolled pyramid with vases. A most dignified and grandly perpendicular effect is produced, but the screen unfortunately is not to remain *in situ*. At Belton (p. 90) the railings to the main avenue are equally without intermediate horizontals, but

Railings 229

FIG. 71. RAILINGS AT BEDDINGTON, SURREY (FORMERLY THE MANOR HOUSE, NOW THE ORPHANAGE).
(Showing the coat of ar.ns, now taken down, see also Plate xxviii.)

the pilasters of varied lyre designs do not rise above the top horizontal, though having wide pyramids of scrolls arched over vases now surmounted alternately by the Brownlow coronets and crests. The spikes are moulded and the arrow-pointed dog-bars have button and twist points, the first appearance of this distinctive feature. The Courtyard railings are lower with pilasters of lyre design next the gates, and of scroll-ended bars and ovals beyond, with similar dog-bars and a fine pyramid cresting of G scrolls, etc., between. The Wilderness railing has leafy arrow-points, and the same dogs with the addition of a bead to the shaft, and lyre pilasters. The railings flanking the entrance to Grimsthorpe Castle are imposing, recalling Belton, but with the lyre pilasters rising above the top horizontal, and alternately capped by a large gilt vase and a scrolled pyramid. The alternate bars are arrow-points sheathed in leaves, and there are no intermediate rails or dog-bars. The date is probably about 1720 and the work may be by Robinson. The western screen at Beddington (Fig. 71 and Plate XXVIII) has high railings with a splendid cresting and central pilaster of scrolled and foliated bars, scrolled border at the height of the lock-rail, fringe of husks and button-points, and arrow-pointed dog-bars. The railings at Harrowden, though plain, are imposing in their height and simplicity (p. 91). There are railings at Arbury Hall (p. 105) which may be Robinson's work, and those which form such fine sweeping lines flanking the gates at Wootton (Plates XXVI and XXVII and p. 89) with numerous pilasters of scrolled and foliated bars are perhaps his though the water-leaf husks with waved tongues taking the place of dog-bars appear so far unique.

A railing which may more safely be attributed to Warren is that at Clandon Park (Plate XXXV), with its fine cresting of dolphin scrolls, etc., terminating in very bold buttress brackets with waved branches of laurel leaves in clusters. The grand pilasters (Fig. 32) rise high above the upper horizontal, with rich and

Railings

delicately worked lyre panels, having acanthus capitals and foliage and lofty pyramids of scrolls and tendrils. The railings are about 9 feet high on a low stone kerb, with arrow-pointed dog-bars, and a mid horizontal with a fringe of twisted spikes between

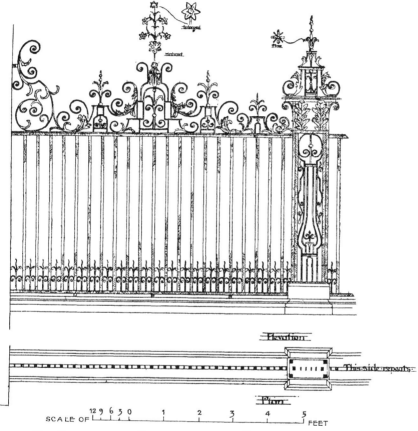

FIG. 72. RAILING, "PRIORY GATEWAY," BELL STREET, REIGATE.

thrown-over leaves and scrolls. The fine screen at Kirkleatham Hospital comprises a range of high railing on each side of the gates, divided into four bays by lyre pilasters, each bay surmounted by a wide pyramid of dolphin scrolls with spiked finials and thrown-over leaves. Between each vertical is an **S** scroll, and a short spike with lateral scrolls at the base.

The finest existing is probably that at Erdig, near Wrexham, richly worked with horizontal borders, forming a screen with modern gates. They rival those to Powis House. There were also crested railings to Lord Archer's House in Covent Garden. There are crested railings in Stamford, particularly on Barn Hill.

The pilasters to the fine railing of the Priory in Bell Street, Reigate (Fig. 72), are of lyre design and richly worked, continued above the horizontal, with a large acanthus capital and pyramid and finial, terminating in an erect bell-shaped flower and moulded spike. The railing has a lower horizontal, with dog-bars of leaves and scrolls and wavy points, with a fine pyramid cresting, the centres rising high above the rest with several large flowers on stems, and scrolls and acanthus connecting with lesser pyramids. the whole ending in fine buttress brackets.

Pilasters must frequently have been carried above and through the horizontals of the railings in the spacious fore-court screens that have been destroyed in such numbers in the northern, southern and eastern counties. The fine effect that resulted must have been fully appreciated in those artistic days, and our illustration of the old courtyard of High Street House (Fig. 40) is a case in point. In some cases these have been preserved, for at Inwood, near Templecombe, a pergola is supported by a number of very high pilasters of fine design, and others are used to support arches and for various purposes about the extensive grounds. One or two are in the Museum at Nottingham. A church railing of late date at Bedford is remarkable for the lyre pilaster which is carried through the horizontal to almost double the height of the railing, with spreading buttress scrolls on each side and wide-scrolled exaggerated pyramids.

Other crested railings are at North Pallant House, Chichester, said to be modern; and on each side of the gate at Marlow (Plate LX),

Railings

and coming nearer to London, at Ormeley House, Ham Common (Fig. 35, p. 110), with richly worked pilasters, probably by Robinson. A pilaster is seen in the illustration of a railing in St. Giles' Churchyard at Reading, with oversailing pyramid (Fig. 73).

In London we have Robinson's work in the railings to Queen's House on Cheyne Walk (Plate XXXVI, p. 106). They only extend 13 feet 6 inches on either side of the gate piers with a central lyre pilaster of delicate work, one shape within another, which rises above the top horizontal with a scrolled

FIG. 73. ST. GILES' CHURCH, READING.

pyramid. The railings are about 6 feet high on a wall, with richly worked heads of two thrown-over leaves, and two scrolls with a short central spike over a button. It is no doubt contemporary with the building of the house in 1715. Another railing by Robinson, whose works were not far distant, is at No. 24, Kensington Gore (Plate LII). It is light with plain moulded spikes, alternating with leafy arrow-heads on a low wall, with three pilasters, the salient feature of which is the use of bars bent over like U's inverted of various dimensions, and the peculiar recurved scrolls to the pyramids. The railings to 15, Cheyne Walk (Plate LI), may be his, with plain moulded spikes, a pyramid of scrolls to mark the centre without pilaster, and finely-ramped scrolls at either end. That to No. 4 is plain, each alternate spike having scrolled barbs.

The railing illustrated in the Spring Gardens Sketch Book

234 English Ironwork of the XVIIth and XVIIIth Centuries

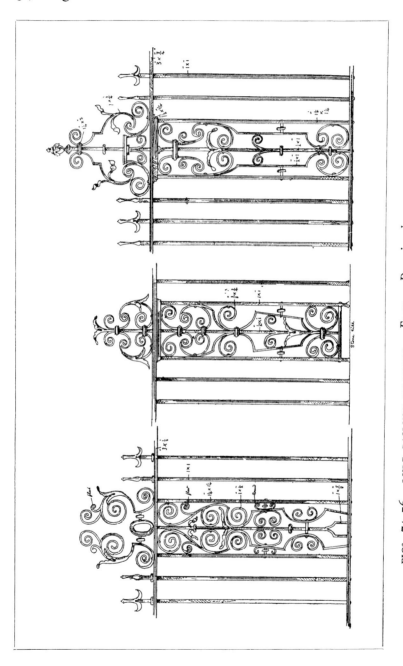

FIGS. 74–76. LYRE RAILING PILASTERS. *From a Drawing by* MR. G. D. STEVENS.

Plate LXXI.

GATE, LAMP HOLDERS AND AREA RAILINGS IN GREAT ORMOND STREET, BLOOMSBURY.

Plate LXXII.

 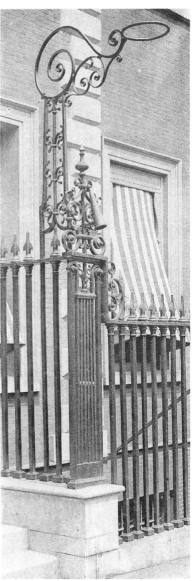

RAILING AND LAMP HOLDER
44 GROSVENOR SQUARE.

RAILING AND LAMP HOLDER
12 GROSVENOR SQUARE.

at Manor Street, Chelsea, must long since have disappeared. It had fine lyre pilasters, the lyre outline repeated concentrically one within the other, with leaves, scrolls, and a beaded centre bar, and pyramid of **G** scrolls. The heads were forged separately, alternately a leafy arrow-point and moulded spike, fixed by tenons to the verticals below. Our illustrations (Figs. 74–6) drawn in 1875 present three rather late and considerably modified examples of pilasters. That on the left, at 6, Hanover Square, is the sole survivor of several panelled railings which remained until a few years since. Fig. 76 was also formerly in Hanover Square, and Fig. 75 is from the Old Manor House in Stoke Newington.

The pilaster type is more abundant and is seen in many engravings of old London, as in the charming view of the old Fountain Garden in the Temple (Fig. 77), in which the finials of the pyramids over the pilasters are carried up in an unusual manner with moulded swellings and arrow-tops. A drawing by Hunt in the Victoria and Albert Museum shows that this was altered subsequently, for there are heavy square sectioned piers with caps and bases, and a semicircular recess in the railing. Another with the pilaster type of panel is seen in Bowles' engraving of the statue of Charles I at Charing Cross, 1753, and again in his view of Powis House, Lincoln's Inn Fields. Among actually existing specimens that on a dwarf wall on the south side of Richmond Green is one of the best. Its panels are wide, of scroll-ended bars, beaded centre bar with thrown-over leaves, and a pyramid of **G** scrolls ending in an open heart-shaped finial of four twisted bars meeting in a point. This, though more quaint, is not very dissimilar to that with oval centres at Walpole House, Chiswick Mall. A more graceful specimen is at Hall Place, Bexley, probably by Robinson, with a beaded centre to its **G** scroll pyramid and button and twist finial. The best known example is probably that in Great Ormond Street (Fig. 78 and Plate LXXI), in which the four bars filling the panel diverge slightly towards the centre where they are suddenly bent and brought together and welded with C scrolls. They are scrolled above into a heart shape with water leaves, and more simply to form a base, and the pyramid of two stages is graceful with moulded centre and cast flask-shaped finial. The panels are 4 feet 6 inches apart, and the railing heads forged separately and fixed by tenons, alternately a leafy arrow and moulded spike drawn into a slender point, with a fringe of two scrolls and broadly twisted spike between each vertical.

Grosvenor and Berkeley Squares still preserve a few finely panelled area-rails. The striking pilasters in the former (Plate LXXII), apparently adopted from the French, are formed of a group of slender and closely set vertical bars beneath heavy volutes, with moulded abacus under a pyramid formed of two G scrolls with leaves, supporting a vase. The verticals have cast javelin heads, fixed by tenons and rivets, and cast caps and bases. These are at Nos. 43 and 44 and probably date from about 1725 when the Square was completed, or later. A pilaster in Serjeant's Inn is on the same lines, with simpler cap and flask-shaped vase.

James Gibbs published designs for railings at about this time, his pilasters rather affecting the lyre type, with rich pyramids of dolphin scrolls. In one the pilaster is carried higher than the horizontals, which rise towards it (Fig. 45, p. 130); in another the verticals and dog-bars are arrow-pointed (Fig. 46); the third has a scrolled cresting (Fig. 47); and the fourth is in the French manner, with spear-heads and tassels, intended to be cast, and a border of circles at the base.

The design for the railings of the still existing screen to the Horse Guards, built by Vardy about 1753, appears in Isaac Ware's *Body of Architecture*, 1756, the opened-out spear-heads apparently taken from Tijou's book of designs. His Plate 9, devoted to railings, is reproduced (Figs. 79–82). The first (Fig. 79) is described " as a plain railing leaded into a stone curb. The second (Fig. 80)

FIG. 77. THE OLD FOUNTAIN GARDEN IN THE TEMPLE, LONDON.

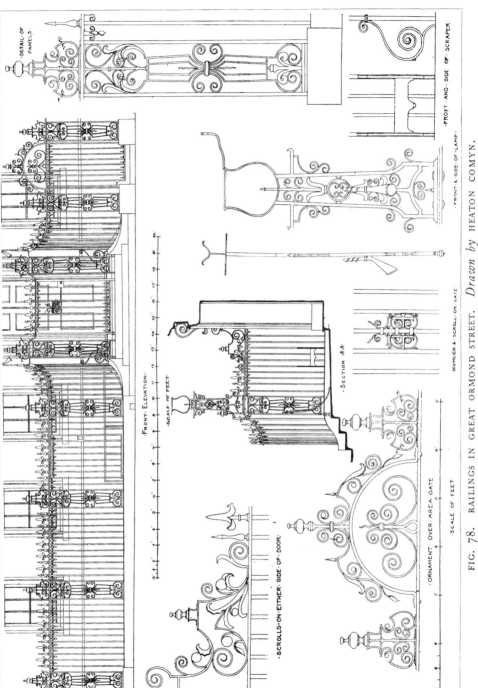

FIG. 78. RAILINGS IN GREAT ORMOND STREET. *Drawn by* HEATON COMYN.

is of somewhat richer kind, framed with flat bar at bottom let into a groove in stonework." The third (Fig. 81) is " of more ornamental kind, the bottom bar supported by balls, and thus the frame is kept out of wet and is safer from rusting and rotting." The fourth (Fig. 82) is a " railing of a slight kind with pilasters and the bar let into a shallow groove." Ware advocated wooden gates to the forecourts of town houses. Plain rails then cost $3\frac{3}{4}d.$ per lb.

London continued throughout the eighteenth century to make great demands on the smith for railings, generally of severe type.

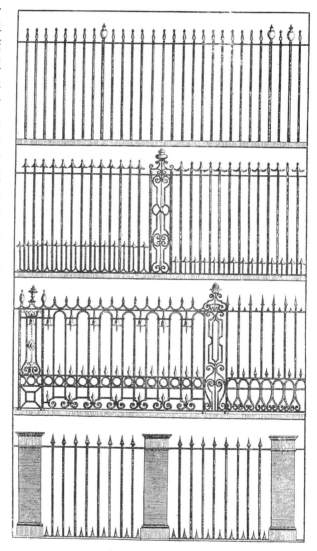

FIGS. 79-82. DESIGNS FOR RAILINGS BY ISAAC WARE, 1756.

In the suburbs houses were set back from the road, and railings, while preserving an agreeable out-look, provided sufficient privacy and protection to insure their popularity. London building was no less propitious, for houses set back but few feet from the line of frontage, with domestic offices in the basement, required the space in front to be dug out to afford light and air, and to be bridged by the steps leading to the entrance, the whole needing the protection of iron railings. Stowe notes that the houses in Crosby and Devonshire Squares had iron palisades in front in 1754, and when such extensive estates as the Bedford, Portland, Grosvenor, Berkeley, Portman, and Northampton were being laid out in

FIGS. 83–86. COMMON FORMS OF CAST-IRON VASES ON RAILINGS.

streets and squares, immense quantities of area railings were needed. These were massive and protective, of vertical bars, spaced some 5 to 6 inches apart, spiked or barbed, and held together by a single wide horizontal above, and each let separately into the stone kerb at the base. Perhaps being more easy to climb, decorative panels were usually avoided, and standards took their place. Few departures were made, and the different dates are partially denoted by the forms of the cast-iron vase-shaped finials to the standards; but the old flask-shape (Fig. 83), the pine-cone (Fig. 84), and a vase wide and gadrooned above (Fig. 85), all perhaps originally taken from designs by Wren for the towers and parapets of his churches, continued in favour side by side with the more classic forms introduced later by the Adams (Fig. 86), which were numerous but not very varied.

Railings

The central areas of the London squares were at first left as open spaces, or merely railed off by posts on wood palings. Lincoln's Inn seems to have been one of the earliest provided with iron railings, for the *Daily Journal*, July 9, 1735, states that plans for the four gates and iron palisades on dwarf walls were then before the Duke of Newcastle, and a subscription to replace the wood palings with iron railings was made in 1748. These still exist and are of spiked inch bars with heavier standards, bearing cast flask-shaped heads, and preserve the original supports for the quaint basin-shaped lamps, about forty paces apart, since supplemented by intermediate lamp supports of " Adams " date and design. Lindsey House had a forecourt at that time with six spacious brick piers, " with curious ironwork " between them and handsome gates. Cavendish Square was laid out in 1717, but there is no reference to iron railings till 1780. Soho Square was fenced in with iron in 1748, at a cost of over £800,* with four iron gates and eight lamps at the angles, the squares being still thoroughfares. Golden Square was similarly treated later. It is only in 1787 that a view of Hanover Square shows iron railings with high and severe pilasters carrying lamps. Here when building St. George's Church, James II had also built two stone houses with fine ironwork and link extinguishers on each side of the door. The centre of St. James' Square was laid out as an octagon, with obelisks at each angle, and plain railings and standards bearing flask-shaped vases; while Grosvenor Square had a circular inclosure with railings between stone pillars and four handsome double gates. The railings enclosing Westminster Abbey are of plain bars with moulded spikes, interrupted on the north side by stone obelisks formerly carrying lamps, and on the east by square piers now without pyramids. Iron railings were introduced in the parks still later. Pennant states in 1790 that Green Park was bounded by a wall along Piccadilly,

* The original contract for the work is printed in *Soho and its Associations*, London, Dulau, 1895. Peter Vandercombe undertook the contract, and Wm. Yates supplied the lamps, etc.

" but in many places are rows of benevolent railings which afford a most elegant view of the park." George IV had Hyde Park closed in with iron railings, and it was at the instance of Loudoun, the eminent horticulturist, that the wall to Kensington Gardens was replaced by railings in the reign of Victoria.

The first railings wholly of cast iron, except the horizontals, were, with the seven massive gates,* it is now well known, produced for St. Paul's Churchyard at a cost of upwards of £11,000. A baluster design in the Spanish manner was selected, and the Lamberhurst foundry was commissioned to produce it, but apparently sublet a part to other foundries in the vicinity. Some underhand dealing took place, for Wren, when petitioning the House of Lords for payment of arrears, stated : " As to the iron fence, it is so remarkable and so fresh in memory, and by whose influence and importunity it was wrested from me, and the doing of it carried in a way which I venture to say will ever be condemned." The cost, 6d. or 8d. per lb., was, in any case, excessive, the usual price of castings being 2d., and no others are recorded as having been made in Sussex. Gibbs had introduced cast balustered standards into one of his designs for railings, published in 1728 (Fig. 47, p. 130), and in 1726 used a cast baluster pattern for the existing enclosure of St. Martin's Church. Another example is in Cambridge, round the Senate House, where cast balusters and wrought bars alternate. Its introduction was at first gradual and tentative. Isaac Ware remarks in his *Body of Architecture*, 1756, p. 89, " that cast iron is very serviceable to the builder and a vast expense is saved in many cases by using it ; in rails and balusters it makes a rich and massy appearance when it has cost very little, and when wrought iron much less substantial would cost a vast sum. But, on the other hand, there is a neatness and finished look in a wrought iron that will never be seen in cast, and it bears accident vastly better."

* One is now in the Hastings Museum.

Railings

Sites were taken up in the best squares by speculative builders, and a good deal of cast iron is seen to have been used, possibly for economy. Later it was often used from choice, and under the Regency, when the severely classic taste introduced by Napoleon became a fashion in England, wrought iron was almost excluded for decorative purposes.

Some of the most decorative of the London area rails were designed by Robert Adam. The house on the east side of St. James' Square, built for Sir W. W. Wynn in 1773 by him, still preserves its handsome railing (Fig. 87). The verticals finish in mace-heads, and there are fleur-de-lis and honeysuckle borders. The pilaster is a lyre with fan and honeysuckle enrichments. In the finished drawing of the elevation in the

FIG. 87. RAILING, BY ROBERT ADAM, ST. JAMES' SQUARE, 1773.

Soane Museum the four pilasters are surmounted by rich lamps, apparently removed with the fan-light grille when the iron porch was installed. The house built for Lady Home by Robert Adam on the north side of Portman Square also preserves the original railing

(Plate LXXIII), with its lamp standards complete. It was completed only a year or two later, in 1775. The vertical bars are spiked with borders of ovals and arrow-points, and lozenge centres, and the lamp standard is an obelisk with fan, honeysuckle, and looped ornament. At this time designs for rich railings and gates were being published in Carter's *Builders' Magazine*, an illustration of railings for the year 1774 being especially remarkable. The railing to Chandos House in Queen Anne Street, Cavendish Square (Plate LXXIII), formerly Chandos Street, is very similar, with borders of arrow-points and rosettes and rich honeysuckle pilasters supporting lyre pattern pedestals for lamps to correspond. Winchester House, next door to Sir W. W. Wynn's, in St. James' Square, has a railing of javelins and borders of ellipses, retaining its dignified scrolled obelisk lamp supports. The fine mansion forming the corner of Cavendish Square and Harley Street, once Princess Amelia's, has a relatively plain railing with javelin heads and diagonal border and several lyre-shaped lamp pedestals with delicate lozenge and honeysuckle enrichments, a turned baluster beneath taking the place of the usual enriched pilaster. The railings to the house in Burlington Gardens, built in 1792 by Vardy for the Marquis of Anglesey, are principally cast, with javelin points and C scrolls, and arrow-points between; and no fewer than eight lofty honeysuckle lamp supports. These recall the still later examples in Hamilton Place, facing the Wellington Statue, which also comprise honeysuckles and are principally of cast iron. In contrast with these are the delightfully simple railings of Adam's date to Boodle's Club in St. James' Street, and others as good which have recently disappeared from Lincoln's Inn Fields.

Plate LXXIII.

AT CHANDOS HOUSE,
QUEEN ANNE STREET.
By Robert Adam.

AT No. 1 PORTMAN SQUARE.
By Robert Adam.

BALUSTRADES, BALCONIES, STAIR RAMPS AND GRILLES

Balustrades, Balconies, Stair-ramps and Grilles

Balustrades

THUS far the works we have considered, both gates and railings, have been devoted to one definite purpose, to shut out intruders, and therefore however beautiful they may be in design or execution, they only appear completely satisfactory when difficult to climb. Gates and railings are usually of considerable height, and their silhouettes as uninviting as possible to such as would climb them.

The much smaller section now to be considered is designed for safety and convenience. Thus while railings hitherto considered are lofty and spiked, these are low, seldom exceeding 3 to 4 feet in height, and generally end above in an invitingly broad and horizontal rail for the hand. They bear various names, according to position; but the designs for all are similar, and all are comprised in the one comprehensive term "rail." This consists of one or more horizontal bars with supports, but if the latter are decorative and the more important part of the design, they are known as balustrades, unless custom, as in the case of altar or communion rails, excludes the use of the term. The same design may be applied as a balcony rail, or to a roof or bridge as a parapet rail, while used for a garden terrace or flight of stairs it becomes a balustrade. Few of the latter survived the destructive rearrangements of gardens by Lancelot Brown. The term balustrade is Italian in its origin, but reaching us from France, the French form has been retained. Great use of balustrades was made under Louis XIV, when they were richly and superbly wrought, the *Mercure* of the period continually chronicling the erection of masterpieces. Our example, from Tijou's book (Fig. 88), furnishes designs conceived in this sumptuous style, probably never to be

FIG. 88. DESIGNS FOR BALUSTRADES, BY TIJOU.

executed, though one of the four on the left hand has clearly sug-

FIG. 89. BALUSTRADE TO LONG WATER, HAMPTON COURT.

gested the beautiful balustrade over the Long Water (Fig. 89) in the Fountain Garden, which presents panels of reversed fleur-de-lis in open work alternating with horizontal C scrolls impaled by short vertical bars. The design is interrupted at intervals by panels of vertical bars and joined by a broad and moulded handrail. Much simpler railings are shown in Kip's view, which were probably replaced when the garden was extended to the water's edge. This or one of the following may be the work of William Bache, who in 1689 was employed in taking down a balcony by the water-side and refixing it in a new position at the Water Gallery. The cost, with additional scrolls, rails and standards, amounted to £197 2s., by the " Declared Pipe Roll Accounts," the work extending over several years. If not this, it may be the rail to the south front of the Palace (Fig 90), which seems to have originally closed the garden end, and required considerable

FIG. 90. BALUSTRADE AND GATES TO THE SOUTH FRONT, HAMPTON COURT.

Plate LXXIV.

BALUSTRADE AT MELBOURNE HALL, DERBYSHIRE.
By Robert Bakewell.

Plate LXXV.

BALUSTRADE IN FORECOURT OF CHESTERFIELD HOUSE, MAYFAIR.

Balustrades

additions when shifted to the present position. This comprises pairs of gates of G scrolls and water-leaves, framed in borders of circles and centring in an ellipse; between low pilasters of scroll-ended bars with beaded centre and pyramid tops of turned vases upon scrolls. The rest is of vertical bars, the spikes separately forged, and swelled into spheres at the base, tenoned through the single wide horizontal, with C scrolls and low-arched dog-bars with

FIG. 91. QUEEN'S HOUSE, CHEYNE WALK.

button tops between them, and heavier standards with solid turned finials at intervals.

An exceptionally rich balustrade by Bakewell of lyre-shaped balusters on open work pedestals, with embossed shell centres and geometric border, overhangs the road by Melbourne, and is reproduced for the altar rail of All Saints' Church, Derby, where there are also magnificent grilles and railings (Plate LXXIV).

In the fore-court of Chesterfield House there still remains perhaps the most magnificent balustrade in England (Plate LXXV). On each side is a central panel of two foliated C's supporting a garter, between palms with a mask and festoons above, tasselled drapery below, and scrolls with acanthus on either side. The pilasters are massive with lions' heads and medallions, and the railing of elongated ovals united by circles, rosettes, and acanthus caps (Plate LXXV). A spiked cresting has been added, and the balustrade may have been brought, with that to the staircase,* from Canons, both being evidently by the same hand. Tradition ascribes it to Tijou, but the design is conceived in a bolder and broader spirit. It could not have been placed in position till the colonnade was built in 1747, when the Earl wrote that his house was "*finie à la française.*" A rich balustrade occupies a similar position in the fine engraving of the French Embassy in Great Ormond Street as rebuilt at the expense of Louis XIV after its destruction by fire (Fig. 43). The balustrade is panelled with lyres and pilasters at intervals, with a large panel enclosing a circle of radiating design on each side of the entrance. No clearer detail exists. A short but remarkably interesting balustrade at Queen's House No. 16, Cheyne Walk, described by W. H.

FIG. 92. THE MASK FROM THE PILASTER OF FIG. 91.

* Illustrated in *The English Staircase*, by W. H. Godfrey, uniform with this volume.

Balustrades

Godfrey in the *London Survey* monograph on Chelsea, is illustrated by permission of Mr. Percy Lovell. The large centre panel is formed entirely of the initials, repeated in reverse and interlaced, of Richard Chapman, who built the house in 1717, ably treated and with very good effect. The pilasters are lyre-shaped under a

FIG. 93. BALUSTRADE TO THE STRAND FRONT OF SOMERSET HOUSE.

remarkably bold satyr's mask (Fig. 92). The Strand front to Somerset House (Fig. 93) presents another handsome and interesting balustrade, no doubt designed by Sir William Chambers, and probably not erected before 1776). It consists of eight rather massive panels of scrolls with fan-shaped centres between stone

252 English Ironwork of the XVIIth and XVIIIth Centuries

obelisks, formerly surmounted by imposing lamp holders separated by lengths of spiked vertical bars between elongated ovals and leafy fringes. A fine drawing of this is in the Soane Museum. In the centre and west court is another interesting balustrade, having a panel of two rectangles and a circle with honeysuckles, pyramid top, and all spaces between the verticals converted into ellipses by half circles of iron, almost entirely wrought, and probably designed by Chambers. The balustrades designed by the brothers Adam were like the railings already noticed, often rich and always refined. A drawing in the Victoria

FIG. 94. DESIGN FOR AN ADAM BALUSTRADE IN THE VICTORIA AND ALBERT MUSEUM.

and Albert Museum (Fig. 94) presents one of Greek honeysuckles between fret borders, with pilasters to match bearing lamps, the whole terminating against a carved stone sphinx and pedestal.

Flat roofs with parapets seem survivals of ancient English tradition, for our mediaeval castles, unlike the high pitched roofs of France and Germany, were flat roofed, providing fighting platforms with crenelations for parapets. Some of our stateliest Elizabethan houses, as Castle Ashby, Burleigh, and Audley End, have stone parapets carved most effectively into mottoes, and later they have stone balustrades of Italian design, as at Whitehall and Chatsworth. It was enacted after the Great Fire of London that

Plate LXXVI.

CROWLEY HOUSE, GREENWICH, NOW DESTROYED.
From an Old Drawing made in 1821.

Balustrades

iron rails might be put round the roofs of houses, permission to do so being first obtained, and old views show some in London streets of plain vertical bars, and to several of the houses on old London Bridge, which enjoyed commanding views.

The old drawing (Plate LXXVI) of Crowley House, Greenwich, shows a raised forecourt with gates and railings, and a good balustrade to a flat roof which may have commanded a view of the shipping and park.

When in accessible situations, London parapet walls are often elaborately defensive, and even picturesque with their rich clusters of barbed spikes. They are far from uncommon, and examples may be seen in Old Palace Yard, Gray's Inn Square, St. Stephen's Coleman Street, the Horse Guards, Abingdon Street, Marylebone Lane, and so on. The dwarf rail on a low parapet of Chiswick Mall has standards with unusually defensive clusters of spikes. Some in Old St. Pancras' Cemetery are very fine, a small arch needing upwards of 100 welds. Similarly defensive brackets and spikes protect exposed angles of walls, cornices, copings, etc., as at the Mansion House, Waterloo Bridge, St. John's, Westminster (Fig. 95), and so on.

There were, in rare cases, iron parapet railings to bridges, when old barrel staves were usually thought sufficient for the purpose. That at

FIG. 95. CHURCH OF ST. JOHN THE EVANGELIST, WESTMINSTER.

Rochester seems the earliest and most notable instance, mentioned in 1543-4. According to Stow's Survey, 1603, the stone bridge over the Fleet was "fair coped on either side with iron pikes"; but this as well as that of Holborn were beautified after the Fire with iron "grates." Some few bridges over the Thames have in more recent years been "beautified" with iron parapet rails, as Hungerford and old Vauxhall Bridges, both demolished, and the railway bridges.

It may be of interest to mention in this connection that the first bridge in England to be constructed entirely of iron is over a brook at Kirklees, Sir George Armytage's seat in Yorkshire. The Coalbrookedale Bridge was not constructed till 1779 or ten years later.

Balconies

Gateways of feudal buildings were picturesquely overhung by machicolations, and either these or the lead flats of Oriel windows with their parapets might have suggested the later overhanging balconies. They appear however only to have reached England with Italian architecture, and, as the name proves, direct from Italy.

It may well be that the overhanging balcony originated in Venice, where they give a distinctive character to the architecture. The Grand Canal, thronged with stately barges and gondolas, and the scene of magnificent water pageants, presented a moving and brilliant spectacle. The superb palaces rose sheer from the waterway, and balconies supplied points of vantage to the inmates from which to overlook the canal, and thus they became not merely luxuries but necessities. The strength, lightness, and transparency of iron, the ease with which balconies of iron could be added to existing buildings, and the small space required for them, presented advantages, and they are found in Venice as early as the fourteenth century, constructed of panels of small quatrefoils fastened together by collars, in rectangular frames. From Venice their use probably spread to Verona, where are early specimens of balconies of plain and twisted vertical bars, sometimes with braziers at the angles, and from thence they no doubt passed to other mediaeval towns in Italy. Thence they also must have reached England, for our earliest form differs little from those of Verona. One of these is at Kirby Hall, Northants (Fig. 96), supported on stone console brackets in front of a window inserted over the door-

Balconies

way by Inigo Jones. It is wholly of plain and rather closely set vertical bars, fixed between horizontal bars, the upper being heavily moulded with stouter standards at the angles, surmounted by balls.

Other examples of balconies over the entrances to Inigo Jones' houses are at Hutton in the Forest and Thorpe Hall, Peterborough, but these are of florid design and probably replace plainer originals.

FIG. 96. KIRBY HALL, NORTHANTS, BY INIGO JONES.

Lord Arundel is credited with having introduced the fashion for balconies into England in 1650, and speaking in 1659 of houses in Covent Garden, Richard Broune notes that every house had one of them. The first appears to have been put up at the corner of Chandos Street, when country folk were wont to gape at it. Houses possessing them needed no other sign; a house in Bedford Street was distinguished as "the Bellconey," and one in St. Martin's Lane as "Ye Balconey" in 1667; the "Blue and Gilt Balcony" was the sign of a house in Hatton Street in 1673, and the "Iron Balcony" stood in St. James' Street in 1699. Pepys relates how a man leapt over a first-floor balcony into the garden below at Lord Sandwich's in 1661, and that he got into a balcone over against the Exchange in 1662. A great appreciation of balconies took place in London, when it was enacted among the building rules after the Great Fire that all houses in the principal streets should have balconies 4 feet wide with rails and bars of iron extending for two-thirds of the frontage with a roof above. These

256 English Ironwork of the XVIIth and XVIIIth Centuries

in some degree replaced the overhanging stories and eaves then abolished. The balcony at Bow Church, put up by Wren immediately after the fire, is of plain vertical bars. Those to the second Royal Exchange were of plain vertical bars but with narrow scrolled panels bordering the angle standards, which were surmounted by balls. This was probably the ordinary type of the seventeenth century. Two such still remain over the gateway to the Middle Temple, erected by Sir Christopher Wren in 1684. A beginning of decorative panels is seen in a balcony over the entrance to a large house in St. Peter, St. Albans, which has four panels of C scrolls between the vertical bars and four twisted standards surmounted by balls. In the balcony to Cupola House, Bury St. Edmunds, every second vertical bar is twisted with a central panel of C scrolls, much dilapidated, and very large balls over the standards and buttress scrolls at the angles.

That to the Town Hall at Wallingford (Fig. 97)

FIG. 97. TOWN HALL, WALLINGFORD.

Balconies

repeats the twisted verticals and extra standards with ball finials and three scrolled panels in front, more or less restored. Those at Guildford, dating from 1683, are finer. In the large balcony to the Town Hall the vertical bars are alternately plain and twisted, and the standards twisted and surmounted by faceted balls, with a central panel, the scrolls terminating in thistles, repeating four ways with simpler and corresponding panels on each side. A

FIG. 98. BALCONY AT GUILDFORD, DATE ABOUT 1683.

smaller balcony in the same street (Fig. 98) has the central panel of quainter design with two terminal thistles, four scrolls ending in leaves and spiral twists; and perhaps the modern addition of cressets in place of balls at the angles. The principal front of Caroline Park, Granton, N.B., has a quaint looking balcony over the porch, but not of much earlier date than 1696, with the initials of George Mackenzie, Lord Tarbat, and his wife in monogram under a viscount's coronet, forming a central panel : the two crests and a rose and thistle forming centres to the four scrolled panels at the sides.

The use of balconies spread to Spain and Germany during the Renaissance, but in France they do not seem to have been the fashion until the time of Louis XIII. Under Louis XIV they became more richly worked—in fact, of the most sumptuous and costly description. The introduction into England of such balconies is certainly due to Tijou, and his designs for these are even more in the French manner than usual and follow closely those

FIG. 99.   DESIGN FOR A BALCONY AT CHATSWORTH, BY JEAN TIJOU, 1693.

by Daniel Marot, the celebrated French designer who had also fled to Holland in 1685, and held the appointment there of architect to William III. The balcony (Fig. 99) shows one of the remarkably fine works executed by him for Chatsworth and displays the serpents, arms, and coronet of the Cavendishes, amidst scrolls and acanthus foliage, and pilasters of intersecting circles. Another by Tijou, in his book of designs, for an even richer balcony, might have been intended for Versailles itself, with lyre pilasters enriched with dolphins and festoons surmounted by masks of Phœbus Apollo,

Balconies

and for centre a large panel with the Royal Crown and monogram, W.R., masks, and the heads of a lion and unicorn.

Tijou's earliest work in England, as already noticed, was the balcony to the Water Gallery at Hampton Court, overlooking the Thames, in which Queen Mary was wont to sit and work with her Maids of Honour, and to receive visitors. A design in Tijou's book probably suggested the balcony of curiously scrolled lyre

FIG. 100. BALCONY AT SEATON DELAVAL IN NORTHUMBERLAND. BUILT BY VANBURGH IN 1720. ARTHUR STRATTON, *del*.

panels (Fig. 100) at Seaton Delaval in Northumberland, built by Vanburgh in 1720. In 1739 Batty Langley reproduced and published designs for balconies by the French artist S. Le Clere, for use " where the slightest balustrades would be too massive." Of two balcony designs by Gibbs, one is of heavy vertical bars fringed with C scrolls, with lyre panels at the ends, and the other of scrolled panels between massive turned balusters at the ends. The examples of balconies given by the Welldons and by Jores are chiefly on French lines and French designs may have prevailed for a time since there were several good specimens in Spring Gardens, and a few remain in Mayfair, designed in the style of François Babin, who worked in Paris about 1750.

FIGS. 101, 102. FROM "GENTEEL HOUSEHOLD FURNITURE," ETC., BY A SOCIETY OF UPHOLSTERERS, ETC., 1763.

There was relatively little change till well after the middle of the eighteenth century, as contemporary designs sufficiently demonstrate. Two are reproduced here from Part IV. of the book oddly entitled *Curious New Designs of Household Furniture in Genteel Taste*, by a Society of Upholsterers, Cabinet Makers, etc. (Figs. 101 and 102). The design of these, though poor, are on the old lines. It was not until the brothers Adam began to effect their great change of style and taste that the light and graceful balconies, generally somewhat geometric in design, came into vogue. Almost every house erected on the London estates during their period, which lasted nearly to the close of the century, and for at least a decade after their deaths, were provided with balconies, the designs for which, though varied, are similar and belong to relatively few types. Those illustrated in Figs. 103 and 104 at Boodles Club in St. James's Street are somewhat early, probably of the date of the Adelphi, about 1770, partly cast and with spikes, a rare feature in balconies. The type, in the main an arrangement of light and closely set vertical bars with a border above, and narrow panels at the ends, remained in favour for many

Stair-Ramps

years. Another favoured design consists of diagonally crossing trellis-like bars with border, interrupted by small vertical panels, generally filled with some scheme based on either lozenges, rings, ovals, or the Greek fret. This type dates from before 1770, and occurs in Grosvenor Place and Lincoln's Inn Fields, and there are similar balconies to Grosvenor House, with slender panels erected no doubt when occupied by the Duke of Gloucester.

FIG. 103. THE BALCONY OVER THE PORTICO, BOODLES CLUB, ST. JAMES'S STREET, LONDON.

STAIR-RAMPS

The wide flights of steps in large mediaeval churches and halls, and approaches to them were, when necessary, protected by iron handrails, when other interior stairs between walls were

FIG. 104. BALCONY TO FIRST FLOOR WINDOW, BOODLES CLUB, ST. JAMES'S STREET.

without. They are represented in illustrations to ancient manuscripts, and consisted of iron rails supported at intervals by wrought vertical bars. The steps and pulpits in Spain and Germany were furnished with handsome balustrades of iron so early as the sixteenth century. The double flight of stairs at the west end of Burgos Cathedral have really magnificent iron balustrades of that date. In England Tudor and Jacobean staircases and their balustrades were of wood, and possibly none is existing of iron of earlier date than that at Holyrood Palace, a bold design of crowned thistles in plate iron with the monogram of Charles II. Iron stair-balustrades were as little used in France until about 1676, when Delorme, Lescot, and Bellin began to show the architectural possibilities of staircases and to devote large spaces to them in central positions in their buildings. Under these artists French smiths first revelled in magnificently costly *rampes d'escalier*, and *chefs-d'œuvre* exist at Versailles, the Palais Royal, Chantilly, and many other French chateaux. At least one superb example is in England, the stair balustrade at Hertford House, brought from the Paris *Bibliothèque*.

The earliest produced in England of a grandeur approaching the French is that by Tijou, to the King's staircase at Hampton Court, designed for William and Mary before 1693, but not carried out until 1699.* The handrail of this is in moulded iron, mahogany not having been introduced for this purpose till a later date under Louis XIV. In France a stair balustrade fixed in the sides of the steps, or treads, was known as a *Rampe Anglaise*.

With interior stair-balustrades we are not now concerned however, and those to terraced garden steps or to flights of stairs conducting to important entrances merge almost imperceptibly into the balustrades already noticed. Among fine existing examples are those at Chatsworth (Fig. 105) to the double flight of steps leading to the West terrace. The broadly moulded handrail is carried by alternately plain and twisted vertical bars, with four-sided newels of scroll work having concave covers surmounted by vases, and on the

* Illustrated in *The English Staircase*, by W. H. Godfrey, uniform with this volume.

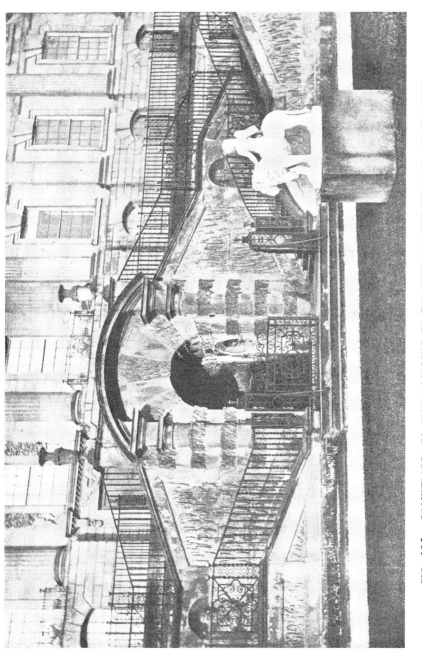

FIG. 105. BALUSTRADES TO STAIRS LEADING TO THE WEST GARDEN TERRACE, CHATSWORTH.

half landings broad panels of diagonal scrolls and honeysuckle centring in medallions. The terrace balustrades have narrow panels of scrolls between pilasters of intersecting circles, their standards surmounted by bronze balls. This no doubt by Oddy, the Chatsworth " gatesmith," once surrounded the house but has alone survived the destructive landscape gardening so fatal to the large stately ironwork seen in Kip's views. Oddy was no doubt influenced by Tijou's work at Chatsworth, and his work resembles the magnificent staircase and terrace balustrades to the paved court and formal garden at Drayton House, which may be the work of Tijou himself. These are illustrated in Plates LXXVII and LXXVIII. Here also the newels to the paved court are four-sided, of rich scrollwork with concave covers and balls as at Chatsworth, and the balusters are handsome and of lyre pattern. The landings to the formal gardens have wide panels of scrolls with laurel and water-leaves, acanthus, and in one case a ducal coronet, their designs being curiously reminiscent of those by Daniel Marot. The standards are surmounted by balls, and the rest of the balusters are of lyre pattern.

More majestic but somewhat on the same plan as those at Chatsworth are the terraces and stairs at Donibristle in Fife, a seat of the Earls of Moray. These have been drawn by R. S. Lorimer, and more recently by Baily Murphy, who records the tradition that the ironwork was presented by William III to Anne Countess of Moray, whose monogram it bears. The balusters to the stairs are rectangular panels of two twisted vertical bars and a quatrefoil with scrolled cap, and the newels are four-sided, as at Chatsworth and Drayton, with moulded concave tops surmounted by balls. A centre panel bears the bold monogram A. C. M. and coronet. The balustrade to the terrace is of vertical bars, every alternate one bearing two scrolls and arrow-pointed dog-bars between. At intervals are four-sided pilasters, some surmounted by tulip flowers and buds, and others by aloes. The

Plate LXXVII.

STAIRS TO THE FORMAL GARDENS, DRAYTON HOUSE, NEAR THRAPSTON.

Plate LXXVIII.

STAIRS TO FRONT ENTRANCE, DRAYTON HOUSE.

Plate LXXIX

TERRACE STEPS, STONELEIGH ABBEY, KENILWORTH.

Plate LXXX.

STEPS AND BALUSTRADES, HIGH HEAD CASTLE, CARLISLE.

Plate LXXXI.

STEPS AND BALUSTRADES, WENTWORTH WOODHOUSE, YORKSHIRE.

approach, as at Chatsworth, is closed by low gates, but these are under a high double arch of C scrolls and laurel, surmounted by a lofty pyramid of masks, a coronet, and the initial M under flower spikes of tulip and lily. The resemblance to the work at Chatsworth and Drayton, and the presence of arrow-pointed dog-bars, is against Mr. Murphy's suggestion that the work is Flemish, and the flowers, though reminding us of earlier work in Belgium, seem distinctive of early eighteenth century ironwork in Scotland. Defoe records in 1769 that both at Pinkey and Yester, seats of the Marquis of Tweeddale, the stone staircases were balustraded with iron, which must have been of striking design to have attracted his notice, but neither now exist.

Terrace steps at Stoneleigh Abbey (Plate LXXIX) with lyre balusters have a landing panel with the Leigh arms and unicorn supporters, crest and motto, between vertical panels and pilasters with acanthus. This is said to have been brought from Watergall, an old mansion near Southam, dismantled a century ago. The imposing balustrade to the steps in the courtyard of Kimbolton Castle comprise landing panels with coronet and monogram, and other panels and balusters of rich work. There appears to be a somewhat similar but less rich example at Ledstone Hall, York. The double steps and landing at High Head Castle, Carlisle (Plate LXXX) have lyre balusters, and the landing panel is of four repeats of a scroll diverging from a circle. The handsome steps to Wentworth Woodhouse (Plate LXXXI), and those at Carshalton, have balusters of lyre design. Many grand flights of stairs have somewhat plain balustrades, as at Stoke Edith, but as a rule the balustrades to the terraces and wide flights of steps of country mansions remained handsome and almost entirely of wrought work till the beginning of the reign of George III. A fine example of geometric design of the latter reign is at Easton Neston, near Towcester.

The balustrade to the spacious terrace and steps to the garden, owned by Lord Thurloe in 1704–5, remained till recently in the

FIG. 106. STEPS TO LORD THURLOE'S HOUSE, GREAT ORMOND STREET (NOW DEMOLISHED), 1704–5.

Grilles

rear of 44, Great Ormond Street. The design is of bent over bars alternating with verticals, all with diverging scrolls (Fig. 106), with panels and newels of scrolled vertical bars, with flask-shaped finials over the standards.

The usual flights of steps to the entrances of smaller mansions rarely present balustrades calling for notice, though examples are very numerous. That to the Deaf and Dumb Asylum at Clapton, illustrated in Belcher's "Later Renaissance" is typical, with alternate lyre balusters. The steps to the Manor House at Wandsworth had a balustrade of scrolled S's, and others are at Great Marlow Place, Bucks, and Kirklees in Yorkshire. A handsome example of rich lyre panels and plain verticals maintains its position at 24, Kensington Gore; but the one sketched and published in 1876 by Norton to 10, Upper Manor Street, Chelsea, has disappeared. A curious geometric design suggesting Chippendale is at No. 65, Lincoln's Inn Fields, while the fine double flight of stairs at its north-west corner has a plain balustrade with an early example of a half-round iron handrail.

The balustrade to the Chapter House of St. Paul's, which must at least have been approved by Wren, is of plain verticle bars with scrolled panels at intervals. A remarkably fine balustrade of the time of William and Mary is seen on the steps of Nos. 39 and 40, Stepney Green, with a rich landing panel of four scrolls repeating round an oval.

GRILLES

Though window grilles are more protective than shutters and readily become a decorative feature, relatively little use has been made of them in this country. Elsewhere their use must be almost coeval with architecture, for remains of window grilles have been discovered amidst the ruins of Pompeii, and is general in the East, in Italy and Spain, where it continues to the present day. The Victoria and Albert Museum abounds with decorative specimens of Renaissance and later days from Italy and Germany; but few, if any, English examples are there. With us, while windows were without glazing, and indeed until the end of the Tudor period, window grilles were purely protective, usually of rectangular bars threaded at right angles, one through the other, as we see them in the old manor houses, such as Compton Wynyates, Penshurst, Hever, or Knole. We learn incidentally that John Coneway was paid for such work by Elizabeth, Queen to Henry VII, in 1502, at the rate of 1*d*. per lb.; while John à Guylders was paid in 1534 for the gratings to Henry VIII Great Hall at Hampton Court at the rate of 1½*d*. per lb. Though this form is of immense strength, all the bars are represented in a fourteenth-century manuscript to be broken through by Sir Lancelot to reach his lady's chamber. Contemporary window grilles in France often aimed at a decorative effect, but the only departures here were in the cases of a few church windows, as at Canterbury, where the bars followed the leading of the windows in the French manner.

These early grilles were of the same construction as the iron doors described (pp. 13–15) among "mediaeval gates." Vertical and horizontal bars of the same sections were made to pass through each other at right angles. To permit the passage without loss of strength one or other had to be thickened at the intersection, usually the horizontal, where a short piece of wider iron with the necessary hole neatly drifted through, and the angles carefully hammered, was welded in by the smith. Generally the bars were set with their face parallel to the window opening, but sometimes they were placed diagonally, when the smith's task became more difficult. These swellings, or "blockings," as the smiths term them, present a picturesque appearance, and their use is continued to the present day. They were frequently used by Wren, as at Trinity College, Cambridge, where the bars are bent over above to form concentric arches, their decorative effect being enhanced by scrolls; and for the crypt of St. Paul's, where the verticals,

Grilles

and not the horizontals, are blocked 100 times in each window. Gibbs, Dance, Soane, and later architects used grilles of this kind where protection was required.

Though decorative grilles had been familiar for centuries to rail off or close choirs and chapels in the interiors of churches, they had rarely, if ever, been used for the exteriors of buildings in England, and we probably owe their introduction to Wren, but only after Tijou had settled here. The openings beneath the library of Trinity College, as already mentioned on p. 36, were closed with decorative grilles by Partridge, a London smith, the scrolled panels introduced in them differing from contemporary work. It is curious to find an original sketch for a much richer but less artistic grille, perhaps for this very site, among the Wren drawings at All Souls', Oxford, in which the same panels occur associated

FIG. 107. PROTECTIVE GRILLE AT THE MANSION HOUSE.

with other work more in the manner of Tijou. The great windows to St. Paul's Cathedral are practically grilles, though arranged to take the glass, with arabesqued borders, forged by different smiths at from 5d. to 6d. per lb. Later examples of protective grilles rendered more or less decorative may be seen at the Mansion House (Fig. 107), and the Bank of England, those radiating from a lion's head on the north side being particularly effective. Windows in the areas of Bloomsbury and elsewhere sometimes have grilles forged to produce a large quatrefoil diaper, but usually they are of plain spiked verticals, and horizontals.

Tijou includes only one grille in his book of designs, but the many fine examples over doors and elsewhere in St. Paul's Cathedral are certainly by him. To him might be safely ascribed a beautiful grille over a doorway of Corpus College, Oxford, and an oval grille in Clare College, Cambridge. At a much later time decorative window grilles must have been used generally in the city, though all have now disappeared: sketches exist of some in Newgate Street, Mark Lane, Leadenhall Street, Addle Street, Fenchurch Street, and Printing House Square. Several appear to be by the same smith, and take a scrolled and partly geometric form, centring in an oval or circle, in the richer examples enclosing an interlacing monogram. One still lingers *in situ* in Idol Lane, a rather

FIG. 108. GRILLE IN THE POSSESSION OF MR. E. B. I'ANSON.

late example, with No. 3 quaintly rendered in the centre; while a few others have been removed and preserved, such as the one possessed by Mr. I'Anson (Fig. 108), and another at Padstow, erroneously believed to be part of a London sign. Plenty of contemporary and later grilles must still exist in the interiors of eighteenth-century houses, as that to a staircase window of 28, Bedford Square.

Grilles of early eighteenth-century date over entrances are not common, though there may be many over doors invisible to the passer-by. We are indebted to Mr. Godfrey for our knowledge of one of these, the beautiful example at No. 6, Cheyne Walk, with its fine horizontal treatment of scrolled bars centring in an oval with the arms of Danvers impaling Babington. One or two are visible in Westminster, one at 52, Devonshire Street, Bloomsbury, and another at Birch's, Cornhill, where there is also an excellent scrolled pyramid over a bar with hooks. Grilles over the west entrance to St. Martin's Church by Gibbs are of good design, and boldly executed, 1726. Quaint designs are seen in Dutch settlements, as at Sandwich, where fanlight grilles are still numerous. Some approximate in style to "Chippendale," of which a few examples remain in London and Westminster, but generally of wood. A few designs for iron, "Window Lights and Door Lights," in this manner will be found in W. and J. Welldon's *Smiths' Right Hand*, 1765, "in the Gothic, Modern, Ornamental, and Italian tastes," several being purely geometric. J. Jores' *New Book of Ironwork*, London, 1759, also includes a few "Door Lights and Gratings." He claims that these designs are useful to other trades, besides the smiths', and the price is 3*s*.

A larger number of grilles were required for the wooden gates and doors (see p. 17), with panels of ironwork, which were used where iron gates were undesirable, and these may be recognized by heavier weight and closer workmanship. The square panel designed by Tijou is undoubtedly intended for a wooden gate, and Carter reproduced two on exactly the same lines but with more modern details about sixty years later. Many of this form are still extant in the suburbs of London and in country towns. They were used for the larger pairs of gates, while those for wicket gates and doors were more elongated and of less dimensions. Several of these have been published, and the Victoria and Albert Museum possesses two good specimens, one from the Manor House at Tottenham, and the other from Foresters' Hall, Canterbury.

Grilles were largely required for stall boards under shop fronts to ventilate the basement areas. Rich designs for these were made by Carter and others and a few still exist, as at Birch's on Cornhill, Fribourg & Treyer's in the Haymarket, Lamberts, Widdowson & Veal, silversmiths, Strand, but all rather plain.

An entirely different treatment for grilles over doorways was brought into fashion by the brothers Adam, who were working in association from about 1760 to the time of their deaths in 1792 and 1794. Robert, one of four sons, held the appointment of architect to George III from 1762 until he entered Parliament a few years later, and was the author of many splendid publications and an artist, and with his brother James was well supported by His Majesty and extensively employed in building and decoration at Windsor Castle, and by a large number of the nobility and gentry. The style they inaugurated became extremely fashionable and practically carried all before it, and was indeed so much approved by contemporaries that their designs, as in the case of John Yenn, R.A., dating from 1769 to 1780, cannot, unless signed, be easily distinguished.

The reason for the complete change in the style of window and door grilles is set out in the advertisement of Joseph Bottomley, who published a now extremely rare book of designs, from his manufactory, No. 42, Wood Street, Cheapside, some time after 1794. The windows, door grilles, etc., had been so "crowded" for the

Grilles

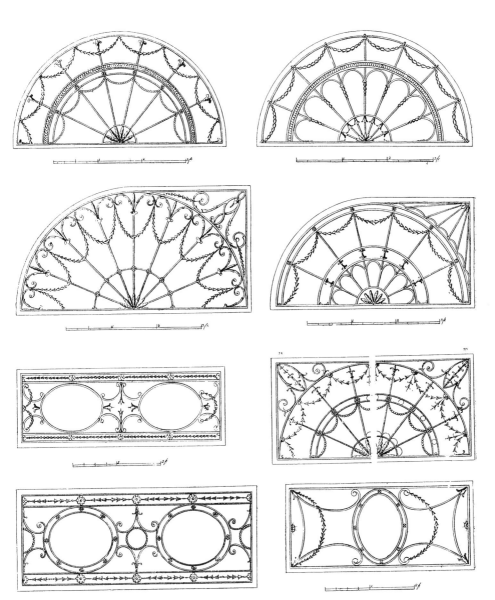

FIGS. 109–116. GRILLES FROM JOSEPH BOTTOMLEY'S BOOK, 1794.

274 English Ironwork of the XVIIth and XVIIIth Centuries

FIGS. 117–121.   FROM AN ANONYMOUS SERIES OF ENGRAVINGS, UNDATED.

Plate LXXXII.

DOORWAY IN MANSFIELD STREET
Built by Adams Brothers about 1770.

Grilles

past half-century with wood as to require double the space to admit the same amount of light and air. The change now taking place, for sashes, sky- and fan-lights, and staircases, " from wood to metal has besides the elegance of material its advantages of strength and durability." The difference in cost was in many cases inconsiderable, and in curvilinear designs metal had the advantage. The writer concludes: " Let any one look at the old Chinese and other railings and balconies, etc., and compare them with present work, and they cannot but admit the taste of present professional gentlemen." Figures 109–116 give a selection of door grilles and " fanlights " from this book, the latter term being obviously derived from designs which bear strong resemblances to fans. A grille at Sandwich is almost a facsimile of that in the left hand lower corner of the group. Figs. 117–121 are taken from a smaller, perhaps slightly earlier, anonymous and extremely rare series of engravings.

Earlier designs may be found in Carter's *Builders' Magazine,* an example of which is seen in Fig. 122 of the date 1774. Plate LXXXII shows a doorway in Mansfield Street, built by the Adams about 1770, which, unlike later examples, is intersected by an arch of wood and plaster. The drawing by Robert Adam for two very rich grilles for Drapers' Hall (Fig. 123) is not only interesting as bearing his memorandum that it is of wrought iron and brass, with the approximate price thirteen guineas, but for the fact that two are still in existence, though shorn of some ornament, in the warehouse of Messrs. Feetham, Clifford Street, and the

FIG. 122. FROM CARTER'S "BUILDER'S MAGAZINE," 1774.

FIG. 123. FANLIGHT FROM THE ORIGINAL DESIGN BY ROBERT ADAM FOR DRAPERS' HALL.

central part of the other in Grosvenor Square. Portland Place, built by the Adams in 1778, still presents a large number of excellent fan-lights, the designs for which must be credited to them. There are two fine examples on the north side of Portman Square, and many in the adjoining streets on the Portland and Portman estates. The original designs for several of these, signed by Robert Adam, are to be seen in the Soane Museum, some comprised in elevations, such as that of the house in St. James' Square for Sir W. W. Wynn, and for Lady Horne's house in Portman Square, 1773; and others sketched and often without localities. Several delicate and graceful designs for window guards were published by John Taylor in 1800.

LAMP-HOLDERS, BRACKETS, SIGNS, VANES

Lamp-holders, Brackets, Signs, Vanes

Lamp-Holders

THE picturesque old lamp-holders which rise from the area railings on either side of doorways are among the more notable survivals of other days. These are to be seen in most of the London squares and streets, especially about Mayfair and Bloomsbury. They yet carry at times the extinguishers and forks for mending the link-boys' torches.

The simplest form of lamp-holder is a plain bar reinforced by a scroll, supporting a cradle and ring, and rising either from an area railing or a post. They were in common use and are introduced into paintings by Hogarth and De Loutherberg, and lighted such spots as the corner of Park Lane or Tyburn turnpike; and they still exist forty paces apart in the railing round Lincoln's Inn Fields and to some of the houses there.

The supporting bars are, however, more usually duplicated and the space between filled in with scrolls or geometric designs. The earliest of these, perhaps, date from about 1700, and generally take a bulbous, or lyre, or flask-shaped outline and are richly scrolled. The cradle either rests directly on the standards or it is bracketed out to overhang the pavement or the steps. When lamp-irons are in pairs a light arch is sometimes thrown over between them to carry the lamp. These handsome supports are conspicuous objects on the west side of Berkeley Square, especially those to No. 45, the old stone-fronted house which still bears the original brass plate of the Earl of Powis, a relic from the days before houses were numbered.

Plate LXXXIII.

LAMP HOLDER AT 45 BERKELEY SQUARE.

Plate LXXXIV.

LAMP SUPPORTS, 41, CHARLES STREET, MAYFAIR.

Plate LXXXV.

LAMP HOLDERS.

37 GROSVENOR SQUARE.   35 BERKELEY SQUARE.

Plate LXXXVI.

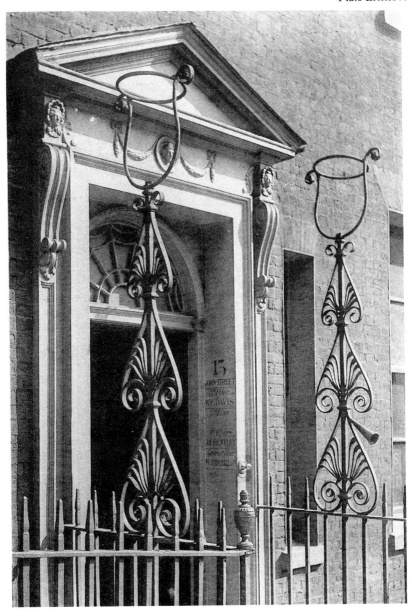

PAIR OF LAMP HOLDERS IN JOHN STREET, ADELPHI.
By Adams Brothers.

Lamp-Holders 279

They are of intercrossing scrolls and leaves (Plate LXXXIII), recalling French rococo or Chippendale design. Similar holders were formerly in Portman Street, and a smaller pair still remains to No. 13, Chesterfield Street. A finely scrolled design with husks and tendrils, and arching support for the lamp, is at No. 46, and a lyre-shaped pair at No. 49, Berkeley Square. No. 41, Charles Street possesses a particularly fine pair (Plate LXXXIV), richly scrolled with water-leaves of flask-shaped outline, carrying scrolled brackets and rings. The design, without the brackets is almost repeated at No. 89, Curzon Street. Others, of lyre outline and rather massive, have rich intercrossing scroll-work and tendrils descending on either side from the cap, at No. 34, Portman Square. A design formed of a lyre within a lyre with florid work was formerly in Berkeley Square, and duplicates still exist in Portman Square, Curzon Street, and St. James' Place. A lyre lamp-holder, with intercrossing scrolls recalling Chippendale design, is not infrequent on the Bedford and neighbouring estates, as in Bedford Row, Queen Square, etc. One of simpler outline with a centre bar enriched with scrolls and leaves in pairs seems characteristic of the Portland estate, and may be seen in Cavendish Square. A Grosvenor Square example of simple lyre form, at No. 37, supporting a bracket and ring for the lamp is illustrated on Plate LXXXV, together with a second lamp-holder in Berkeley Square, No. 35. Another example of this outline is seen in Plate LXXII, in Grosvenor Square, associated with the railings described on page 236. Examples of the obelisk outline and scrolled centre bar opening into a lozenge are or were also to be seen in Great George Street, Guildford Street, Queen Anne Street, and Serjeant's Inn, and examples without the lozenge centre are still more numerous. A more cone-shaped type is carefully depicted by Hogarth and is far from uncommon, existing in Montagu Square, Charles Street, Great College Street, in Bloomsbury and in Edinburgh. Richer variations are in Portman Square. A lofty specimen over a scrolled pilaster, sketched and published, and long a landmark in Whitehall, has disappeared. There are still good examples in Harley Street, Great Ormond Street (see Plate LXXI) and one in Hanover Square, and a rare example of the geometric Chippendale is in George Street, close by. Late examples are sometimes wholly filled in with a repetition of lozenges, ellipses, or circles, dating perhaps from about 1760 to 1765. In contrast to these formal designs, and of about the same date, are those with scrolls and thrown over leaves worked with unusual freedom to some of the houses in Stratford Place, built about 1775.

Belonging rather to the Adams' period is the lyre design of simple graceful outline so frequently seen on the Portman estate and in Great Cumberland Place. An outlying specimen surmounted by a vase and carrying an extinguisher but no lamp was a picturesque addition to Spring Gardens (Fig. 124). There are even simpler forms. An Adams' design of obelisk—the drawing for which is in the Soane Museum—exists in Great Cumberland Place and its vicinity, formed of four slightly converging bars with three transverse bands of rings and spikes, supporting scrolled brackets.

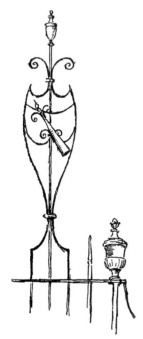

FIG. 124. EXTINGUISHER FORMERLY IN SPRING GARDENS.

Some of the Adams' designs are of great richness. The well-known pair in John Street, Adelphi (Plate LXXXVI), of three Grecian honeysuckles on a central stem, are entirely of wrought iron and unique. The fine lamp supports designed by Robert Adam for Lady Home's house (Plate LXXIII) on the north side of Portman Square (page 243), dating from 1773, are still in perfect condition, of obelisk outline filled in with a pattern of vesica over honeysuckle and fan. No less rich but of slender classic lyre outline, with honeysuckle, scrolls, and rosettes, (Plate LXXIII) are those to Chandos House at the east end of Queen Street, Cavendish Square (page 244). Those to Sir Watkyn Wynne's house, also designed by Robert Adam (page 243), on the west side of St. James' Square (Fig. 87) have, unfortunately, been removed in the course of alterations, but the original design is preserved in the Soane Museum. Good lamp supports remain, however, to Winchester House next door, of 3 bars, the two outer being scrolled, and forming an obelisk, united by collars and balls. A fine series rise from the railings of the large house occupied by Princess Amelia at the corner of Cavendish Square and Harley Street, of an elongated classic lyre shape filled in with a lozenge design supported on scrolls, delicately worked and enriched. A no less extensive series of eight lamp supports give dignity to the railings of the house in Burlington Gardens, built by Vardy for the Marquis of Anglesey in 1792, now in part the Bank of England. These are not very dissimilar to the lamp-holders fronting Piccadilly at the south-west corner of Hamilton Place, of heart shape enclosing a cast honeysuckle under a scrolled vesica.

In addition to those already noticed in Portman Square there are two of elegant obelisk design on the south side, the one at No. 40 with a small fan, mask, honeysuckle, and lozenge borders. On the west side of Lincoln's Inn (Nos. 59 and 60) is a tall obelisk enclosing husks between beaded borders, over a honeysuckle. Nor should the even higher obelisk lamp support be overlooked, of picturesque aspect and geometric design in the east or King's College Courtyard of Somerset House. The design by Chambers is in the Soane collection. Among the Adams' drawings there is an ambitious design (Fig. 125) for a pyramidal lamp-holder with terminal cupids at the base holding torches, and scrolls and honeysuckle above, rising from a richly panelled railing. Three designs

FIG 125. DESIGN FOR RAILING AND LAMP-HOLDER, BY ROBERT ADAM, IN THE SOANE MUSEUM.

Plate LXXXVII.

ARCHING LAMP HOLDER AND RAILINGS, 10 DOWNING STREET.

Plate LXXXVIII.

PORCH AND LAMP PEDESTAL, CHESTERFIELD HOUSE.

Lamp-Holders

published by Carter in 1750 (Fig. 126) are less constructive and would have been difficult of execution. A series of 11 with vesica filling rise from the railings of the Trinity House. The latest examples are those on Carlton House Terrace.

The high lamp supports just described frequently take an arching form, especially when they are of rather late date. A

FIG. 126.   DESIGNS FOR LAMP-HOLDERS PUBLISHED BY CARTER IN 1750.

fine example in Essex Street, Strand, bends over without a break and tapers to a scroll; but more often two lamp-holders unite to complete the arch which carries the lamp. Our illustration (Plate LXXXVII) shows the doorway of the historic house, No. 10, Downing Street, with its early Georgian railings and lamp-holders, to which the arch may have since been added. Such arching

284 English Ironwork of the XVIIth and XVIIIth Centuries

supports are no doubt less characteristic and less interesting than those we have been considering, but there are still a few restrained and pleasing examples, as in Audley Square, and one of an earlier type that has disappeared from Spring Gardens. Bedford Square possesses one presumably by the Adams, and there are others in Lancaster Place and Lincoln's Inn, a charming specimen in Austin Friars, and another until recently in Lombard Street, all of delicate Adam type. One dating from about the end of the eighteenth century and chiefly of cast iron is at No. 28, Buckingham Gate. Many earlier examples have disappeared with the demolitions in Spring Gardens, Great George Street, Whitehall Place and so on; but, on the other hand, specimens may yet be seen in old country towns. At Carlisle there is quite an important and distinctive local group, and there are many in Edinburgh, Bath, and Bristol. Our illustration (Fig. 127) shows a lamp supported on an arch and pilasters intended for a gate.

FIG. 127. ARCHED LAMP SUPPORT OVER GATEWAY.

Stone obelisks for holding lamps appear to have been popular for a brief period towards the middle of the eighteenth century, when they formed conspicuous features in the railings on the north side of Westminster Abbey. The higher of these carried lamps, and the others much lower still take the place of pilasters and stays to the railings. Stone obelisks may be seen on the east side of Berkeley Square, in Clifford Street, Savile Row, and elsewhere about Mayfair. A pair still lingers in St. James' Square, and another in front of St. George's, Hanover Square. In 1752 there were high stone obelisks and lamps to the railings in front of the Mansion House, when Ware complained that "the heavy ironwork crowds on the very flights of steps." Stone obelisks formerly carrying handsome lamps are used effectively in the low railings of the Strand front of Somerset House (Fig. 93, page 251).

Iron posts with lamps bracketed from them were formerly set up at street corners, and higher and more commanding posts were erected at important turnpikes and much frequented cross-roads in the approaches to London. A careful drawing by Rowlandson represents one at Hyde Park Corner, lofty and with three lamps, and a later aquatint by Ackerman shows the same lamp railed round, with four supplementary lamps at a lower level bracketed from wood posts. On the conclusion of the peace of Aix-la-Chapelle in 1748 a dozen very high posts, each with ten or more brackets holding lamps were set up for the benefit of the crowds viewing the fireworks in Green Park. Small lamps in clusters were no novelty in London, for Stow relates that in the time of Henry VIII hundreds of glass lamps with oil burning in them, suspended on curiously wrought branches of iron, were hung out on festival nights in some streets of the city. Thousands were used in Ranelagh, Vauxhall, the Surrey and other public gardens, and not discontinued till long after the introduction of gas.

Perfectly unique in their magnificence are the four-sided newels, bearing short scrolled standards and four-sided lamps with richly worked tops, on each side of the steps in the courtyard of Chesterfield House (Plate LXXXVIII). The bases are enriched with lions' masks and garlanded and festooned with acanthus flowers over scroll-work. Even the torch extinguishers take the unusual form of dolphins, the head forming a cover which has to be raised. The balustrade is described p. 250, and illustrated Plate LXXV.

Probably the most ambitious structure in iron to support a lamp was that designed for Chelsea Hospital, to resemble a lighthouse. At the base was a railing with panels and massive cast balustered standards at the angles. Over this was a domed support of scroll-ended bars designed in panels, sustaining a large cylindrical column of eight richly worked panels of scrolls opening into vesicas, ovals, and lozenges, between plain vertical bars with Ionic caps. This supported a square cradle or cage which held a four-sided lantern. Probably the only existing representation of this remarkable structure is the drawing by George Winter. There are two fine four-sided wrought iron obelisks of openwork design to a house in Market Place, King's Lynn, probably made in London, which may have been simply honorific, like the sheriffs' posts, or intended, like the stone obelisks which are so important a feature of a few London houses, to support lamps as those at the Foundling Hospital.

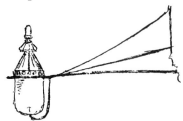

FIG. 128.   BRACKET IN SACKVILLE STREET.

FIG. 129.   REMAINS OF A BRACKET NEAR SAVILE ROW.

The street lighting was mostly from brackets fixed to the houses, as may still be seen in Sackville Street in the West End, and in many of the narrower streets, squares, courts and alleys of the east and west central districts. At first lanterns of sheet iron glazed with horn were suspended from the brackets, but early in the eighteenth century a new and better form of lamp was introduced, still known in France as *Anglaise*. This consists of a deep blown-glass bowl slightly constricted below the rim, seated in a ring support at the end of the bracket, and a removable domed or conical wind-proof cover, under which a simple oil lamp without chimney was

Lamp-Holders

suspended. The brackets for public lighting were plain, as may be seen in Sackville Street (Fig. 128) and in old prints, but many of a more decorative character were put up privately. One interesting example in a dilapidated condition has quite recently been removed

FIG. 130. LAMP BRACKETS IN THE COURTYARD OF THE ADMIRALTY, 1726.

from a house near the north end of Savile Row (Fig. 129). A curious example with the fork for mending or snuffing links and a rectangular panel of scrolls is still to be seen in the cloister at West-

288 English Ironwork of the XVIIth and XVIIIth Centuries

minster. A complete set of six remain in and are probably contemporary with the building of the forecourt of the Admiralty, Whitehall, by Ripley, in 1726 (Fig. 130). These are of two stout horizontal bars riveted to a back-plate, and bent upward and welded together in a swan-neck to support the ring. A panel of an oval and water-leaves and finely worked supporting scrolls above and below, give them a rich effect. One in Micklegate, York, which might well be by the same hand, has been sketched and published (Fig. 131). They are more often found in the older provincial towns than in London, where they have no doubt been improved out of

FIG. 131. LAMP BRACKET AT MICKLEGATE, YORK.

FIG. 132. LAMP BRACKET AT TOTTENHAM CROSS, SKETCHED BY J. NORTON.

existence ; but seldom being conspicuous objects, they need to be looked for. An unusually rich example made to receive a rectangular lamp was sketched at Tottenham Cross in 1877 by Norton and published (Fig. 132). Many

Lamp-Holders

examples, some of them of great interest, may be discovered in the courts and passages of University towns, and the closes and cloisters of cathedrals. Sketches of three at Carlisle have been published by Benwell, and they are far from rare in Edinburgh and elsewhere in Scotland. Quaint examples may be found in old English towns, the finest perhaps in Somerset, where they are always worth noting.

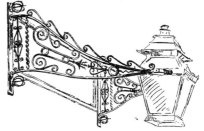

FIG. 133. A DOUBLE BRACKET AT "THE RED LION," STRATFORD.

The old inn lamp brackets, frequently doubled are usually more modern, we give an example from Stratford (Fig. 133). There are good examples at the *Red Lion* and *White Hart*, Salisbury, the *Portobello* at Kingsdown in Kent, the *Neville Arms* at Audley End, and so on. Eight designs in the Chippendale and the French manners for lanthorn irons were published by W. & J. Welldon, smiths, in 1765. Two original designs for Drapers' Hall by the Adams' brothers are reproduced (Figs. 134–5). Finer and better preserved examples, such as those supporting the glass lustres in the old ballroom and the lantern over the staircase, in the Mansion House, must still exist in the interiors of many eighteenth-century houses.

The load on brackets, when heavy, is relieved by stays or bars, which also mitigate the force of the wind. Stays decorated with clustered scrolls and thistles help to carry the clock which projects so conspicuously on a beam from the Guildford Town Hall. Brackets carrying Inn signs are nearly invariably strengthened by stays, and are seen in immense numbers, in old drawings of the principal streets of the city.

Doorway Brackets.

Richly wrought brackets were also much used in the eighteenth century to support the heavy and picturesque weather-boards over

FIGS. 134—5. DESIGNS FOR LAMP BRACKETS, BY THE BROTHERS ADAM, FOR DRAPERS' HALL.

the front entrances to houses and even cottages. A large number have found their way into museums, for there are no less than twelve at South Kensington which have probably served this purpose. They may yet be met with, as at the *White Hart* at Salisbury, which not only retains its pair of supporting brackets to the weather-board, but boldly wrought G. R.'s with scrolls as stays above. Fine brackets support the shelters to doorways at Kingston, Woodstock, Evesham, Blandford, Ludlow (Fig. 136), and Lancaster, some being

FIG. 136. BRACKET FROM A COTTAGE NEAR THE STATION, LUDLOW.

extremely good in design and richly foliated. The richly worked bracket (Fig. 137) is one of several that were in the possession of Messrs. Trollope, while that shown in Fig. 138 is only less elaborate but scarcely inferior, from a cottage at Frensham in Surrey. They appear to be by

FIG. 137. BRACKET AT MESSRS. TROLLOPE.

FIG. 138. FROM A COTTAGE AT FRENSHAM, SURREY.

the same smith and both are designed with a view to carrying a certain amount of weight. They sometimes follow the lines of the finely scrolled ramped ends to railings where these end against walls or gate piers. Simpler iron brackets support lead gutters and spouts. The books of Jores, the Welldons, and others contain numerous design of brackets, in later styles for these and other purposes.

Inn Signs.

From remote times inns and ale houses were distinguished by a bush or a hoop garlanded with ivy or laurel suspended on a pole, every passer-by recognizing the symbol, which had existed with us since the Roman occupation, most inns even in the seventeenth century being content with these, as in the case of three of the five inns of Oxford in 1636. The signs of the cock and of the chequers or lattice were almost as ancient, but the more important hostelries supplemented them with others more peculiar and distinctive. Their numbers and great projection in the city and especially in Cheape so impeded traffic that an edict limited their projection to seven feet. The ale stakes as they were termed not only impeded riders and others, but by their excessive weights deteriorated the houses they were fixed to. It was therefore enacted that in future no stake bearing either a sign or leaves should project more

Inn Signs

than the prescribed limit at most. Richard II was perhaps the first to make it compulsory for innkeepers to hang out signs, leaving other traders to do as they pleased. The rules were frequently altered, and the privilege of projecting them from the frontages of houses was alternately conferred and withdrawn. Thus though Charles I restored it, Charles II withdrew it after the Fire; but later they again became almost universal. A French traveller, Misson, notes in 1719 that while they are of small dimensions in Paris, in London they almost met in the wider streets, and stretched across to the opposite houses in the narrow, many of them with their painted and gilt iron supports having cost, he supposed, over 100 guineas. A later French traveller believed that they had reached an apogee of magnificence, forming veritable triumphal arches, in 1765, when all were again condemned.

Androuet du Cerceau, or Andrew of the Hoop, published designs for iron sign brackets so early as 1570, and we know from an example existing in Bruges that they must have been in use in Flemish towns from at least about 1500, but so far there is no evidence as to the existence of metal sign-brackets in the sixteenth or even the early seventeenth century in England. Du Cerceau's designs in the Renaissance style are graceful and restrained, but difficult or impossible of execution by a blacksmith. Designs, more florid in style, were published by Mathurin Jousse, a smith, in 1625. Magnificently florid and impossible designs for sign brackets were published in England by Tijou in 1693, but no smiths seem to have been inspired by them. A few eighteenth-century iron signs by village smiths are quaint enough to pass for mediaeval. One at Great Mongeham in Kent, suspended from a wooden bracket and dated 1735, has three horseshoes and possibly did duty as a blacksmith's sign, like an equally quaint example in the Nottingham Museum dated 1752, exhibiting blacksmith's tools. A drawing of a curious sign, the Harrow and doublet, of excellent design and dated 1700, is the earliest we have as yet met with. An illustration to Stowe, in 1720 and Maitland in 1772 show fine signs to the *Rising Sun Inn* in Fish Street Hill, and the "neat ironwork" supporting the sign of the *George* in Fleet Street is mentioned. Hogarth represents public-house signs in several pictures, and a particularly rich bracket and stay to the *King's Head* in his "Lord Mayor's Show," 1747.

FIG. 139. "THE BULL" INN, REDBOURNE.

An extensive sign at Canterbury, with finely scrolled bracket and stays, commemorates Sir John Falstaff, perhaps because he gifted the *Boar's Head* in Southwark to Magdalen College. The scrolls and tulip flowers decorating the sign of the *Bull* at Redbourne, near St. Albans (Fig. 139), suggests an early date; and the curious sign of the *Iron Pear Tree* at Appleshaw and Redenham opens out possibilities, or may commemorate some past triumph of the smith.

The *Market Inn* and the *Black Swan* signs in Romsey are hung from plain brackets, with a rich effect due to the scrolled stays, which also have tulips. The few iron signs about the Weald district are not remarkable, but all are picturesque, as in Essex, where there must have been good local smiths, some

FIG. 140. "THE OLD BULL," BRUTON, SOMERSET.
From a Drawing by E. GUY DAWBER.

few, like he of Plashey, being excellent. The West Country is undoubtedly the richest, Wimborne possessing three and Wareham a fourth, by the same hand, handsomely scrolled, three of them arched and drooping. In Somerset is a fine example to the *Bull Inn* at Bruton (Fig. 140) with a quadrant-shaped support and scrolled stays, and another at the *Crown Inn*.

FIG. 141. "THE SHIP" HOTEL, MERE, WILTS.

FIG. 142. "THE MAGPIE," HARLESTON, NORFOLK.

Inn Signs

The large one at Mere in Wilts (Fig. 141), with its complicated system of scrolls and stays, is of poor and late workmanship, something in the style of an equally large one at Thame. One of no less spread is at Wylie in the same county. The *Magpie* (Fig. 142), is interesting as a Norfork specimen, being from Harleston.

FIG. 143. "THE ANGEL INN," AYLESBURY.

At Much Wenlock an oval representing the ancient hoop, supported from bars and twined with hop or vine leaves, supports a smaller ellipse of honeysuckle design, on which is perched a raven. This is no doubt due to the vicinity of Coalbrookedale, where there is a more pretentious one of less uncommon design and the same workmanship. Another of exceptional interest, being of workmanship so far peculiar to certain London churches, is at Wendover, Bucks, and another supported by a dolphin bracket with acanthus leaves almost worthy of Tijou is at the *White Hart*, Stanton, Northants. Both these probably belong to the early part of the eighteenth century.

In addition to being bracketed from houses, signs are frequently elevated on high wood, or wood and iron posts, forming conspicuous and welcome objects by the roadside, and denoting some good old inn to be near. To the post is firmly secured a frame of iron, usually of well-wrought scroll-work, and often comprising bunches

298 English Ironwork of the XVIIth and XVIIIth Centuries

of grapes, inside which a picture swings in the wind. One of charming design, on a post mainly of slender iron fixed over a wooden base, bids the wayfarer to the old *Angel Inn* at Aylesbury (Fig. 143). The post supports a rising and arching bracket of delicate and

FIG. 144. A DISMANTLED SIGN FORMERLY AT "THE FOUNTAIN INN," BEDFORD.

interesting work, from which the unframed picture swings. Plenty of inferior workmanship on the same principle are met with. In the 1720 Stowe one is shown on a similar iron post on Fish Street Hill, but stayed and bracketed to the frontage in addition, an

Inn Signs

arrangement of which probably no example is extant. It stands on a massive balk of timber with moulded cap and supports, an obelisk of open ironwork and finial, and the sign, a large star in rectangular frame depends from it as a flag might.

Of more ordinary type the most refined is at the *King's Arms*, Melksham, suggesting work of Louis XVI, arching over to receive a bell. There is or was an excellent one at Farnham, framed by scrolls from which numerous leaves and three large tulips depended which had partly perished, with a small delicate double arch over the board. The example from Bedford (Fig. 144) is framed in scrolls, and was photographed at a local blacksmiths. The *Bear* at Woodstock provides a sturdy example with an arched top to the lace-like fringe of ironwork. The *White Hart* (Fig. 145), with its large and realistic bunch of grapes, provides a striking and decorative object slightly reminiscent of a Chippendale design. An old drawing of Chelmsford, 1762, shows one of finer character. A most noted example is on Highgate Hill, where a post is caged round by iron bars which are carried upward and diverge into spandrel brackets supporting a cresting, one end of which is extended to carry the sign.

FIG. 145. THE SIGN OF "THE WHITE HART," BLETCHINGLY.

While iron supports frequently hold wooden signs, iron signs may rest on wood trusses. Occasionally the decorative brackets of cranes survive, like that to the old Italian Consulate in Old Jewry, of the Adams' design, and a very graceful example at King's Lynn.

Weathercocks and Vanes.

Weathercocks were in use in England long before the Norman Conquest, when almost unknown on the Continent. They surmounted our important buildings, and invariably took the form of a cock elevated on plain rods, and are so represented in contemporary manuscripts, such as Cædmon's *Ark*, about A.D. 1000, St. Ethelwold's *Benedictional*, about 1024, an English Pontificale in the Rouen Library, about 1056, and in the Bayeux Tapestry. Wulfstan's *Life of St. Swithin* possibly carries them even farther back to the end of the tenth century, containing a paneygric on the resplendently gilt weathercock on Winchester Cathedral. The Bayeux Tapestry represents that on Westminster Abbey. They were made of copper gilt usually on plain iron rods, though one of the stems in the Harleian MS. 603 in the British Museum is handsomely scrolled. In these illuminations other finials to gables are shown, which could also only have been of iron. The cocks were not at first confined to ecclesiastical buildings, but later some religious significance became attached to them. The fashion appears to have remained exclusively English until many years after the Norman invasion, so much so that when the cock on the Cathedral of Coutance was destroyed by lightning the bishop sent for an English plumber to replace or repair it. The fact is commemorated to the present day in our term weathercock, which has no equivalent in French.

Records are silent as to whether our great Cathedral of St. Paul's, built by Ethelbert and burnt in the time of William I, was surmounted by a weathercock. The new Cathedral was planned on so grand a scale that it was thought impossible ever to complete it, and its spire was not dedicated till the reign of Henry III, 1240, when it had reached the prodigious height of 520 feet from the ground. It was surmounted by a large cock over its gilded cross and ball. It is recorded that this was renewed in 1273, 1314, 1420, 1455, 1461, when the vane was called an eagle, and a man was killed in attempting to fix it; and in 1498, when the steeple was burnt by lightning, as set forth in various contemporary chronicles. It appears as a conspicuous object in the Cottonian MS. Nero, 'D. II, in the British Museum, A.D. 1307, completely dwarfing the very large gilt cross and ball. The dimensions of the latter are carefully noted in a Lambeth MS. of 1314. The cross was then 15 feet 6 inches high and 5 feet 10 inches wide, made of wood, covered with lead, and sheathed in copper stained red; the ball of copper gilt measured 9 feet 6 inches in circumference, and held 10 bushels of corn. In a later account it was said to hold 8 bushels. The ball was filled with relics of saints destined to protect it from storms, and these were examined and renewed from time to time with much ceremony. The weathercock, called in the narrative an eagle, was blown down in 1505, the year the Archduke Philip was driven by stress of weather to land on our south coast; and it was considered ominous that it smashed in its fall the sign of the black eagle in St. Paul's Churchyard. For some reason a new weathercock, which measured 4 feet in length and 3 feet 6 inches over the wings, was set up by Peter, a Dutchman, in 1553: its weight, 40 lb. of copper gilt. Advantage was taken of the scaffolds, to give an acrobatic display at the height of 500 feet from the ground, when eight streamers of the City arms were displayed to call attention to the performance. The man stood on the cock and then knelt on its back, a feat till then believed to be impossible. The spire was struck by lightning in 1561, and burnt downwards to the roof. The upper part with the cross and vane fell unconsumed, but the spire was never rebuilt.

The frequency of the renewals and repairs in the case of this important weathercock, three of them within intervals of only about forty years, may serve to warn us how few of those we see can have any real claim to antiquity. A small one in the vestry of York Cathedral, fashioned from an old monumental brass, which surmounted the lantern turret built in 1666, and saved when this was destroyed in 1803, shows the actual construction at that time, which was sufficiently rude.

The desirability of rebuilding the steeple was frequently discussed, but its liability to damage by lightning and the great cost were deterring. Evelyn relates that a strong committee met on August 27, 1666, to settle this question, when the majority favoured building the steeple anew on the old foundations, while himself and Wren " had a mind to build it with a noble cupola, a form of church building not as yet known in England." A fortnight later the mighty Cathedral lay in ruins.

It was debated in the Commons whether the cupola of the new building should be covered in lead or copper. The vote of the Commons was for the latter, which increased the cost by £550, but the Lords threw it out. The diameter of the ball is 6 feet 2 inches and it is said to hold 8 persons, and the cross weighs 3,360 lb. Jane Brewer, coppersmith, supplied the pine cone finials for the western turrets for £354. The cross of gold surmounted Eastern churches according to Bede from the beginning of the eighth century, and it was associated with the ball in England as a finial for churches in the thirteenth, and probably long before.

The term VANE, now commonly used as a synonym for weathercock, had in its inception a totally different origin and significance. By old writers, like Chaucer, and until about the time of Elizabeth, it is written *fane*, and later this became assimilated with the Dutch *vaan*, though its more proper equivalent is the old Saxon fæna or fana and the modern German *Fahne*, flag. When hoisted over a building it denoted the rank and family of the owner, as perhaps did the Norman flags when carried at their mast-heads and in battle. A pair of flags, indented in three points like most of the pennons in the Bayeux Tapestry, supposed to symbolize the Trinity, and waved as if fluttering in the breeze, are seen in a twelfth century drawing, surmounting the two eastern turrets of Canterbury Cathedral, the rods

Weathercocks and Vanes

crowned by archiepiscopal crosses, while over the west end turrets are two cocks, the two forms thus being used synchronously on the same building. A century or so later a royal licence was required for the use of vanes, as it was to crenelate, when they were in effect restricted to the nobility, though any hero who had first planted his banner in the breach might claim to be admitted to the privilege.* When later it became a fashion to adorn the roofs of chapels and banqueting halls with numerous pinnacles and turrets, each was surmounted with a small metal flag, or pensel, supported, in the time of Henry VIII, by some image or heraldic beast. To such the poet alluded in the " Tower of Doctrine, *tempus* Henry VII " :—

> "The little turrets with ymages of golde
> About was set, which with the wynde aye moved."

They were used in vast numbers and of diminutive size at obsequies and for festivals, and were called " pensels " from *pencillus* or the old French *panonceaux*, applied to the small flags carried on the lances of esquires. Each of the towers of Nonsuch

---

* The banner was a rectangular flag, and bore the coat armour of the nobleman in command, and practically represented his shield borne aloft. The present Royal Standard is properly a banner. The following were furnished to the Duke of Suffolk for his expedition into France in 1523 by John Browne, the King's painter:

"Item, a standard wrought with fyne golde and sylver apon dowble sarsnet, and frynged with sylke iijl." This was an immensely long triangular flag, 17½ yards in the case of a Duke, slit at the ends and never reproduced in vanes.

"Item, ij. banners of your armys wroght with gold and sylver apone dowble sarsnet, and fryngyd with sylke, vl. vjs. viiid." Square, used for the larger kind of vanes.

The Bannerolle was a banner widened to take an impalement of arms.

"Item, x gyttons of dowble sarsnet wroght with gold and sylver, and fryngyd with sylke at viijs. iiijd. the pece." From the French *Guide-homme* variously spelt, originally the smaller standards allowed to esquires. These are the guidons of mounted troops, triangular flags richly fringed and emblazoned, generally used for single vanes.

Pennons were also small standards, but rounded at the ends.

"Itcm ij. doseyne and iiij. flaggis and pencellis " "at xijd. the pece." These are the flags used in quantities for vanes on turrets.

was surmounted by a vane cut in the form of a banner, surrounded at a lower level by a forest of pinnacles, each with a pensel on a balustered stem. Elizabeth had a survey made of several of her distant castles, when those not hopelessly ruined are seen to have been repaired and brought up-to-date. Some plans of these in the Duchy of Lancaster office have been reproduced in *Vetusta Monumenta* by the Society of Antiquaries. The elevations of Melborne, Lancaster, Pontefract, Sandal, and Tickhill, show that a principal feature of these restorations was the emplacement of a finial on every coign of vantage. These were not like the older vanes, but lofty spikes of scrolled iron, apparently 8 or 9 feet high, in the design of which mediaeval tradition was wholly cast aside. On the roof of the small church close by Lancaster Castle they occur over the gables and buttresses, some sixteen in number; about eighteen seem to cluster round the lantern tower of the castle church of Pontefract, the central tower being surmounted by a high cross over which is a cock. There are fewer to Tickhill Castle, and they include some with banners, but the great church in the town and its lofty spire was not exempt from this adornment. It is recorded that there was a tall ornamental vane of ironwork over Queen's College in 1510, so that all these may possibly date back almost to the accession of Henry VIII.

It is questionable whether any of these had to do with indicating the direction of the wind, except incidentally, and they were probably only made of metal for the sake of durability. A brief experience of the behaviour of such objects when fixed under high wind pressure would suggest the expediency of making them revolve. They were gilt and armorially emblazoned, and their production entrusted to the hands of the goldsmith, a term which even in the sixteenth century by no means implied that the craftsman's work was restricted to the precious metals. Of existing specimens the earliest is an almost square banner-shaped flag of gilt copper pierced with the *fretté* coat of the De Etchynghams,

Weathercocks and Vanes

over the tower of Etchingham Church, which Lower claims in his History of Sussex to be the original vane. It revolves on a perfectly plain rod, and is a solitary and precious surviving example of the early and severe mediaeval banner vane.

Of much later period is the heraldic vane of Oxborough Hall in Norfolk (Fig. 146) which consists of a banner of copper gilt, on a plain rod, vandyked in four large and four smaller fleur-de-lis, and in the centre a shield pierced with the arms of the Pastons, Earls of Yarmouth, six fleur-de-lis—three, two, and one, and a chief indented or. The companion vane with the arms of the Bedingfields was blown down and never replaced. Sir Henry Bedingfield fixes their date as about 1661, when the two families intermarried.

FIG. 146. HERALDIC VANE OF OXBOROUGH HALL, NORFOLK, ABOUT 1661.

FIG. 147. VANE FORMERLY AT BUTLEIGH, SOMERSET.

The vane of the seventeenth century was more usually a square or nearly square banner, fretted at the angles into fleur-de-lis, as in our illustration (Fig. 147) once at Butleigh in Somerset. A little later we find an additional fleur-de-lis on each of the free sides of the flag, as in that to Barlborough Hall, near Eckington, pierced with I.R. under a scroll for John Rodes, about 1616 (Fig. 148). Another of the same design, unpierced, maintains its position, though much battered by weather, on the north-east pinnacle of the staircase of the picturesque ruins of Cowdray, the interesting survivor of many which surmounted its pinnacles and towers. In these cases the stem is partly twisted and decorated with button swellings, two four-way knots, and an openwork finial. Vanes at Charlcote, perhaps not original, on shorter stems, are painted with the arms of the Lucys. One on Ruscomb Church, five miles north-east of Reading (Fig. 149), is pierced with the royal crown and C.R. under the date 1639, with the stem partly twisted and scrolled, and surmounted by an orb and cross. A vane taken down and preserved from Street Church, pierced W.D. under date 1636, is of gilt copper, illustrating the rather rude construction of the then prevalent type and the fleur-de-lis cut out separately and riveted on. More or less contemporary with these are guidons, swallow-tailed and waved. The well known Blickling example is pierced with the Hobart Star of eight points, with the stem like that at Cowdray, and dating from about 1628. Two sketched at Bourton-on-the-Water have fleur-de-lis in addition, but may possibly no longer exist.

FIG. 148. VANE AT BARLBOROUGH HALL, DATE ABOUT 1616.

FIG. 149. VANE ON RUSCOMB CHURCH, NEAR READING.

So far the vanes noticed have been destitute of pointers, and not until these appear can we be certain that vanes were intended to point to the direction of the wind, and not merely to flaunt the exalted status of their owners. It may

Weathercocks and Vanes

be doubted whether pointers came into use before the reign of Charles I. Old forms appear with this addition, as at Hatfield and Cobham, but have probably been reconstructed, and not by antiquaries. The important and probably original vane over Lambeth Palace can hardly be later in date than about 1663, when the roof and lantern were completed by Archbishop Juxon's executors. The guidon, swallow-tailed with waved points and six fleur-de-lis, is pierced with the arms of the See of Canterbury impaled with those of Juxon and prolonged into the broad pointer, which terminates in a small bulb and broad

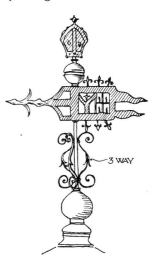

FIG. 150. VANE AT LAMBETH PALACE, ABOUT 1663.

FIG. 151. TURRET OF THE LUCAS ALMSHOUSES, NEAR WOKINGHAM.

arrow. The stem seats in a sphere, as it did in Anglo-Saxon days, and carries three scrolls, while a second sphere over the flag is crowned by the archiepiscopal mitre (Fig. 150). The vane to the Lucas Almshouses, near Wokingham, bears a banner with a single fleur-de-lis point, inscribed with the date

1665; the pointer perfectly plain, though the stem and finial are decorated with scrolls (Fig. 151). A banner bordered with seven fleur-de-lis, without piercing, is over St. Nicholas's Church, Rochester, with spoon-shaped pointer, scrolled stem, and acorn finial.

FIG. 152. VANE OF RYE CHURCH DATED 1703, COMMEMORATING THE ACCESSION OF QUEEN ANNE.

Vanes pierced with A.R., like that on Rye Church dated 1703, commemorates the accession of Queen Anne (Fig. 152), and G.R. may mean no more than a popular expression of good-will on the accession of monarchs with those initials. Certain churches share with royal palaces the privilege of surmounting their vanes with royal crowns, like St. Martin's-in-the-Fields and old Chelsea Church, a practice which mediaeval days may have superstitiously discouraged, as when the crown falling from Dover Castle shortly before the Battle of Northampton provided an omen unlucky to Henry VI. Two sparrow hawks dashed themselves against the crowns on the White Tower about the time of the death of Charles II. The iron crown on the turret of the Council House at Salisbury was blown off on the arrival of James II there, when William had landed. A vane with a large gilt crown surmounted the unfortunate Eddystone Lighthouse, destroyed in 1703, three years after its completion. Crowns surmounting vanes in the country have the practical inconvenience that birds build in them, rooks even deserting neighbouring trees in their favour; while storks delight to take possession of them, wherever they are large enough, as in the case of the great Imperial Crown at San Pablo. Carrion crows nested a century ago in the dragon vane of Bow Church, and falcons in Spitalfields. Two ravens built in the weathercock at Bakewell.

Weathercocks and Vanes

Vanes very frequently rise from balls. The swallow-tailed guidon was favoured by Inigo Jones, with or without the ball at the base, and sometimes with the pointer. The vane to Guildford Town Hall, 1683, appears to be an early example of a ball midway on the stem (Fig. 153), and has small clustered scrolls as well in the old manner. Wren followed Inigo Jones in his predilection for the small guidon swallow-tailed in two points, either waved or rigid. He adhered to the small-barbed pointer either simple, or supported by a bent bar, half hoop, or some form of scrolls, and central to the flag; frequently the stem appears to penetrate through the flag, part of which appears in front. The stem in his hands became of bulbous or balustered outline by means of dressed or cast lead or copper, with spheres, discs, buttons, and so on applied over the central rod, and gilt. Perhaps avoiding the triple indentation of the earlier vanes which symbolized the Trinity, may have been in deference to religious feeling, the days of "Blue Dick," the destroyer of superstitious vanes, not being then very remote.

FIG. 153. VANE OF THE TOWN HALL, GUILDFORD, 1683.

FIG. 154. PRINCIPAL VANE TO ST. STEPHEN'S CHURCH, WALBROOK. SIR C. WREN.

Typical vanes are seen to surmount most of the City Churches, as St. Stephen Walbrook (Fig. 154), St. Margaret Patterns, St. Margaret Lothbury, St. Martin Ludgate, St. Benet Thames Street, etc., as well as those erected elsewhere in London in the reign of Queen Anne, as St. Martin's, St. James' and St. Giles'. Occasionally the stems are surmounted by a cross, as in St. Magnus, St. Michael College Hill; St. Benet Gracechurch Street; St. James' Garlick Hill, and a few others, but these are often found to be modern additions. Saint Bride's, however, seems to have maintained its cross for 150 years. Though these look so insignificant in their lofty positions, they are really important objects. That removed from above the vane of St. Margaret Patterns and now preserved in the church is 2 feet 6 inches high, weighing over half a cwt. of hammered copper gilt. The vane when complete was 15 feet in height, and elevated 215 feet above the ground on the lead-covered spire. The vane over the dome of Greenwich Hospital (Fig. 155) emerging from a ball and crowned above, would be almost typical, but for the curious strap with trefoil ends intended for buckles. Even St. Paul's Cathedral was to have been surmounted by one of the typical vanes according to Wren's first design.

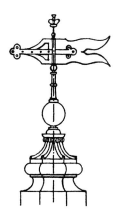

FIG. 155. VANE ON THE GREENWICH HOSPITAL DOME.

The obviously simple barbed and feathered arrow is rarer than might be anticipated; St. Helen's Bishopsgate and St. Botolph's Aldgate being among the few seen in the City. There was one on Westminster Abbey, and several on secular buildings in London at the close of the eighteenth century. They should appropriately surmount churches dedicated to St. Edmund the Martyr.

Wren occasionally, probably at the wish of incumbent or churchwarden, fashioned vanes in the likeness of symbols of the Saints to whom the churches were dedicated, but they were rarely artistically successful. An example is seen in the gridiron of St. Lawrence Jewry, where the handle forms the pointer. The large key placed on end over St. Peter's Cornhill, the bit forming the flag, probably reproduces a form existing before the

Weathercocks and Vanes

Fire, as the picture of Sir Henry Dunton in the National Portrait Gallery, painted about 1596, shows the central spire of St. Peter's Faringdon, where he was buried, with a large key similarly placed for vane, and the four lesser spires with identical vanes on a lesser scale. The large A over St. Anne's near the Post Office detracts from a vane in which the flag is continued and cut into the semblance of the head of a dove, but its date is uncertain, as no such vane is represented to this church by Maitland. Happier are the emblems pierced in the flag itself, like the crossed swords of St. Antholin, and the anchor of St. Clement's Danes on a shaped flag. Quite different are vanes by Wren worked entirely of bar iron. Kensington Palace was provided with vanes, possibly at the Queen's suggestion, formed, both flag and pointer, of the Royal monogram W.R. and M.R. interlaced. Another unique and more modern departure is on St. Mildred's, Bread Street, the vane, royally crowned, being in the likeness of a rather ragged flag, formed half of a shield bearing a chevron and the Red Hand of Ulster, and the rest of the intercrossing initials P.P.M., all worked in bar iron with a waved pointer, to commemorate some forgotten churchwarden or benefactor.

Wren's form of vane was preserved by his immediate successors, and until the close of the eighteenth century. They were rendered more ornate by Gibbs, but Kent, Thomas, Ripley, Leoni, Dance Chambers, seem to have used them with unvarying monotony, with the fore-part of the guidon projected in front of the stem, finishing in the central barbed arrow-point. As used by Robert Adam, it took a longer and more exiguous form.

The popularity of the swelled and baluster-like stems to vanes seen

FIG. 156. THE VANE AT BOW CHURCH, CHEAPSIDE.

in Wren's City churches may be due to Dutch influence, but it can hardly be doubted that the conspicuous and well-known dragon of Bow Steeple (Figs. 156 and 157) was inspired by the still greater dragon of St. Bavon of Ghent. However we need not forget its city connexion, nor that our Kings from Harold to Henry III had fought their battles under the dragon standard, and that it was a badge and the chief of the supporters of the arms of the Tudors and formed their principle standard, so that Wren may have patriotically wished to see it on his chef-d'œuvre. It is of gilt copper, 8 feet 6 inches long, on a short rod proceeding from a ball 2 feet 3 inches in diameter in the old English manner. Other dragons formerly over the four turrets of the Guildhall, the old Cloth Hall at Newbury and the Guildhall at Faversham, may recall some almost forgotten trading connexion with the Low Countries. The dragon also surmounted old Bethlehem Hospital, and still does that at Kirkleatham. Flitcroft fixed one over the ordinary guidon vane at Wentworth. However this may be, the presence of the Gresham Grasshopper in large quantities and as a vane on the first Royal Exchange is clearly attributable to the Dutch influence. The shape satisfactorily lends itself to the purpose, like the dragon, and the first building, finished in 1570, was designed by a Flemish architect, and built on the lines of the Antwerp Burse. The two engravings by Rogenburg, produced before the building was well begun, show a huge *girella* or grasshopper, resting on a cross and ball, crowning the lofty

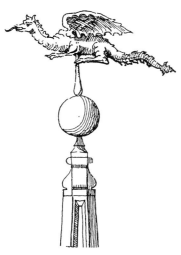

FIG. 157. THE VANE AT BOW CHURCH. FROM AN ENGRAVING BY T. CHRISTOPHER.

bell-tower, and another capping the high Corinthian column on the Cornhill side. Small grasshoppers beset the dormers of the windows and gables. The second Exchange, built after the Fire, had high scrolled vanes to the four turrets, half surmounted by flags and royal crowns, the rest by grasshoppers. Two maintain their places on the present Victorian building, the larger of which measures 6 feet 4 inches in length on a rod 16 feet high.

The outlines of most kinds of fish are suitable to the purposes of a vane, as evidenced by those of the Natural History Museum, and no form could be more appropriate for seaport towns which depend on their fisheries, yet they are conspicuously absent. If we may judge from Thoroton's *Nottingham*, 1677, such vanes were fairly popular in the county, for three churches are surmounted by fishes. A fish points the wind over the Mass house on the bridge of Bradford-on-Avon, and another with wings does duty on Hereford Town Hall, both fairly modern. There is also a snarling dolphin at Maidstone, which looks more antique.

As to birds for this purpose, the domestic cock's monopoly in England has never been challenged. A finely modelled cock fitly surmounted the old College of Physicians in compliment to Æsculapius. It was, however, only used on St. Dunstan's-in-the-East and St. Stephen's Coleman Street by Wren. One surmounts the earlier Church of St. Catherine Cree, and singularly enough there is a fine original design for a vane with a cock, scrolls and the cardinal points, signed by Wren, in the Soane Museum (Fig. 158). Wren also surmounted St. Swithin's Cannon Street with a dove, perhaps connecting the heavy rains that follow the saint's day with floods and the ark.

FIG. 158. FROM A DESIGN FOR A STEEPLE BY WREN.

The birds over St. Mary Abchurch and St. Andrew Undershaft may also be intended for doves. St. Paul's Church Covent Garden was surmounted in 1715 by a graceful swan on a plain stem, possibly by Inigo Jones.

Except such mammalia as are domesticated or connected with sport, the horse, hound, and fox, and rarely a cow or pig, hardly any have soared to such heights. No vegetables and among invertebrata only the *girella* have been so exalted. The most costly and majestic of vanes are the figures of saints and angels turning with the wind, a conceit dating back to remote antiquity. The Tower of the Winds at Athens, erected about 100 B.C., was surmounted by a bronze Triton which turned to indicate the direction of the wind, and Rome is said to have possessed a similar tower. At Constantinople a female figure surmounted a lofty structure of copper and turned with the wind, stated to have been erected either in the fourth or the eighth century A.D. The most celebrated of recent times is the well-known bronze Giralda of Seville, produced in 1568 and 14 feet high, but formerly Granada also boasted its armed Moor over the *Casa del Gallo*, destroyed in 1817, and Astorga had its painted *Maragate*, regarded as a charmed talisman, until the town was taken and the Moors expelled. There was an angel at Milan which turned with the wind bearing a banner, and it is recorded by Evelyn that the figure of an angel over the campanile of Venice served the purpose of a *girouette*. A high tower at Emena in Syria was surmounted, according to an account written before 1651, by a copper horseman which turned with the wind. Whether any of this expensive type ever existed in England is not matter of history, but two high turrets of Canterbury were crowned with figures of saints in the twelfth century, and another dominated the old Castle of Melbourne in Derbyshire. Defoe calls the George I on the spire of St. George's Bloomsbury a weathercock, wondering that the statue of a prince famed for good sense and steadiness should be placed in such a position.

Weathercocks and Vanes

The ship, the *deus ex machina* of seaport towns, could also be costly when reproduced as a vane. With all its countless associations, either prospering in its voyage or cast away, according to the temper of the winds, the ship has been less seen over the buildings of our sea-girt isles than in Holland or the Baltic seaports. The great port of London never appears to have boasted more than four over its scores of churches, and all these have now by some fatality disappeared. There perished in the Great Fire, St. Bartholomew's near the Royal Exchange, its ship vane set up in 1607; St. Margaret's, Lothbury, its vane only supplied in 1637, at the moderate cost of £3 10s., but needing repair at the hands of a smith named Greene, and regilding, in 1651, only fifteen years before it was burnt; St. Mildred's, Poultry, the vane said to have been identical with the former; and St. Michael's, Queenhithe, whose vane held a bushel of corn when this was the staple traffic of the ward. Of these the three rebuilt after the Fire were after a time again surmounted by vanes in the form of ships of copper gilt, but none are shown by Maitland nor do any now exist. The careful delineation by Mr. Niven of St. Mildred's Church, the last of the three to disappear, shows a three-masted barque with the spanker but none of the square sails set and the flags at the mast-heads, seen in Strype's illustrations. When the church was destroyed the vane was passed over to St. Olave's, Old Jewry, which fell in its turn a prey to the house-breaker. St. Michael's possessed, according to an old illustration, a ship which corresponds with Niven's drawing of St. Mildred's in all respects, except the flag at the mast-head; but a still older illustration presents a full-rigged ship with all sails set. Perhaps the older ships perished, and were replaced with more modern and simpler forms.

Fortunately two much larger ships remain in excellent preservation, both men-o'-war and of a date some thirty years later. One surmounts the cupola of the old Town Hall of Rochester (Fig. 159), and is an exact and careful model of Sir Cloudesley Shovel's frigate, the *Rodney*. He commanded the British Fleet in 1705, but was unfortunately drowned only two years later off the Scillys. As he had been a great benefactor to Rochester, the Town Council ordered the vane to commemorate him; but the careful workmanship and fidelity of the detail to the original made the model very costly, and the Council declined to pay for it, and but for the generosity of a citizen it must have been lost. It is three-masted, barque rigged, and under bare poles except the spanker, and measures over 6 feet from stem to stern, and as much in height. There are flags on the main-mast and peak, and a small Union Jack on a short staff rigged perpendicularly over the end of the bowsprit, where the gaff begins. The ship over the old Town Hall of Portsmouth was presented by Prince George of Denmark in 1710, and is identical in rig, except that the spanker seems partly reefed and colours are flying from all the masts and an enormous flag from the stern, no doubt to help the vane to answer to the wind, which otherwise it would hardly do. It measures 6 feet 10 inches over all, and is quainter and with less detail. The small flags over the bowsprits, Union Jacks, in the case of these two vessels, are among the most curious and distinctive features of English and Dutch men-of-war of

FIG. 159. MODEL OF SIR CLOUDESLEY SHOVEL'S FRIGATE ON ROCHESTER TOWN HALL, ABOUT 1708.

Weathercocks and Vanes

their date. The four finely modelled copper ships of the Trinity Almshouses in the Mile End Road, 1686, are worth noting in this connexion. There is a modern ship vane at Greenwich Observatory.

FIG. 160. VANE OF ST. ETHELBURGA'S, BISHOPSGATE.

It is difficult to pronounce positively as to when letters denoting the cardinal points of the compass were added to vanes, but it seems clear that Wren made little use of them, and perhaps disapproved of them. It is remarkable that Maitland in 1762 only shows the cardinal letters to two vanes in the City, St. Catherine Cree and St. Martin's Outwych. St. Ethelburga's, Bishopsgate Street (Fig. 160), provides a very early dated example, which consists of a rectangular frame from which five Maltese crosses and fleur-de-lis project, bearing the date 1673 over the initials of the patron saint, S.E., all worked in bar iron. The pointer dips to accommodate a small cock, and the stem is swelled and scrolled and finishes above in small scrolls and a cross. Four waved bars fixed to a central disc on the stem carry the cardinal letters. The vane to Crowhurst Church is only remarkable for its guidon pierced 1681, under initials

A.W., on a scrolled stem with the cardinal letters. Careful drawings made between 1681 and 1689 by order of the Master of the Ordnance, when the renewal of the vanes to the four turrets of the White Tower was in question, show a fringed banner and pointer on a stem, scrolled to support the bars carrying the cardinal letters, and surmounted by a royal crown, indicated in dotted lines. In Elizabeth's days they were of the simplest banner shape, probably pierced, as they were in the fifteenth century, with the arms of England and France quarterly. Among some sketches of vanes in Lancashire with cardinal points, is a banner with five fleur-de-lis points pierced with the date 1685, the stem surmounted by a royal crown. Another vane treated archaistically is on Charlton Manor House, the flag pierced 1700 over W.A.; and another over Rye Church with date 1703 and A.R (Fig. 152, *ante*). The part of a vane consisting of a monster's head under a crown in the Maidstone Museum is believed to have surmounted the building when it was Chillington Manor, and appears to have been suggested by a vane at Dijon. It probably finished like one at Chingford, in a short pointer, or like that of the not far distant Minster Church in Sheppey (Fig. 161), where a grim looking horse's head forms the flag with a smaller horse above, commemorating the feat of Sir Robert de Shurland related in the *Ingoldsby Legends*. The Church at Queenborough has the

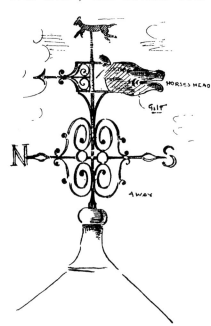

FIG. 161. VANE TO MINSTER CHURCH, SHEPPEY.

Weathercocks and Vanes

swallow-tailed guidon, pierced 1793, with a duck's head or some similar bird's for pointer. On High Wycombe Town Hall is one dating about 1710, in which Sagittarius as a centaur about to loose an arrow from his bow, forms both flag and pointer.

Few vanes are astronomical, but for a brief period comets were in fashion. The King's Mews, where is now the National Gallery, is said to have sported one; and one may be seen on the spire of St. John's Horsleydown. Possibly the vane to St. Mary's Church in the Strand, which remains as designed by Gibbs, may also be intended for a comet.

In later vanes the precise form of the flag is no longer of interest, nor can we implicitly trust the dates on them, since the flag being of copper gilt can often be used again when the wrought ironwork has perished. It may be assumed, as a rule, that much scrollwork between the stem and the bars carrying the cardinal letters indicates relatively modern workmanship. The pointers were usually straight and barbed like arrows, but sometimes twisted into loops and bent downward; or two bars outlining the flag are continued round the spindle and bent and welded together into the point. The pointer may also be supported from below by a scroll, or set between two scrolls. Our illustration of the vane to Hedsor Church, near Clevedon on the Thames, is a relatively simple form (Fig. 162). That at Canons Ashby is much more elaborate with its tapering stem of five almost vertical bars and scrolled arms (Fig. 163). Occasionally it finishes in a small dragon's, serpent's, or bird's head.

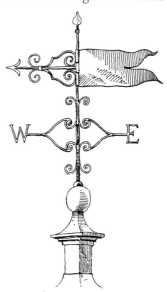

FIG. 162. VANE ON BELL TURRET, HEDSOR CHURCH, BUCKS. T. GARRATT, *del*.

A few eighteenth century vanes were frankly heraldic, like that to the old Swedes' Church in Ratcliff Highway, where a rampant and crowned lion held an escutcheon on a scrolled stem with the cardinal points. The vane on the Danes' Church in Wellclose Square seems to have represented a galley with streamer under the Danish crown. Maitland illustrated these in 1772. Both these are now destroyed. A lion rampant over a banner and plain pointer surmounted the Church of the Trinity Almshouses in the Mile End Road in 1686, but this picturesque treatment has now given place to a flag pierced T.H. for Trinity House. Something like it, but with a griffen, has been reproduced by the Benchers of Gray's Inn. A drawing of a vane perhaps by Hawksmoor in the Soane Museum shows a lion springing and folded ribbon, and over an obelisk clock tower floats a streamer above the star of the garter.

FIG. 163. VANE ON STAIR-TURRET AT CANONS ASHBY, NORTHANTS.
T. GARRATT, *del.*

Vanes, as we have seen, are usually carried on a single vertical stem, whether this be plain or balustered and swelled, or loaded with scrolls; but J. Jores, an enterprising designer, published in 1759 eight designs of vanes in which the stems are built up of several bars joined by handsome scroll work in Chippendale style, the pointers being of open work something like the elaborate hands of contemporary clocks, while the flags are cut into most fantastic shapes. In 1765 the Welldons, two smiths, produced six further designs in the same manner. Only one of these is shown with cardinal points, and but one of the fourteen is surmounted by a cock. Besides vanes, the designs include several finials, but none made to these designs appear to exist now, and probably very few were ever actually executed.

LIST OF SMITHS AND DESIGNERS

SMITHS.

	Page References.	Text Illustrations.	Plates.
A. Guylders, John	268	—	—
Alexander le Imaginator	4	—	—
Bache, William	248	90 (?)	—
Bakewell, Robert	59–63, 86, 130, 226, 249, 308	70, p. 80	VIII–XIII, XIX, LXXIV
Brewer, Jane, coppersmith	302	—	—
Buncker, George	85, 109–115, 189	35–37	XXXVIII–XLI, LX
Coalburn, Thos.	83	—	—
Coneway, John	268	—	—
Edney, William	72–80, 118, 130, 227	26–28	XXI–XXIV
Fardons, The	193	—	—
Greene	315	—	—
Jackson	204	—	—
Jores, J. (designer)	135, 259, 271, 292, 320	—	—
Leghtone, Thomas of	4	—	—
Lewes, Henry of	4	—	—
Matsys, Josse	6, 213	—	—
Oddy, Richard	197, 264	105	—
Patrick	213	—	—
Partridge	36, 83, 269	13	—
Peter the Dutchman	301	—	—
Roberts, the Brothers	63–72, 117, 130, 198, 226	22a–25	XIV–XX, LXIII
Robinson, Thomas	81–95, 118, 130, 204, 206, 227, 230, 233	29–71, p. 58	XXV–XXXI
Shaw, Huntington	50, 51, 58, 197, 223	—	—

List of Architects and Designers

	Page References.	Text Illustrations.	Plates.
Tijou, Jean	33, 37–59, 81, 86, 216–217, 222, 228, 247, 250, 258, 259, 262, 264, 270, 271, 293	14–22, 88–99	III–VII, LXXVII, LXXVIII
Warren	83, 84, 95–109, 160, 206–7, 230	30–34	XXXII–XXXVII
Weldons, The	135, 259, 271, 289, 292, 320	—	—

ARCHITECTS & DESIGNERS

NOTE.—In cases where the illustration is taken from the building and not from the published designs, it is probable that the architect did not actually design the ironwork associated with his building.

	Pages.	Fig. Numbers.	Plates.
Adam, Robert and James	136, 172–4, 240–1, 243–4, 252, 260, 272, 280–4, 311	84	—
Design in Victoria and Albert Museum	252	94	—
Lansdowne House	172	—	LIV
St. James' Square	243–4, 281	87	—
Portman Square, Chandos House	244	—	—
Lampholders	280–1	—	LXXIII
Boodle's Club balconies	261	103–4	—
Drapers' Hall fanlight	275	123	—
Design for railing, lampholders, etc.	281–2	125	—
Lampholders, Adelphi	280	—	LXXXVI
Lamp brackets	289–90	135, 136	—
Bottomley, Joseph (Grilles)	272–3	109–116	—
Carter, J. (*The Builder's Magazine*)	174, 244, 272, 275, 283	122, 126	—
Chambers, Sir William	126, 251, 311	—	—
Somerset House	—	93	—
Dance, G.			
Mansion House Grille	269	107	—

List of Architects and Designers

	Pages.	Fig. Numbers.	Plates.
Flitcroft, H. (designed by)			
Wentworth Woodhouse	265	—	LXXXI
Gerbier, Sir B.			
Hamstead Marshall	30	11	—
Gibbs, James	130–5, 185, 216, 220–221, 236, 242, 259, 269, 271, 311, 319	45, 46, 47, 48, 49	—
Jones, Inigo, Designs by	—	—	—
Kirby Hall balcony	254–5	96	—
Ripley (designed by)			
The Admiralty	288	130	—
Society of Upholsterers	260	101, 102	—
Vanbrugh, Sir J.			
Seaton Delaval	259	100	—
Vardy	133, 236, 244, 287	50	—
Ware, Isaac	133, 201, 236, 239, 242, 285	—	—
Designs	—	50, 79–82	—
Wren, Sir C.*(Buildings designed by or attributed to)	32–8, 48, 115, 130, 217, 240, 242, 256, 267–9, 309–13	—	—
Trinity College Cambridge Library	35–6	—	—
Groombridge	19	5	—
Sheldonian, Oxford	34	12	—
St. Stephens, Walbrook	309	154	—
Greenwich Hospital	310	155	—
Bow Church Vane	311–2	156–8	—
Wynde, Capt. W.			
Buckingham House	107, 124	34	—

* For Hampton Court, *see* Tijou, pp. 37–50.

GENERAL INDEX TO THE TEXT

NOTE.—For references to Subjects Illustrated, see the Alphabetical Lists at the beginning of the book.
Names of Places refer to examples of Ironwork unless otherwise described.
The names of the principal Smiths, etc., are indexed in a separate list which precedes the present one.

Abney House, 106, 152
Acton, 146
Adam Bros., 136, 172, 241, 243, 252, 260, 272, 275, 280–284, 289, 311
Adams, Maurice S., 146
Adelphi, 260, 280
Admiralty, 288
Alcester, 192
Aldermaston, 85, 104
Ale Stakes, 292
All Saints', Derby, 59, 60, 70, 249
All Souls' College, 135, 185, 269
Alton, Hants, 184
Ampthill, 199
Anglo-Saxon Doors, 2
   ,,   Parks, 128–9
Anne, Queen, 45, 49
Arbury Hall, 105, 192, 230
Architects, Influence of, 129–37
Area railings, 240
Argyll House, Chelsea, 155
Ashburnham House, 182
Ashmolean Museum, 34
Atkyn's *Gloucester*, 117
Audley End, 200, 252, 289
   ,,   Square, 284
Austin Friars, 284
Avington Park, 105

Aylesbury, 189, 298
Ayliffe, 86

Badminton, 32
Bacon on Gardens, 16–17
Bakewell, 86, 130, 226, 249, 308
Balconies, 254–61
Balustrades, 246–52
Bank of England, 133, 141, 270
Banner vanes, 304–10
Baptist Chapel, Derby, 61
Barlborough, 104, 198, 305
Barnes, 167
Barrington, Daines, 41, 65
Bath, 284
Bathurst's, Lord, Park, 104
Battersea, 152
Battle Abbey, 22, 214
Batty Langley, 51, 135, 259
Bayeux Tapestry, 303
Beckenham, 139
Beddington, 91, 230
Bedford, 199, 232, 299
   ,,   Row, 279
   ,,   Square, 271, 284
   ,,   Street, 255
Beechwood 199, 204
Beeston Park, 204

General Index to the Text

Belton, 90, 221, 230
Berkeley Square, 237, 278, 279, 284
Berkshire, 188, 189
Berwick Park, 72, 198
Bexley, 91, 235
Bickell, S.W., 109
Birds as vanes, 313-14
Bland, E., 207
Blandford, 291
Blickling, 19, 306
Bloomsbury, 133, 270, 271, 278, 314
Bloxham Park, 94, 204
Bolton House, 170
Boodles Club, 244, 260
Boston, 206
Botanic Gardens, Cambridge, 136, 203
Bow Church, 256, 308, 312
,, Bridge, 214
Bradfield, 192
Bradford-on-Avon, 313
Braintree, 200
Bramham Park, 207
Brentford, 165
Brewers' Hall, 19
Brewill & Bailey, Messrs., 195
Bridesfoot House, 111
Bridewell, 54
Bridgeman, 126-7
Bridges, 254
Bristol, 72, 191, 227, 284
British Museum, 300, 301
Bromley College, 140, 178
Brook Green, 158, 168
Brown (Capability), 41, 126, 247
Bruton, 295
Buck, 65, 224, 227
Buckingham Gate, 284
Buckingham House, 107, 124

Buckinghamshire, 189
Builders' Magazine, 174, 244, 275
Bulwick Hall, 80, 195, 220
Burford, 186
Burgos Cathedral, 262
Burleigh House, 46, 195, 220, 252
,, ,, Enfield, 107
Burley-on-the-Hill, 56, 58, 220, 226
Burlington Gardens, 244, 281
Bury St. Edmunds, 3, 102, 204, 256
Butleigh, 305
Buxted, 183

Caius College, Cambridge, 16
Cambridge, 96, 136, 202, 203, 242, 268, 270
Cambridgeshire, 202
Cannock Chase, 62, 197
Canons, 78, 250
Canons Ashby, 18, 19, 319
Canterbury, 212, 268, 272, 294, 303, 314
Carden Hall, 67, 227, 229,
Cardinal Letters to Vanes, 317-20
Carlisle, 207, 265, 284, 289
Carlton House Terrace, 283
Caroline Park, 257
Carshalton, 92, 219, 221, 228, 265
Carter's Magazine, 174, 244, 272, 275, 281
Cast iron, 240, 242-3
Castle Ashby, 252
,, Bromwich, 192
Castles, flat roofs to, 252
Cavendish Square, 241, 244, 279, 281
Cedar Villa, Enfield, 157
Chadwell Heath, 152
Chambers, Sir W., 126, 251, 311

Chandos House, 244, 281
" Street, 244, 255
Changes of style, 143
Chantry House, 195
Chapter House, St. Paul's, 267
Charing Cross, 235
Charlcote, 306
Charles II, 18, 30, 32, 39
Charles Street, 279
Charlton Manor, 318
Charmouth, 191
Chatsworth, 48, 197, 253, 258, 262–5
Chauncey's *Herts*, 20
Chelmsford, 200, 299
Chelsea, 106, 124–5, 155–7, 163, 168, 170, 233–5, 250, 267, 308
Chelsea Hospital, 139, 285
Cheshire, 63–4
Chester, *see* Eaton
Chesterfield, 226
" House, 249, 285
" Street, 279
Chester-le-Street, 121, 208
Cheveley, 84, 98, 100
Chevening, 118, 217
Cheyne Walk, 106, 140, 144, 163, 233, 250, 271
Chichester, 183, 232
Chiddingfold, 176
Chillington Hall, 198, 318
Chingford, 318
Chippenham, 190
Chirk Castle, 63–5, 221, 227
Chiswick, 101, 102, 146, 150, 157, 158, 235, 253
Christchurch, Oxford, 217
" Newgate Street, 168
Church grilles, 4–5
" house, 155

Cirencester, 22, 104, 118, 190–91
Clandon Park, 85, 101, 102, 221, 230
Clapham, 156, 157, 170
Clapton, 106, 267
Clare College, Cambridge, 83, 84, 96, 220, 270
Clarendon Press, 36, 52, 54
Clark, J. W., 84
Clifford Street, W., 284
Clutterbuck Hall, 208
Coaches, 17
Coalbrookdale, 254, 297
Coats of arms on gates, 24–6
Cocks as weather vanes, 300–302
College of Physicians, 313
Collington, F. E., 195
Colt House, Bristol, 191
Colwick Hall, 197, 220
Compton Beauchamp, 189
Cookham, 188
Cornhill, 271
Corpus Christi College, Oxford, 184, 270
Cote Bampton, 21
Cotman, Grahame, 203
Courtyard Gates, 17
Covent Garden, 123, 232, 255
Cowdray, 22–4, 214, 305
Craigie Hall, 210
Cranford, 164
Crested railing, 221, 232
Cresting to gates, 18
Croome, 173–4
Crowhurst, 317
Crowley House, Greenwich, 124, 253
Crowns on vanes, 318
Cubey, Berkeley, Mr., 208
Culford Hall, 102, 204
Curzon Street, 279

General Index to the Text

Dacre's Almshouses, 139
Dalkeith, 174
Dance, 133, 269, 311
Danes Church, 320
Dates on gates, 139–40
Dawber, E. G., 140
Dawley, 117
Defensive spikes, 253
Defoe, 45, 88, 200, 210, 265, 314
Delille, Abbé, 128
De Loutherberg, 278
Derby, 59–61, 249
Destruction of screens and gates, 127, 128
Devonshire, 150, 191
    ,,   House, 85, 101, 102
Ditchfield's *Manor Houses*, 190
Divinity School, Oxford, 184
Dog-bars, 220
Donibristle, 210, 264
Doors sheathed, 3, 12
Doorway brackets, 291
Dorsetshire, 191
Dover Castle, 308
    ,,   House, 216, 220
Downing Street, 283
Downton, 190
Dragons as vanes, 312
Drapers' Hall, 275, 289
Drawbridge, 11
Drayton House, 54, 83, 84, 117, 219, 220–225, 264–5
Droitwich, 68
Du Cerceau, 29, 293
Dugdale's *Warwickshire*, 127
Dulwich, 85, 109
Dunkeld, 210
Durdans, The, 71, 220
Durham, 208

Dutch gardening, 125
Dyrham, 117

Eagle House, 106, 154, 162
Earlham, 203
East Alton, 146
Easton Hall, 150, 200
    ,,   Neston, 265
Eaton Hall, 43, 52, 63, 68, 227
Ebbetts, 27, 94, 102, 106, 115, 117, 140, 154, 160, 170, 171, 200
Eckington, 104, 198
Eddystone, 308
Edinburgh, 279, 284, 289
Edmonton, 154, 162, 163
    ,,   Lower, 155
Edward I, patron of smiths, 4
Eleanor Crosses, 214
Elm Hall, Snaresbrook, 152
Elm House, 154, 155
Elmsdale, 160
Eltham, 154, 167, 179
Ely, 6, 15
Emral, 63, 66
Elvaston, 116, 216
Enfield, 107, 113, 115, 154, 157
English gardens in France, 128
Erdig near Wrexham, 232
Essex, 150, 199–200
    ,,   Street, 283
Etchingham, 305
Etwall Hall, 62
European iron-work in the sixteenth century, 7–8
Evelyn, 3, 30, 32, 39, 85, 302
Evesham, 199, 291
Exning, 84, 98

Fairford, 117

Falkner, Harold, 182
Fan-lights, 272–5
Faringdon, 311
Farnborough, 174
Farnham, 182, 299
Faversham, 312
Fenton House, 148
Fiennes (Celia) Diary, 33
Figures as vanes, 314
Findlater Castle, 174
Finedon, 195
Fish as vanes, 313
Fitzadam, 125–7
Flags as vanes, 303–20
Fleet Bridge, 214, 254
Flintshire, 65, 66
Foots Cray, 178
Forbes House, 168, 169
Fordrin, L., 51
Forecourt screens, 115–124
    „   „   origin of, 16
Formal gardens, mediaeval, 28
Foundling Hospital, 286
Four-oaks Hall, 127, 192
Fragnall, 121
Frensham, 291
Frognal, 178
Fulham, 158, 164

Garden gates, 17, 18, 28–36
Gardens, 28–36, 124–8
Geometric design, mediaeval, 5
George Street, 280
Gerbier, Sir Balthazar, 30
Gibbs, James, 130–5, 185, 217, 220–1, 237, 242, 259, 269, 271, 311, 319
Gibson on gardens, 33, 39
Glass lamps, 285, 286
Gloucester, 190

Godfrey, W. H., 163, 251, 271
Gogar, 210
Golden Square, 241
Gosford, 173
Gough's Park, 113
Granton, N. B., 257
Grasshoppers as vanes, 312–13
Gray's Inn, 139, 320
Great Cumberland Place, 280
Great George Street, 279, 280, 284
Great Marlow, 189, 232, 267
Great Mongeham, 293
Great Ormond Street, 121, 216, 220, 236–7, 250, 267, 280
Great Yarmouth, 204
Green Park, 242, 285
Greenwich, 124, 253, 310
Grilles, 267–76
Grimsthorpe, 230
Groombridge, 18
Grosvenor House, 261
    „   Square, 216, 219, 237, 241, 279
Grosvenor Place, 261
Grove Hall, 152, 200
    „   House, Seymour Place, 156
Grumbold, 84, 96, 202
Guildford, 257, 289, 309
Guilford Street, 279
Guy's Hospital, 139

Hadleigh House, 188
Hall Place, Bexley, 91, 235
Halton on London gates, 141
Ham Common, 110, 168, 169, 232
    „   House, 26, 27, 217, 220
Hamilton Place, 244, 281
Hammersmith, 146

Hampshire, 183, 184
    ,,   Hog Lane, 159
Hampstead, 148, 158, 170, 171, 220
Hampton Church, 50, 58
    ,,   Court, 32–35, 38–42, 49, 52, 54, 56, 117, 220, 221–3, 248, 259, 262
Hamstead Marshall, 30
Hanover Square, 235, 241, 280
Harleston, 297
Harley Street, 244, 280, 281
Harpenden, 201
Harris' *Kent*, 118
Harrowden, 91, 230
Hatfield, 200
Hatherop, 118
Hatton Street, 255
Hawksmoor, 133, 135, 320
Hedsor, 319
Henry VIII and foreign smiths, 8
    ,,   ,,   ,,   lamps, 285
Henry VIII's gardens, 29
Hereford, 22, 313
Herefordshire, 198–9
Hertford House, 262
Hertfordshire, 200–202
Highgate, 161, 170, 299
High Head Castle, 265
High Street House, 118, 232
High Wycombe, 319
Hinwick Hall, 199
Hoddesden, 201
Hogarth, 127, 278, 279, 294
Holborn Bridge, 214, 254
Holland House, gates near, 33, 79, 115, 155
Holyrood Palace, 262
Honor Row, 169
Hopetoun House, 210

Hornby, 208
Horseguards, 133, 216, 237
Horseheath, 84, 100
Houghton, 204
Huntercombe Manor, 189
Huntingdonshire, 199
Hutton-in-the-Forest, 255
Hyde Park, 82, 173, 242, 285

I'Anson, Mr. E. B., 271
Inigo Jones, 33, 118, 217, 254, 255, 309, 314
Inn Signs, 292–9
Inverness-shire, 210
Iron bridges, 254
Inwood, 102, 148, 152, 191, 232
Irongate Park, 62
Italian gardens, 29, 124
Iver, 111

Jardins anglais, 128
Jesmond, 208
Jesus College, 202, 220
John Street, Adelphi, 280

Kendal, 207
Kennet's *Ambrosden*, 19
Kensington, 155, 157, 311
    ,,   Gardens, 242
    ,,   Gore, 171, 233, 267
Kent, 121, 175–179, 311
  ,, House, 150
  ,, William, 126, 136
Kimbolton, 199, 265
King's Bench Walk, 219, 235
Kingsdown, 289
King's Lynn, 286, 299
Kingston, 291

Kip, 30, 32, 41, 48, 68, 117, 120, 121, 204, 248, 264
Kirby Hall, 254
Kirkleatham, 206, 221, 231, 312
Kirklees, 105, 206, 254, 267
Knole, 176

Laguerre, L., 37, 47, 48, 78
Lambeth, 307
Lamp-holders, 278–89
Lancashire, 207
Lancaster, 207, 291
„ Place, 284
Landscape gardeners, 126–8
Langley, Batty, 51, 135
„ Lodge, Berks, 188
Lansdowne House, 172
Latimer House, 146
Lattice gates, 3
Law, Ernest, 39, 41, 42
Leadenhall Street, 141
Leatherhead, 180
Ledstone, 207, 265
Leeswood, 63, 65, 226
Leicester, 79, 198
„ Square, 62
Leland, 129
Lenôtre, André, 32, 125
Leominster, 79, 198
Lewes, 183
Lewisham, 179
Lichfield, 95
Lid gates, 15
Lincoln, 193, 204
Lincoln's Inn, 124, 219, 235, 241, 244, 261, 267, 278, 281, 284
Lindsay House, 163, 206, 241
Little Cloisters, Westminster, 106, 171

Littlecote, 189
Liverpool, 207
Llandaff, 22
Llangollen, 64
Lombard Street, 284
London and Wise, 125
London Bridge, 253
„ gates, 140–72
„ squares, 237, 240, 241
Longwood, 105
"Lordships, The," Hadham, 201
Lorimer, R. S., 264
Loughton Hall, 93, 200
Lower Lypiatt, 107
Ludlow, 291
Luton, 199
Lynn, 140
Lyre Pilasters, 218–19

Magdalen College, Oxford, 185
Maidstone, 313, 318
Maitland, 294, 311, 315, 317, 320
Maîtres Ornamentistes, Les, 136–7
Malpas, 67
Mammalia as vanes, 314
Mansard, 130
Mansfield Street, 275
Mansion House, 133, 270, 285, 289
Mapledurham, 186
Marlow, 189, 232
Marot, Daniel, 32, 39, 47, 58, 258, 264
Mary, Queen, 37, 38, 47, 259
Maxstoke Castle, 75
Mayfair, 260, 278, 284
May, Hugh, 32
Mediaeval grilles, 268
Melbourne, 59, 60, 249
Melton Constable, 204

Mere, 297
  ,, Hall, 68
Merston Green, Evesham, 199
Merstham, 159
Merton Abbey, 148, 164
Midgeham House, 104
Middle Temple, 256
Milbourne Port, 191
Mill Hill House, 61
Mills, Stead, Mr. 78
Minster, Sheppey, 318
Milton House, 195
Miserden Park, 79, 190
Mitcham, 162
Mold, 65
Monmouth House, 123
Monmouthshire, 74
Montagu Square, 279
Montesquieu, 128
Moot, The, Downton, 190
Much Hadam, 201
  ,, Wenlock, 297
Murphy, Baily, 54, 56, 80, 88, 117, 135, 185, 210, 264-5
Myddletons, of Chirk, 64

Netherhampton House, 190
Newark-on-Trent, 195, 221
Newbury, 104, 312
Newcastle-on-Tyne, 208
New College, Oxford, 82, 88, 221, 228
Newdigate House, 195
Newhouse, Buxted, 183
Newington, 160, 161
Newmarket, 84, 98
Newnham Paddox, 63, 68-70
Nicholls, Sutton, 40, 43
Niven, D. B., 315
Nollet, André, gardener, 30

Nonsuch, 303
Norfolk, 140, 203
Norman castles, 10
  ,, gates, 11
Northampton, Lord, 33
Northamptonshire, 193-5
North Cray, 178
North End, 158
North Runcton, 204
Northumberland, 208, 259
Norton near Sheffield, 226
Norton Conyers, 103, 207
Norton, John, 146, 154, 157, 158, 160, 164, 267, 288
Norwich, 203
Nottingham, 50, 62, 195, 221, 226, 232, 293

Oakley Park, 104, 190, 197
Okeover, 62, 226
Old Divinity Schools, Oxford, 184
  ,, Hall, Aylsham, 204
  ,, Silk Mill, Derby, 60
  ,, St. Pancras, 253,
Ormeley House, Ham, 110, 221, 232
Osterly, 174
Oswestry, 63
Oxburgh Hall, 305
Oxford, 36, 52, 82, 88, 135, 184, 217, 228, 270, 292
Oxfordshire, 21, 184-8
Oxnead Hall, 204

Packwood House, 193
"Pales," 212
Parapet rails, 252-3
  ,, ,, to bridge, 253
Parham, 183
Park Lane, 278

General Index to the Text

Parks, 128–9
Pencil vanes, 303–4
Pennant's *London*, 241
Penshurst, 62, 176
Pepys, 32, 255
Percy House, Tottenham, 163
Peterborough, 193, 195, 255
Petersham House, 169
Piers, 18
Pilasters, 217–19
Pinkey, 210, 265
Plashey, 295
Poddington, 199
Pointers to vanes, 306–7
Ponders End, 154
Pontefract, 207
Portcullis, 11
Portland Place, 276
Portman Square, 243, 276, 279, 281
   ,, Street, 279
Portsmouth, 315
Poston, G. G., 150
Powis House, 121, 220, 221, 235
Preston-on-Stour, 193
Price, Sir Uvedale, 128
Primitive construction, 21
Priory, Reigate, 180, 220–1, 232
Pritchard, J. E., 72
Puritans, destruction by, 30

Queen Anne Street, 279, 281
Queenborough, 318
Queen's College, 304
   ,, House, Chelsea, 106, 233, 250
   ,, Square, 279
Quemby Hall, 78

Radcliffe Library, Oxford, 133, 185, 215

Ragley Hall, 192, 207
Railings, 18–20, 212–244
   ,, ancient use of, 212
   ,, cast iron, 242
   ,, construction, 214–16
   ,, crested, 232
   ,, mediaeval, 212–3
   ,, origin of term, 212
   ,, passage of wood to iron, 20
   ,, roof, 253
   ,, tomb, 212–13
Rainham, 150
Rampe Anglaise, 262
Ramsbury, 189
Ramps, scrolled, to railings, 221
Raphael Park, 152, 199, 221
Ravenscourt Park, 158
Reading, 233
Redbourne, 294
Reigate, 180, 220–1, 232
"Remnants," Marlow, 189, 232
Rendcomb, 117
Repton, 126–7
Rice, Garraway, 50, 58, 162, 179
Richmond, 159, 168, 169
   ,, Almshouses, 140
   ,, Green, 156, 169, 235
Ripley, 288, 311
Ripon, 207
Rochester, 179, 214, 253, 308, 315
Romford, 152, 159, 199
Romsey, 295
Rose, gardener, 32
Royal Exchange, 256, 312
Ruscomb, 306
Rutland Lodge, 169
Rye, 308, 318

Sackville Street, 286, 287

General Index to the Text

Saint Albans, 202, 256, 294
,, Andrew's, Holborn, 139
,, Bartholomew's, Smithfield, 141, 315
,, Bride's, Fleet Street, 310
,, Catherine's College, 203
,, ,, ,, Cree, 313, 317
,, Clement's, Danes, 311
,, Dunstan's in the East, 313
,, Ethelburga's, 317
,, George's, Bloomsbury, 133, 314
,, ,, Chapel, Windsor, 5, 213
,, ,, Hanover Square, 285
,, Giles', Reading, 233
,, James's Palace, 32
,, ,, Piccadilly, 172
,, ,, Place, 279
,, ,, Square, 241, 243, 244, 276, 281, 284
,, ,, Street, 244, 255, 260
,, John's College, Cambridge, 202
,, ,, College, Oxford, 184
,, ,, Horsleydown, 319
,, ,, Hospital, Warwick, 73, 227
,, ,, Westminster, 253
,, Lawrence Jewry, 310
,, Margaret's Lothbury, 309, 315
,, ,, Pattens, 309–10
,, ,, Westminster, 220
,, Martin's, 242, 255, 271, 308, 317
,, Mary's, Oxford, 186, 220
,, ,, le-Strand, 220, 319
,, ,, Warwick, 227
,, Michael's, Cornhill, 315
,, Mildred's, Bread Street, 311

Saint Mildred's, Poultry, 315
,, Olave's, Hart Street, 315
,, Paul's Cathedral, 44, 51, 81, 82, 83, 85, 86, 223, 227, 242, 267, 268, 270, 300, 310
,, ,, Covent Garden, 313–14
,, Peter's, Cornhill, 310
,, ,, Faringdon, 311
,, Stephen's, Coleman Street, 313
,, Swithin's, Cannon Street. 313
,, Thomas' Hospital, 139
Salisbury, 190, 289, 291, 308
Sandon Park, 197
Sandringham, 139
Sandwich, 271, 275
Sandywell, 190
Sarsden, 20, 214
Savile House, 62
Savile Row, 284, 287
Scotland, 210, 214
Scraptoft Hall, 75, 227
Seaton Delaval, 259
Senate House, Cambridge, 242
Severn End, 199
Serjeants Inn, 237, 279
Shaw, Huntington, 50-1, 58
Sherborne, 191
Sheldonian, Oxford, 34, 184–5, 217, 223
Ships as vanes, 315–6
Shobdon Court, 79, 198, 227
Shop fronts, 272
Shrewsbury, 198
Shropshire, 198
Silk Mill, Derby, 61
Sion Park, 172
Smith's Right Hand, The, 135, 271
Snaresbrook, 152, 200

Soane Museum, 172-5, 243, 268, 280, 281, 313, 320
Society of Upholsterers, 260
Soho Square, 123, 241
Solihull, 192
Somerset House, 251, 281, 285
Somersetshire, 191, 289, 295
Spiers, Phené, 101, 102
Spikes, defensive, 253,
Spring Gardens, 260, 280, 284
Squares, London, 124, 278
Squerries, 118
Stafford, 197
Stair Ramps, 261-7
" Stakes," 214
Stamford, 206, 232
Stanchions, 212
Standards, 212, 217
Stansted Abbots, 201
Stanstead, 217
Stanton, 297
Stepney Green, 164, 267
Stevenson, G. D., 167
Stoke Edith, 30, 265
Stoke Newington, 102, 106, 152, 154, 155, 156, 160, 171, 235
Stoneleigh Abbey, 193, 265
Stone obelisks, 284, 285, 286
Stow, 214, 253, 285, 294, 298
Strand, The, 251
Stratford, 150, 152, 167, 289
Stratford Place, 280
Street, G. E., 306
Stroud, 107
Studley Royal, 207
Sudbrooke Lodge, 168-9
Suffolk, 204
Sunbury, 102, 204
Surrey, 180-2

Sussex, 115, 182-3
Sutton Coldfield, 192, 227
Swede's Church, 320
Switzer, John, 39
Sydenham House, 150
Symbolic vanes, 310, 311

Tadcaster, 207
Tadworth, 180, 219
Talman, 39, 48, 49, 223
Tamworth, 192
Tanfield, 208
Taplow, 189
Taylor, John, 276
Temple, The, London, 139, 235, 256
Tewkesbury Abbey, 73-4
Thame, 297
Theobalds, 30
Thoresby, Ralph, 41
Thorpe Hall, 195, 255
Tissington, 61
Tiverton, 189
Topiary work, 125
Tottenham, 113, 163, 169, 272, 288
Tower, 308, 318
Traquair Castle, 26, 210, 214
Tredegar Park, 74
Trinity Almshouses, 317, 320
    ,, College, Cambridge, 36, 48, 100, 268-9
    ,,   ,, Oxford, 88, 228
    ,, House, 283
Trowbridge, 190
Trumpington Street, Cambridge, 203
Turnham Green, 101
Twickenham, 115, 148, 170
Tyburn, 278

Umberslade, 119, 217
Uxbridge, 111

Vanburgh, Sir John, 52, 68, 259
Vane, 303–20
Vardy, 133, 237, 244, 281
Vases, cast-iron, 240
Venice, balconies of, 254
Venn, 191
Verona balconies, 254
Verrio, 32, 48
Versailles influence, 30–32
Victoria and Albert Museum, 165, 235, 252, 267, 272, 292

Wadham College, Oxford, 36, 184, 186, 217
Waldershare Park, 118
Wales, North, 63
Wallingford, 256
Walpole, Horace, 125
Walpole House, 146, 235
Waltham Cross, 167
Walthamstow, 154
Wandsworth, 159, 167, 267
Wardle, Rev. J. R., 83
Ware, Isaac, 201, 242, 285
Ware's *Architecture*, 133, 201, 214, 237–9, 242
Wareham, 295
Warkworth, 208
Warwick, 73, 192, 193, 227
Wavetree Hall, 207
Weald, iron working, 182
Weathercocks, 300–20
Welford Park, 188
Wendover, 297
Wentworth, 120, 208, 219, 312
„ Woodhouse, 265

West Drayton, 152, 167
Westminster, 106, 171, 213, 241, 284, 300, 310
West Woodhay, 188
Whalebone Hall, Chadwell, 152
Whitehall, 29, 252, 280, 281, 284, 288
William and Mary, 33, 38, 125, 262, 264
Willoughby House, 62, 195, 226
Wiltshire, 189–90
Wimbledon, 182
Wimborne, 295
Wimpole, 46, 117, 220, 222
Winchester, 105, 183, 300
Winchester House, 244, 281
Winchmore Hill, 207
Windsor, 188, 213, 272
„ gardens, 29
Window guards, 268
Winter, George, 286
Wokingham, 307
Wolverton Park, 188
Woodbridge, 154, 204
Wooden construction, 5, 17, 21, 22
Woodford, 152
Wood gates, 17–19
Woodstock, 28, 214, 291, 299
Woolley Park, 188
Wootton, Bucks, 89, 189, 230
Worcester, 63, 226
„ Park, 30
Worcestershire, 199
Worriston House, 210
Wovington, 45, 115
Wren, Sir C., 32–38, 48, 115, 130, 217, 240, 242, 256, 267–9, 309, 312–13
Wrest, 32

Wrexham, 63
Wylie, 190, 297
Wynde, Captain, 124

Yat, 13

Yenn, John, R.A., 272
Yester, 210, 265
Yetts, 13-15
York, 288, 301
Yorkshire, 206
Young, William, 32